Always I am Caesar

For Angela Aslanska and Robin Seager

ALWAYS I AM CAESAR

W. Jeffrey Tatum

BC116T

Blackwell
Publishing

© 2008 by W. Jeffrey Tatum

BLACKWELL PUBLISHING
350 Main Street, Malden, MA 02148-5020, USA
9600 Garsington Road, Oxford OX4 2DQ, UK
550 Swanston Street, Carlton, Victoria 3053, Australia

The right of W. Jeffrey Tatum to be identified as the author of this work has been asserted in accordance with the UK Copyright, Designs, and Patents Act 1988.

First published 2008 by Blackwell Publishing Ltd

1   2008

Library of Congress Cataloging-in-Publication Data

Tatum, W. Jeffrey.
   Always I am Caesar / W. Jeffrey Tatum.
      p.   cm.
   Includes bibliographical refrences and index.
   ISBN 978-1-4051-7525-8 (pbk. : alk. paper) – ISBN 978-1-4051-7526-5 (hardcover : alk. paper)   1. Caesar, Julius.   2. Rome–History–Republic, 265–30 B.C.   3. Heads of state–Rome–Biography.   4. Generals–Rome–Biography.   I. Title.
DG261.T38   2008
937′.05092–dc22

2007036296

A catalogue record for this title is available from the British Library.

Set in 10.5 on 13pt Minion
by SNP Best-set Typesetter Ltd., Hong Kong
Printed and bound in Singapore
by Markono Print Media Pte Ltd

The publisher's policy is to use permanent paper from mills that operate a sustainable forestry policy, and which has been manufactured from pulp processed using acid-free and elementary chlorine-free practices. Furthermore, the publisher ensures that the text paper and cover board used have met acceptable environmental accreditation standards.

For further information on
Blackwell Publishing, visit our website at
www.blackwellpublishing.com

Contents

Lists of Charts, Maps, and Figures

Charts

Maps

Figures

Acknowledgements

It is my pleasure to thank Tricia Smith, at Art Resource, Jenni Adam and Axellle Russo at The British Museum, Luisa Veneziano at the German Archaeological Institute, Rome, and Heidie Philipsen and Claus Grønne at Ny Carlsberg Glyptotek for their helpfulness. I also owe thanks to Indiana University Press for permission to quote from R. Humphries, *Ovid. Metamorphoses*, and to Penguin Press for permission to quote from D. West, *The Aeneid by Virgil*. I am grateful to Otago University for appointing me its De Carle Distinguished Lecturer in 2005 and to the university's Department of Classics for its unexcelled hospitality during my stay. I am indebted to Al Bertrand, Nancy de Grummond, John Marincola, Marjorie and Keith Maslen, and (especially) Jon Hall. My debts to Robin Seager run deeper, and it is my pleasure to acknowledge that reality in the dedication, a billing he shares, for different (but also profound) reasons, with Angela Aslanska.

CHART 1 THE FAMILY OF JULIUS CAESAR

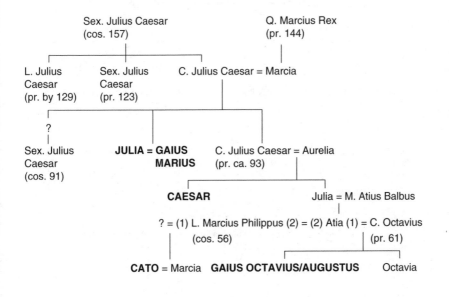

CHART 2   CAESAR AND THE AURELII COTTAE

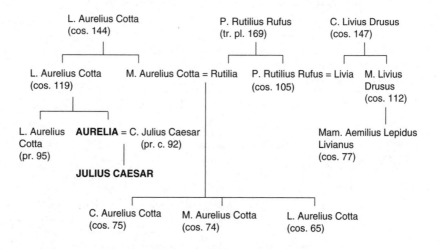

CHART 3   CATO AND HIS CONNECTIONS

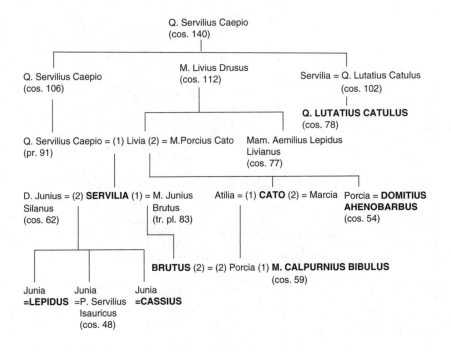

Q. Servilius Caepio
(cos. 140)

Q. Servilius Caepio
(cos. 106)

M. Livius Drusus
(cos. 112)

Servilia = Q. Lutatius Catulus
(cos. 102)

Q. LUTATIUS CATULUS
(cos. 78)

Q. Servilius Caepio = (1) Livia (2) = M.Porcius Cato
(pr. 91)

Mam. Aemilius Lepidus
Livianus
(cos. 77)

D. Junius = (2) **SERVILIA** (1) = M. Junius
Silanus   Brutus
(cos. 62)   (tr. pl. 83)

Atilia = (1) **CATO** (2) = Marcia

Porcia = **DOMITIUS
AHENOBARBUS**
(cos. 54)

BRUTUS (2) = (2) Porcia (1) **M. CALPURNIUS BIBULUS**
(cos. 59)

Junia
=**LEPIDUS**

Junia
=P. Servilius
Isauricus
(cos. 48)

Junia
=**CASSIUS**

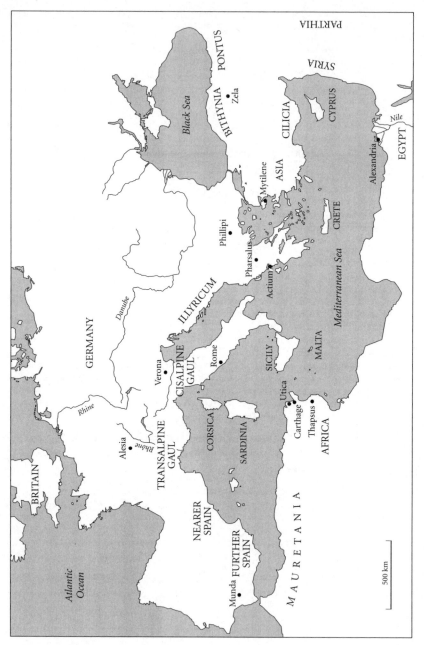

Map 1 The Mediterranean in the time of Caesar.

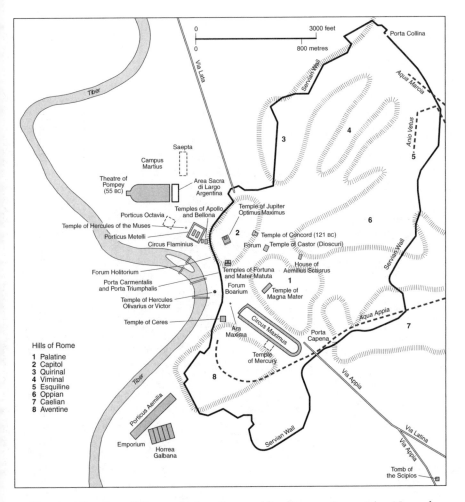

Map 2 The city of Rome during the republic. Source: Rosenstein, N., and Morstein-Marx, R. (eds.), *A Companion to the Roman Republic* (Oxford, 2006).

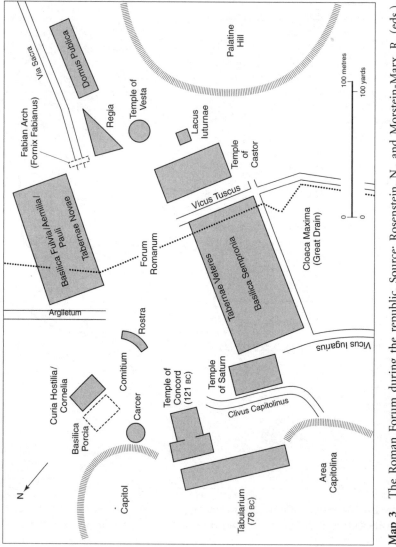

Map 3 The Roman Forum during the republic. Source: Rosenstein, N., and Morstein-Marx, R. (eds.), *A Companion to the Roman Republic* (Oxford, 2006).

Introduction

"The one debt we owe to history," as Oscar Wilde insisted, "is to rewrite it." In the case of Julius Caesar, even if we are not quite prepared to declare ourselves fully paid up, we can hardly be described as falling into arrears. From antiquity to the present day Caesar has remained a favorite subject of biographers, scholarly and amateur alike. And it would be as difficult as it would be remiss to investigate Roman history – or for that matter European history – without at least acknowledging his lasting influence. Caesar abides in all the arts, as a versatile topic and symbol in products of high as well as popular culture, and he remains a potent platform for political discourse about militarism or power or ambitions of an autocratic or hegemonic quality. He is evocative and useful because he is so instantly available to everyone.

Even a legend can be stretched too thin, however. Less accessible than Caesar's reputation is the man himself and the society he both challenged and transformed. Merely to mention Rome, in most circumstances, is to conjure empire – and emperors, of which species Caesar is routinely deemed the author. Hence the familiar transformation of his name into a title: *Kaiser* and *Czar*. This is a reality that does not so much enlarge Caesar as it urges his reduction, making him into an uncomplicated figure – the tyrant who gets his way by force of arms, a representation of Caesar that inescapably diminishes his actual merits as a soldier or a general or a politician. It was this very simplification that made possible the purposes to which Caesar was put in the American Revolution, when every patriot was a Brutus striving to free the colonies from the imperial oppression of a British king who could by no stretch of the imagination be likened to Caesar in any but the most tenuous symbolic terms. By then, however, and long before, Caesar had been diluted to Caesarism, which rendered him available to political polemic in nearly any context. This same impulse

1

Figure 1   Colossal portrait head of Caesar, from the 2nd century AD. Museo Archeologico Nazionale, Naples, Italy. Photo: Scala/Art Resource, NY.

allowed Caesar to cross the Atlantic, where the opponents of Andrew Jackson could attack Old Hickory as a nineteenth-century Caesar whose personal arrogance, contempt for political restraint and imperialist ambitions threatened the American republic with ruin. In our own century, similar complaints, again invoking the image of Caesar, have been aimed at George W. Bush in publications like the *Washington Post*, *Harper's Magazine* and, in an instance of luscious and timely revenge for King George, the *Guardian*. Caesar was a man of great capacity and talent, but not a hint of that is operative when Caesar or his reputation is deployed as a term of abuse. Caesar, there can be no missing it, still stands for imperialism and autocracy.

And also for personal decadence. Here the evidence is all too abundant, from casinos to toga parties to popular television programming. The historical evidence for Caesar's sensuality and prodigality and womanizing is not hard to come by. His political rivals emphasized Caesar's perversities in lip-smacking detail – and the poet Catullus scored multiple successes by lampooning the great general's disgusting license and licentiousness. This Caesar, however, does not always sit comfortably with his imperial reputation. It is as if the ambitious conqueror of the Gauls and or of the Roman republic seems too busy, too efficient or perhaps too valorous to luxuriate in the company of wanton eastern queens or of immoral young men. Even Cicero once said of Caesar that the man was too dissolute to represent a genuine danger to Rome.

Yet this is the same Caesar who was not merely a brilliant military commander but a skillful politician, an eloquent orator, a gifted writer and an inspired reformer. In his own day many saw in Caesar Rome's final opportunity to eliminate its factionalism, to repair its economy, to give lasting order and stability to its empire – in short, they saw in Caesar a statesman blessed with the talent and the will to usher in the fulfillment of Rome's true destiny. This was especially the expectation of the masses. After his death, the common people of Rome began to worship Caesar as a god, idolatry that their betters could do nothing to suppress. On the contrary, the idea of Caesar's divinity caught on and was passed on to his political heirs, becoming one of the essential emblems of the empire and subsisting until Christianity elbowed it out of the way. Christianity hardly spelled the end for the idea of Caesar as something superhuman, however, even if did shunt this article of faith away from the multitude and into the ranks of the elite. Indeed, there has been no shortage of intellectuals for whom Caesar represented nothing less than the perfection of the Roman spirit, the very embodiment of natural superiority, the ultimate Great Man – which are all merely more in the way of simplifications for all their grand and banging formulations. And so we get multiple Caesars: conqueror, autocrat, libertine, god – and *Übermensch*. Not an easy figure to take in all at once. He is instantly available only in smaller bits.

One of the purposes of this book is to examine Caesar's career by way of a selection of different perspectives, such as his professional rise, his political success, his conquest of Gaul, his relationships with women, his elevation to supreme power and beyond that to the condition of a god. Although I begin at Caesar's beginnings and I conclude with the state of affairs established by his heir and successor, Augustus, this is neither a biography nor a linear historical narrative. Instead, in each chapter there is an attempt to understand central aspects of Caesar's life within a pertinent slice of Roman habits, concepts and expectations. There is a reason for this approach. One of the greatest challenges in comprehending Caesar lies in the difficulty of distinguishing the singular qualities of the man from the typical attributes and instincts of his time and class. It is all too easy to regard Caesar as unique, a superman or at the very least a new stage in the evolution of Roman aristocratic politicians, in which case Caesar's historical role more or less explains itself without any reference to its situation. Caesar triumphed because, being Caesar, what else could he do? It is no improvement on this to let Caesar be subsumed entirely by his context, that is, to regard Caesar as little more than a symptom of all that was characteristic, for good or for ill, of aristocratic Roman society in the first century BC. Matters are more elusive than that, and it is hoped that the following chapters will offer some introduction to the problems of sorting out Caesar's individuality and the circumstances in which he asserted it with such enduring consequences.

Caesar matters in the first instance because he was the agent of a cataclysmic political transformation that forever altered the politics, and the society, of Europe and the Mediterranean. From end of the sixth century BC until Caesar crossed the Rubicon, Rome was a republic. Each year magistrates were elected by the people, and all legislation in Rome was enacted by popular vote. Government relied on the executive capacities of magistrates and on the guidance of the Roman senate, a body composed of all former magistrates. The senate, the magistrates and the people, in their dynamic combination, constituted the Roman republic – and it was this state that dominated Italy and soon thereafter gained mastery of much of the Mediterranean world. And it was this state that Caesar overthrew. Caesar made himself master of Rome and dictator for life. He gathered into his hands all meaningful sources of power and prestige, which he held until he was slain on the Ides of March in 44 BC. It is for this reason that later generations designated him the first of Rome's emperors, though in actuality that distinction belongs to his heir, Augustus, who, like his predecessor, emerged from another civil war as a permanent autocrat. Augustus, unlike Caesar, was not assassinated, and on the occasion of his death imperial power passed seamlessly to his adopted son, Tiberius. Thereafter Rome was the Roman empire, the durable imprint of which persists in Europe and, by extension, everywhere in the world that has been shaped by a European presence. This shift from republic to empire is one of the very few historical episodes that can fairly be called epoch making, and, although the event was not entirely of Caesar's doing, it was certainly Caesar who was the essential catalyst of this upheaval, a reality that was understood immediately in Rome. Since that time, Caesar has not dropped from the discourse of political theory or of political polemic.

Caesar and Roman Society: A Very Brief Introduction

Inasmuch as what follows is not a biography of Caesar, it will be useful to offer here a very concise summation of Caesar's life and career, if only to give us a framework on which to hang the chapters to come. Specifics and their dates are recapitulated, in tabular form, at the end of this book. I should also explain a few of the more conspicuous peculiarities of Roman culture that will recur in almost every chapter. The most obvious of these is that the Romans employed Latin (and Greek): exhibits of either language are translated whenever they are alien to our own usage (and most are listed in the book's index along with any other technical terms necessary for describing Roman society). I will not often refer to dates in accordance with Roman practice, the sole exception being the Ides of March, which is simply March fifteenth. More frequently, however, I will discuss money in terms of Roman currency. The Romans in our period, although they employed coins in a variety of weights, tended to rely on the *sesterce* (*sestertius*) as their basic unit of reckoning. It is not really possible to convert ancient currency into modern amounts, owing to the deep differences between their economic systems and our own. For our purposes it will perhaps be enough to observe that in Rome an ordinary laborer could be expected to earn three to six sesterces for a day's effort, on the basis of which income he could only just barely scrape by, that Roman soldiers were paid a salary of 1,200 sesterces each year (of course this does not include their share of the spoils of war and other depredations), that a fortune of 40,000 sesterces sufficed to make one eligible for the First Class in Rome, which comprised Rome's most prosperous citizens, and that the super rich in Rome were the Knights, whose minimal worth was set at 400,000 sesterces (though many were vastly wealthier than that), and the senators, whose wealth was expected to (and regularly did) exceed a million sesterces.

Roman names require some explanation, not simply because their system of nomenclature was different from ours, but also because it was so unimaginative that Romans are easy to confuse (this was true even for the Romans themselves). Every Roman man bore at least two names, his first name (*praenomen*) and the name of his clan (*nomen*). The Romans had very few first names, many of which were simply based on numerals, and so this name was infrequently used on its own (when it was so used, it usually indicated a degree of intimacy). Many Romans also had a third name, called a *cognomen*, some of which were hereditary, others of which were honorific. Unlike the first name, the *cognomen* was often used on its own to indicate a specific Roman. Naturally, there were various protocols for particular situations. In the case of Caesar, his name was Gaius Julius Caesar. We call him Caesar, as did his contemporaries, but his family were the Julii, the Julians. In practice, Romans are sometimes referred to by their *nomen*, sometimes by *cognomen*, sometimes more fulsomely. Some Roman names have been anglicized by custom. Consequently, instead of describing Caesar's great rival as Gnaeus Pompeius we usually refer to him as Pompey, or as Pompey the Great, inasmuch as he immodestly gave himself the *cognomen* Magnus ('the great'). Similarly, Marcus Antonius (who did not have a *cognomen*) is more familiar in English as Mark Antony. Because Roman families recycled the same names, including first names, so routinely, we sometimes distinguish individual Romans by referring to the highest office they reached in politics (e.g. Sextus Julius Caesar (cos. 157) indicates the man who was consul in 157 BC and not any other Sextus Julius Caesar). This is the practice observed in the genealogical tables that appear in this book. Women in Rome generally had only one name, the clan name in its feminine form: consequently, Caesar's daughter was named simply Julia. For the sake of ease and clarity, in the index to this book all Romans are listed both by *nomen* and by their more familiar designation (if they have one): for instance, Marcus Porcius Cato can be found under the heading *Cato* as well as under *Porcius*.

Let me turn now to a very rapid and entirely basic run through Caesar's life. Caesar was born in 100 BC to an ancient patrician family. Romans were unevenly divided between plebeians (the bulk of all Romans) and patricians. In early Rome, the patricians had been a privileged caste. By the late republic, however, although patrician status carried a degree of social cachet, not least because by then there were fewer than twenty patrician families who subsisted, it carried nothing like its original importance. More important, as we shall see, was *nobility*, descent (and especially recent descent) from a forebear who had won the consulship, Rome's highest magistracy. This was a category that included plebeians, and it outshone patrician rank. Caesar's family had in any case not distinguished itself in recent generations. Never the less, as we shall see in the first chapter, Caesar enjoyed important family connections, and they helped to see him through the first great crisis of his life, the civil war between Gaius Marius and Lucius Cornelius Sulla.

Marius, who was Caesar's uncle, was a great military hero. He had triumphed after his victory in North Africa and, far more important, he had saved Italy from invasion by powerful Germanic tribes, in recognition of

Figure 2 Portrait of Pompey, a first century AD copy of an original dating to the fifties BC. Ny Carlsberg Glyptotek, Copenhagen. Photo: Ole Haupt, Ny Carlsberg Glyptotek, Copenhagen.

which he garnered six consulships, an unprecedented achievement and one never replicated in the republic. In the eighties he came into conflict with Sulla, his former lieutenant, which resulted in Rome's first civil war. In the end, Sulla emerged supreme, an outcome that threatened young Caesar, owing to his Marian link, but who was spared on account of the Sullan supporters related to him on his mother's side of the family (we shall return to this in the opening chapter). What needs to be registered here is that Sulla's victory in the first civil war nearly obliterated Marius' memory in Rome. The new establishment comprised Sulla's partisans, men like Lucius Licinius Lucullus, Quintus Lutatius Catulus, Marcus Licinius Crassus (very soon the richest man in Rome) and the youthful Pompey the Great (Fig. 2).

After surviving the civil war, Caesar spent the next decade in typical aristocratic pursuits. He studied in the east, he exerted himself in military service, winning the distinction of a civic crown, and he conducted public prosecutions in Roman courts. In 73 BC he was co-opted as a *pontifex*, a priest in Rome's civic religion, and in 71 BC he was elected to the modest post of military tribune. He reached his first important magistracy, the quaestorship, in 69 BC, which post he filled in Spain. After his return to Rome he became a political supporter of Pompey the Great, then Rome's most distinguished general. At the same time, he established a close political link with Marcus Crassus. Elected an aedile for 65 BC, Caesar produced dazzling public games that won him great popularity even as they plunged him into great personal debt. In 63 BC, to the astonishment of many and to the chagrin of some senior senators, Caesar was elected *pontifex maximus*, the chief of Roman civic religion, a major political coup that marked him out as a man on the rise. He was easily elected praetor for 62 BC, a major post that entailed an independent military command.

Before taking up his magistracy, however, Caesar was involved in the debate surrounding the Catilinarian Conspiracy. In 63 BC, Lucius Sergius Catilina and his followers had plotted to overthrow the government. Their schemes were uncovered by the consul of that year, Marcus Tullius Cicero (Fig. 3), who arrested the remaining coup plotters after Catiline had fled Rome. It was urged by a majority in the senate that these men be executed without trial, a resolution that Cicero enacted. Caesar alone spoke against this action, which was of questionable legality, and his speech left him susceptible to the (false) imputation that he had been involved with Catiline. In the next year, while praetor, Caesar cooperated in a vain attempt to have Pompey recalled from the east to defeat Catiline, who remained in the field. This affair turned violent and Caesar was temporarily suspended from his office, until he yielded and let himself be reconciled with the senate. In the same year there was a public scandal in his own home, the official residence of the *pontifex maximus*, which added to his difficulties. He suffered the further indignity of being harassed by his creditors, which necessitated Caesar's further obligation to Crassus, who covered his enormous debts.

In 61 BC Caesar governed the province of Further Spain, where he waged unprovoked war on local tribes in an attempt to secure enough in the way of spoils to restore his solvency and to acquire a reputation for military glory sufficient to merit a triumph. He returned to Rome in 60 BC, where he applied to the senate for a triumph and prepared to stand for the consulship. Although his hope of celebrating a triumph was frustrated, Caesar succeeded in winning election to the consulship for 59 BC. Now a leading figure in his own right, Caesar capitalized on the political needs of both

Figure 3 Portrait of Cicero, an imperial copy of a late republican original. Musei Capitolini, Rome, Italy. Photo: Bilderarchiv Preussischer Kulturbesitz/Art Resource, NY.

Crassus and Pompey (who disliked one another) and on his own friendship with each of them to forge an alliance known to modern scholars as the First Triumvirate. The resources of the three, in terms of status, wealth, adherents and, in Caesar's case, executive power, rendered them a formidable combination.

As consul, Caesar exerted himself to secure legislation that would satisfy his allies, but he could succeed in doing so only by resorting to shocking domestic violence, which soon made the triumvirs unpopular, with all Romans but especially with the Roman nobility, whose obstructions Caesar had simply steamrollered. Consequently, he remained hated by the likes of Marcus Porcius Cato (Fig. 4), Marcus Calpurnius Bibulus and Domitius Ahenobarbus, a powerful group regularly referred to by modern historians as the *optimates* ('the best men'). At the same time, and before any optimate backlash was possible, Caesar secured the passage of a law that made him

Figure 4 Portrait of Cato in bronze, from the 1st century AD. Galleria Nazionale d'Arte Moderna, Rome, Italy. Photo: Erich Lessing/Art Resource, NY.

proconsul for five years of Illyricum and Cisapline Gaul, to which province Transalpine Gaul was soon added.

For the next ten years Caesar remained in Gaul as its Roman governor (in 55 BC Caesar's tenure was extended for a second five-year period). During this time he conquered the whole of the Gallic territories and introduced Roman armies into Britain and Germany. In the meantime, by way of his allies and other political connections, he remained an important factor in the affairs of the city. Caesar's victories in Gaul made him rich and brought him an abundance of military glory, all of which made him more dangerous in the eyes of his political opponents. Roman politics during the fifties were especially violent and the city was racked by riots and the occasional breakdown of government. In 54 BC, Crassus perished while invading the kingdom of Parthia, a loss that could not fail to affect the dynamics of Caesar's continued alliance with Pompey. Their relationship was further altered when, in 52 BC and in reaction to frightening perturbations in Rome, the senate turned to Pompey to rescue the city. At the urging of the *optimates*, Pompey was appointed sole consul of Rome, an unprecedented honor, which he followed up with the rapid restoration of law and order. Subsequently, Pompey, although he in no way cut his ties to Caesar, began to associate himself more readily with the *optimates*, who were looking for ways in which they might recall Caesar from Gaul and frustrate his expectations of triumph and of a second consulship.

The years 51 BC through 49 BC witnessed a complex sequence of political maneuvers on the part of the *optimates*, of Pompey and of Caesar, all employing the threat of civil war in order to suppress the aspirations of their rivals. In the end, Caesar invaded Italy in an illegal pre-emptive strike. This action precipitated civil war, between Caesar and the followers of Pompey, who now included the *optimates*. This war was waged throughout the Roman world. For the remainder of the year Caesar fought against the Pompeians in Spain. In 48 BC the theater was shifted to Greece, where Pompey was defeated at the Battle of Pharsalus. He then fled to Egypt, where he was assassinated. Soon afterwards Caesar arrived in Alexandria, placed Cleopatra on the Egyptian throne, then proceeded to guarantee the security of the east, most famously by defeating the eastern potentate Pharnaces II at Zela, the occasion of his boast, *veni, vidi, vici* ('I came, I saw, I conquered'). Republican resistance persisted, however. In 46 BC Caesar campaigned in Africa, winning victory at the Battle of Thapsus, a loss that prompted Cato to commit suicide rather than surrender to his enemy. Finally, in 45 BC, at the Battle of Munda, in Spain, a contest that Caesar very nearly lost, the bulk of the remaining republican forces was annihilated.

Throughout the years 49 BC until his death in 44 BC Caesar made himself master of the Roman state. He consistently held the offices of consul and of dictator, and he gathered into his own hands almost absolute power, which he deployed in an attempt to resolve many of the social crises that had come to plague Rome in the late fifties and during the civil war. Examples include Caesar's efforts to solve the crushing problem of Roman indebtedness and his correction of the hopelessly out of season Roman calendar, thus bequeathing to Europe the Julian calendar that is more or less the one employed today. But Caesar gave no sign that he intended ever to resign his powers, even after restoring order and stability. He accumulated privileges on an enormous scale, even allowing himself to receive divine honors, and he openly paraded his superlative status with little sensitivity to the reaction of the senatorial order. In 44 BC, at which time he was preparing a large-scale military expedition against the Parthians, he proclaimed himself dictator for life. In March of the same year he was assassinated, by the very men who had put him in power.

After Caesar's death Rome was again plunged into brief civil war, from which three men emerged, each with a share in supreme power: Mark Antony, Marcus Lepidus and Gaius Octavius, Caesar's great-nephew and heir, who assumed Caesar's name, becoming Gaius Julius Caesar Octavianus. This was the Second Triumvirate, which governed Rome for more than a decade. Soon Lepidus was dropped, and eventually the new Caesar and Mark Antony fought a final civil war that was settled at the Battle of Actium in 31 BC. Victorious, Caesar imitated his namesake in seizing sole power but soon proved that he could exercise it with greater skill than his predecessor. His success was facilitated by the fact that the Romans were exhausted by so many years of civil strife and had been tamed by so many years of autocratic government. A grateful Rome accepted its deliverance and named its new master Augustus Caesar. Augustus boasted that he restored the republic, but in actuality he ushered in a new era, the Roman empire, and in so doing brought the Romans a lasting domestic peace. Not until AD 69 would they return to the habit of civil war.

How Do We Know Any of This?

The chapters in this book originated in a series of public lectures, the De Carle Lectures, which I delivered at the University of Otago in 2005. They have been somewhat revised: most of the jokes, tasteless and topical alike, have been removed, as have references so local to New Zealand that their effect in this context would be to obscure rather than to clarify. Still, the (perhaps too) rambling quality of each lecture persists. And each chapter remains unencumbered by scholarly apparatus like footnotes or citations. Which means that, despite the qualified or controversial status of the research lying behind my assertions, the reader is more or less forced to take my word for it – unless she or he wishes to dig a little more deeply, additional study which I hope to stimulate by appending to each chapter a very brief list of texts for further reading. Professional classicists will of course recognize at once how extensively I have relied on the erudition of others.

In all candor, the reader must remain aware that much of what we believe we know about the first century BC can only ever be tentative and even speculative. Our principal sources – be they literary or documentary or archeological – present profound difficulties of interpretation and, in any case, are severely exiguous. The gaps in our knowledge are extensive and, in many instances, unrestorable. This is not a condition that prohibits genuine scholarly progress. But it does require a high degree of caution, few expressions of which will actually appear in the chapters to follow.

By the standards of ancient historians, however, the age of Caesar is unusually well documented. Inscriptions and coins, for instance, convey the texts (always fragmentary) of decrees and legislation, information about identities and careers, clues regarding chronology and architecture and even topography, along with evidence for the imagery and slogans of propaganda and civic self-fashioning. Our most vital sources, of course, are literary texts, which for this period are diverse and abundant (again, these terms can only be employed in a qualified sense). We possess contemporary histories, orations, correspondence, essays and even verse. Every scrap of information from these writings is precious and can only be retrieved by way of close readings that appreciate the bias – and respect the genius – of their creators. It must not be forgotten that the writers we refer to as our primary sources were clever men with their own points to press: they are not *authorities* but rather authors who must be interrogated.

First amongst contemporary authors is Caesar himself. Of all his literary productions – the versatile Caesar even composed a treatise on grammar and diction – two, and these two the most important, remain, the *Gallic War* and the *Civil War*, each left incomplete at the time of his death. The former is an extensive and detailed narrative of Caesar's campaigns down to 52 BC, the latter an apologetic account of the civil war from 50 BC until it breaks off in 48 BC, when Caesar is involved in Egyptian affairs. One of Caesar's lieutenants, Aulus Hirtius, who later became consul in 43 BC, wrote a continuation of the *Gallic War* that bridged the gap between it and the *Civil War*. He is also the likely author of a continuation of the *Civil War* that extends the narrative of Caesar's eastern campaigns to their conclusion (the *Alexandrian War*). Two more authors, who remain unknown, added two further works to Caesar's histories – the *African War*, covering 47–46 BC, and the *Spanish War*, dealing with 46–45 BC. Caesar's narrative is elegant, remarkable for constantly treating its author as simply another character (though by far the most impressive one) in the story, and extremely tendentious. Still, it offers us the authentic voice of Caesar himself.

Another contemporary is Sallust (Gaius Sallustius Crispus), himself a follower and admirer of Caesar, but hardly an uncritical one. In his *Catilinarian War*, composed after Caesar's death, Sallust includes, along with his account of Caesar's role in this episode, an extensive character study-cum-assessment of Caesar and of his enemy, Cato, each of whom is deemed the epitome of excellence, a treatment so ostensibly and unnaturally balanced that it remains perplexing. A blunter appraisal of Caesar can be found in the poems of Catullus (Gaius Valerius Catullus), a brilliant young equestrian from Verona in the province of Cisalpine Gaul. During the fifties, Catullus so excoriated Caesar's lack of integrity in private and in public life, in verses at once learned and obscene, that his victim feared they would prove an indelible stain on his reputation (such was the power of poetry in a different age, though it is perhaps worth observing that history has proved Caesar right in this matter). Consequently Caesar put pressure on the poet's father, whose estates after all were located in the very province over which Caesar exercised proconsular authority. The result of this exertion was public reconciliation that obliged Catullus to find other subjects for his acid pen.

Our single most influential informant for this period is unquestionably Cicero (Marcus Tullius Cicero). Cicero's was a profound talent: he was a skillful and successful politician, the best orator in Rome, a superb literary stylist and an intellectual of prodigious capacity and energy. His speeches let us grasp the tenor of Roman political discourse in the senate, in the assemblies and in the courts. His essays cover subjects like rhetorical theory, constitutional law, civic religion and moral philosophy. And, most treasured of all, are his letters. Because anything written by Cicero became an instant classic (his literary genius was recognized in his own lifetime – not least by Cicero himself), his correspondence was preserved, edited and ultimately released (after his death) to an adoring and inquisitive readership, thereby initiating a category of publication that persists to this day. Not everything survives – far from it, alas – but we have a large selection of Cicero's letters to his closest friend, Atticus, as well as letters to Cicero's family and to a range of his associates – including Caesar. A few letters from these correspondents (again including Caesar) are transmitted to us along with Cicero's. All of these letters are immensely informative. They allow us to observe Cicero (and occasionally his contemporaries) in moments of embarrassment, hypocrisy, dishonesty, fear and resentment, all of which tells us a lot about this single man, but also a lot about his society and its inclinations. For brief periods these letters exist in such quantities that we can recover an almost daily account of Cicero's view of events. Especially valuable for our purposes is his exchange of letters with Marcus Caelius Rufus (a witty and perceptive younger senator, a fine orator, and, like Caesar, a victim of Catullus' invective) during the months leading to the outbreak of civil war. It can only appear ungrateful to observe that the sheer bulk and quality of Cicero's writings constitute something of a mixed blessing. It is all too easy for us to confuse Cicero's attitudes and opinions for the standard or typical Roman perspective, to forget that his is a single and often a contested point of view (again, he is an informant and not an authority who cannot be queried). This happens, of course, because Cicero is consistently so convincing: it was ever his desire to persuade not merely his contemporaries but also posterity to trust him to be sound and correct. More often than not he succeeds, which is why we so often must make an effort to read *through* Cicero to get at the views and even the facts he wishes to distort or eclipse.

Amongst our most useful accounts of Caesar's career are those of later writers – still ancient, to be sure, but separated from the events they describe by decades and sometimes even by centuries. Velleius Paterculus was an officer and a senator during the reigns of Augustus and Tiberius. His brief, one might say skimpy, history of Rome devotes a disproportionate share of its space to Caesar, Augustus and (naturally) Tiberius, sometimes reporting facts not known from elsewhere. Far more informative, however, are the biographers Suetonius (Gaius Suetonius Tranquillus) and Plutarch, rough contemporaries writing in the early second century of our era. Suetonius was an equestrian active in the administration of Trajan and Hadrian, whereas Plutarch was a Greek intellectual from Chaeronea, a priest at Delphi, and a Greek connection to several distinguished Roman senators (he was also a Roman citizen, whose Latinized name was Lucius Mestrius Plutarchus). Each composed a full-scale biography of Caesar, with remarkably different literary results, but regularly reporting corroborating or complementary information (Suetonius had access to official sources that were unavailable to Plutarch, for whom the particularities of Roman politics are sometimes unclear). Even later than these are the narrative histories of Appian, an Alexandrian Greek of the second century whose career in Rome as an advocate enabled him to retire to historical composition, and of Cassius Dio, a Greek senator who was consul with the emperor Severus Alexander in AD 229. Dio's history, not all of which is preserved, is extant for the period of Caesar's career: its author was an intelligent student of the late Roman republic and the product of his labors is detailed, often confused – and invaluable. Plutarch, Appian and Dio make clear the Roman historian's debt to Greek writers.

It is obvious to us from these later accounts how many more sources were available to them than remain for us. One example is Gaius Asinius

Pollio. Pollio fought alongside Caesar in the civil war, supported Mark Antony after Caesar's assassination and rose to become consul in 40 BC. In the subsequent year he celebrated a triumph, after which he retired from politics and devoted himself to literary pursuits, becoming a distinguished historian and poet. In his youth he knew Catullus, and in his senior years he was well acquainted with Horace and Virgil (he appears in the poetry of each). Pollio was especially highly regarded for his history of the period from 60 BC to 42 BC (the creation of the First Triumvirate to the Battle of Philippi). This work was the product of independent judgment – Pollio had a low opinion of the veracity of Caesar's *Civil War* and never bothered himself with trying to satisfy the political sensibilities of Augustus. This work was exploited by Plutarch and by Appian, and its loss is extremely unfortunate. That Pollio and other lost works appealed to later writers enhances the value of these same later writers for our own historical research. We are not, alas, always or even often in a position to assess how competently later writers put their own historical resources to work in their efforts to recover what was by then *their* past. Which obliges us to use an author like Cassius Dio or Plutarch with an additional layer of care: not only can these writers be willfully grinding an ax, but they can, even with the best of intentions, make blunders that are far from easy for us to diagnose.

In the chapters that follow I will not cite ancient authors (or other ancient documents) by chapter and verse, though I will regularly refer to them and often quote them (and, naturally, I will *rely* on them constantly). The curious reader can easily find excellent and annotated English translations of these writers in series like Oxford World Classics or Penguin Classics. An exception, for our period, is Cassius Dio, though he (like the others) can be read by way of the Loeb Classical Library of Harvard University Press. These volumes include Greek and Latin texts along with an accompanying English translation.

Further Reading

Excellent introductions to almost every aspect of late republican history and society can be found in Flower 2004 and Rosenstein and Morstein-Marx 2006. Denser and more thorough coverage is provided by Crook, Lintott and Rawson 1994. The most readable narrative of the fall of the republic and the establishment of the Augustan age remains Syme 1939, even if the book assumes a good deal of familiarity with the facts on the part of its reader. The influence of Caesar on art and political polemic, from antiquity to the present, is explored in knowledgeable and accessible terms in Wyke 2006. The methods, historical and literary alike, of ancient historical writers are examined in Marincola 2007. Recent and excellent studies of Caesar's writings include Welch and Powell 1998, Batstone and Damon 2006, and Riggsby 2006.

1

Caesar the Politician: Power and the People in Republican Rome

Of the many antique representations of Caesar that we possess, none is more familiar than the (very likely contemporary) portrait now residing in the Castello d'Aglie in Turin (Fig. 5). Middle aged, and showing the wear, but still chillingly handsome, this Caesar gazes at us in an expression that for some, like the young officer who composed the *African War*, was a look radiating energy and confident bonhomie. This was plainly not, however, the view of men whose sensibilities were less assured or more prone to jealousy – like the spirits of Marcus Porcius Cato or Cassius Longinus – to whom Caesar could only appear sardonic, contemptuous – and gloating. Which in turn left them feeling despised and despicable. Which is why they hated him, struggled against him and, ultimately, knifed him to death. The face itself will not give us the means to judge between these competing perceptions. Indeed, the ambiguity of this Caesar's visage, like the controversies attending his reputation, is provoking, and it remains sufficiently perplexing to induce a good deal of squirming in the soul of any modern student of the late Roman republic and the age of Caesar.

Not that past historians have registered many doubts. For them, Caesar was very much one thing or the other. From the moment of his death, he became a symbol. To the mob, he was their idol, literally, inasmuch as they began to worship him as a god. For the troops, he was their peerless leader. Amongst the political classes, he was now a concept to be deployed or to be reckoned with, be he tyrant or liberator or benefactor. And this engagement with the significance of Caesar was hardly limited to antiquity. In the Middle Ages, he was simply synonymous with empire, whereas, in the Renaissance, owing to the recovery of classical literature and its detailed portrait of late republican society, he emerged as a personality. As the man and his age became more intimately known, Caesar became complex as well as great. He appeared a man of decisive action, a brilliant soldier, a

18

Figure 5 Caesar, a contemporary portrait. Castello d'Aglie, Turin, Italy. Photo: Koppermann, Neg. D-DAI-Rom 1965.1111.

ruthless conqueror, a politician of Machiavellian proportions, and a statesman of historic stature. His clemency, his erudition, his love affairs – here was inspiration for prince and poet alike. But there were unavoidable blemishes. The sheer scale of the historical Caesar's violence (his battles cost the lives of more than a million men), as well as his unrepublican tyranny, could only disturb the most sensitive minds of the Enlightenment. Goethe, to take a single instance, found Caesar repellent. He was no more attractive to the authors of the French Revolution, who found inspiration not in Caesar but in Spartacus, though Napoleon I thought otherwise, as did III, and Caesar's place in the symbolism of twentieth-century totalitarianism is too well known to require rehearsal here.

On the topic of Caesar, historians remain disputatious. For the greatest of all historians of Rome, Theodore Mommsen, the only classicist to win the Nobel Prize, Caesar was the culmination of Roman history, in his words, "the sole creative genius produced by Rome, and the last produced by the ancient world." For Mommsen Caesar's every action, even in his youth, was calculated to raise himself to a station wherein he could rescue the destiny of Rome and of posterity. He united Greece with Rome, East with West, "he worked and created as never any mortal did before or after him." Even for those who condemned the Roman, he remained a figure far larger than life. In 1901, to cite a single instance, Guglielmo Ferrero, though he acknowledged Caesar's talents, described him as no statesman but rather "a great destroyer," indeed, "the archdestroyer." The controversy persists, though admittedly in this century, like the last one, it is the good Caesar who seems regularly to get the better of the dark one.

To no small extent this reflects the dominant position of Mommsen amongst all Roman historians, but it is also an effect of the most important and influential of modern biographies of Caesar, *Caesar: Politician and Statesman*, by Matthias Gelzer, first published in German in 1912, the English translation of which remains the standard account in our language. Gelzer's admiration for his subject, although less hyperbolic than Mommsen's, is never the less as unmistakable as it is unapologetic. This enthusiasm is shared by Christian Meier in his own massive contribution to Caesarian biography, which first appeared in 1982. Meier sees Caesar differently from his predecessors, however. In his telling of the story, the decline of the Roman republic was a process that generated *Outsiders*, none of whom brought a solution to the republic's ills, but each of whom reacted against the baleful dimensions of the system into which they refused to be integrated. Caesar was the supreme Outsider, who not only despised the republic but struggled to replace it – with Himself. For Meier, it is impossible to think of Caesar as a "mere desperado." He remains a colossus of world-historical proportions. Not that I want to give the impression that every continental historian has felt obliged to write about Caesar in characters so large and so cosmic. Herman Strasburger, who has written more than one good book about Caesar, remains unswayed by the legendary properties of his subject.

The urgency of this debate has generally been lost amongst Anglophone historians, who are mostly suspicious of ideological controversies and who tend to reject the very possibility of principled motives on the part of any ancient Roman inhabiting the late republic. We tend to view all politics, clearly if simple-mindedly, as sharp practice, it being assumed that no politician ever says what he really believes not least because he doesn't actually believe in anything. The approach possesses an obvious appeal. However, it often results in a "just-the-facts-ma'am" approach to the past.

J.P.V.D Balsdon's elegant and readable biography includes next to no discussion of Caesar's character or historical significance. The tale having been told, it is enough to observe that "his achievement was secure," by which Balsdon means mainly Caesar's conquest of Gaul. As to world-order, Caesar seemed ready enough to sweep aside the republic owing to its hampering uselessness, but, in the event, he mattered mostly because his career and its failures paved the way for Augustus. Similar sentiments pervade the recent and detailed view of Caesar's life by Adrian Goldsworthy. Again Caesar's attractions lie in the actions themselves: "few fictional heroes have ever done as much as Caius Julius Caesar." Indeed, "it is hard to imagine that in any way his life could have been more dramatic." Although Goldsworthy suffers from no illusions where Caesar's foibles are concerned, Caesar none the less emerges as "a patriot and a very able man" who "used victory for a wider good as well as his own." Even in the Anglophone tradition, then, after the ripping yarn has been retailed and the puzzles of the evidence have been satisfactorily solved, when it comes time to take in the larger picture, it is usually regarded as a good thing that the outmoded practices of the republic gave way under Caesar's pressure to the orderliness of the empire. This is regularly made clear to pupils. As H.H. Scullard put it in 1959, in what is still a standard university textbook on Roman history, "The days of the city-state were over. That Caesar's mind must have been moving toward monarchy as the only practical solution of the constitutional problem is obvious enough. But an outraged group of nobles prevented Caesar from revealing to the world the solution." This sounds a tad eerie nowadays. But you shouldn't suppose that British dons of the second half of the twentieth century were keen on autocracy. They just thought it was good enough for Italians and other Mediterranean types.

In this chapter I want to look at Caesar before he became a Great Man, when he remained at the early stages of his ultimately brilliant career and when it was by no means a certainty that he would manage to avoid failure or even to attain to mediocrity. These were the necessary, and in no respect automatic, phases through which any ambitious Roman was obliged to pass in his rise from office to office, all in the hope, for the most successful of the lot, of reaching Rome's highest and most splendid magistracy, the consulship. It was Caesar's accomplishment at this more or less mundane level, after all, that made possible his final elevation to superhuman status, be it good or terrible, which means that our understanding both of the man and of his historical moment requires an appreciation of the system in which he, despite the odds, made it – not yet to the top, but instead to his place amongst the other winners at the top reaches of Rome's political design.

21

In Rome a citizen's status, determined by a combination of his wealth and his reputation, was publicly proclaimed, and frequently contested, every five years, during the census, which means that everybody knew his place. The Roman hierarchy was unsubtle and transparent. At its top were the senatorial families, of which there were only a few hundred. The senators were rich men who had won their position by election to a high public office – the quaestorship – and who remained in public service as privileged advisors to Rome's magistrates and to the Roman people. The most energetic and capable of senators endeavored to rise to higher offices – the aedileship, the praetorship and, the final object of their career, the consulship. Of even the most able of senators, most would fail in the pursuit of the consulship (there were only two consuls in each year). Never the less, all senators had in common their tenure of a significant magistracy, the Latin word for which is *honor*, which will give you a hint of their attitude toward the electorate – and toward one another.

Below the senators were the *equites*, the knights, also very rich. A few equestrian types plunged into senatorial politics. Such a senator was called a new man, and his intrusion into higher offices could be resented by the senate and by the general public alike (who tended to believe that there was a place for everyone and that everyone should remain in his place). The bulk of the equestrian order, true to this principle, remained unwilling or unable to endure the costs or the exertions associated with sustaining a political career. The knights sought dignity, to be sure, and many of them sought profits. Although there was little, and in many instances nothing at all, to distinguish the wealth or the culture or the patriotism of a senator from an equestrian, in every instance, on account of the senators' lifelong commitment to public service, the equestrian order conceded the superior majesty of the senatorial order. After the knights came our aforementioned First Class (in whose number senators technically belonged), followed, in the typically imaginative Roman fashion, by the Second, Third, Fourth and Fifth Classes. At the bottom were the *proletarii*, quite literally 'the baby-makers', too poor to offer society any other contribution.

By the first century BC, according to Cicero and to Dionysius of Halicarnassus, each of whom was an eye witness to the Roman assemblies in action, the lowest classes greatly outnumbered the higher ones (the First and Second Classes). The Roman multitude was a multitude of have-nots. At this point, it is perhaps worth observing that the city of Rome did not have a police force, even a tiny one. Nor were Roman citizens permitted to bear arms within the city. Nor, despite the impression made by Hollywood films, were soldiers allowed, except under very specific conditions, to enter the city under arms. For me this is beyond question the most amazing thing about Rome. How could a city of perhaps a million inhabitants, most of them poor, manage without a well-equipped police force? Or at least a robust interpretation of the Second Amendment? In America, after all, we have to hire people and give them guns and insist that they shoot us in order to keep us from breaking the law. If you could eliminate the police from my home town and could assure me that my neighbors are unarmed (I *do* live in the USA after all), then I can promise you that I should possess a much nicer television and drive an infinitely more elegant car than is now the case.

So why, you are asking, did the poor not simply rise up, seize the wealth and keep it for themselves, not least in a society where swords constituted the cutting edge of weapons technology and in which there was, in any case, no police force to suppress the revolution? The answer is not merely bread and circuses, though the idea lying behind that expression is undoubtedly a part of it. Instead, we need very briefly to take up three gross but very useful over-generalizations about the Romans. Say what you will, gross over-generalizations are crucial for learning about other societies, and, in the tradition of their manufacture, I shall give you three of them.

First, Romans prized conformity. It was regarded as positively wicked to be different from everyone else. That was a situation crying out for *invidia*, the evil-eye, jealousy, hatred. In the Romans' mentality, consensus, pure and simple, was on its own a powerful argument for the veracity of any proposition. The lone voice, by contrast, was suspicious, and potentially dangerous. Now I don't want to push this too far. Just as we in modern societies value our commitment to individuality, we tend all of us to want to be individuals *together*. Amongst ourselves there is not in practice a significant degree of diversity in houses, cars, attitudes toward private property or fashion (most men still go to the office in jackets and ties and not in ball gowns). Likewise the Romans were not clones of one another, but they valued their tendency toward conformity, not least because it promoted social stability.

It was also instinctive for Romans, and this is my second gross over-generalization, to be deferential. Plainly this quality is not unrelated to conformity. Romans tended to do what they were told, when told to do it by someone in authority. This is the very opposite of our natural response (though, in reality, we usually *do* do what we're told, unless we can get away with it). For the Romans, this inclination toward deference was a source of strength. It was why, amongst other things, they made such good soldiers.

Finally, then, we come to over-generalization number three: Romans were devoted to tradition, to *mos maiorum*, the custom of their ancestors.

For the Romans, all actions, including all innovations, must not merely defer to the manners and institutions of the past, they must actually be formulated as continuations or recoveries from the past. In Latin, *new* is something of a bad word. A new man was an oddball likely to attract *invidia*. *Res novae*, new things, signalized revolution in its scariest configuration. Again, the difference between them and ourselves becomes patent.

These principles can be seen in action in the Romans' own appreciation of their past. It is not insignificant that, when debating current affairs or seeking moral or political guidance, the Romans relied on exemplars from their national history. Roman heroes, not unnaturally, set the pattern for Roman excellence. One such celebrated model, from Rome's earliest history, was Titus Manlius Torquatus, three times consul, three times dictator, victor in a celebrated single combat against a gigantic Gaul, and triumphant general. During his third consulship, when Rome was at war with the Latins, Torquatus gave the order that no Roman should leave his post for any reason whatsoever. His own son, however, replicating his father's valor, left the ranks and defeated an enemy commander, again in single combat. For this violation of military discipline – what we should call this display of initiative – Torquatus ordered his son put to death, as a grim but salutary example for posterity. Here we see conformity, deference and tradition in earnest action. And for this unattractive demonstration of Roman constancy, Torquatus was celebrated in prose and in poetry, from the epic of Ennius to Horace's odes. Now one can learn a lot about a society from an examination of their heroes. The Romans did not lionize mavericks or revolutionaries or eccentrics. With unforgiving severity they prized men who kept intact the existing order. *Status quo* is a Latin expression, and that's no accident.

The Romans' habits of thought and action were inculcated and preserved in the basic forms of intercourse between the elite and the many. It was built into the regular routines of the urban poor, for instance, to visit and to seek material assistance from the powerful: the lowly Roman had his patron, and he could also seek aid from any grandee to whom he could find access. The most common circumstance for this was the morning greeting, the *salutatio*, when modest Romans would gather, before the first hour of the day, in the atrium of a great man's mansion (the homes of the elite, remarkably enough, were regularly kept open). There they awaited the appearance of their patron, who, after revealing himself, would wait to be greeted by his inferiors, who took their turn addressing him as *dominus*, seeking his advice and, especially, his aid – in exchange for which he was entitled to expect their gratitude, which was best delivered in the shape of energetic and loyal submissiveness. The mansions of the great were monumental, and the scale and decoration of an atrium, filled with family trophies and representations of one's ancestors, each annotated with a resumé of his offices and glories, all combined to make a poor citizen feel very small indeed. He was inferior – that was the inescapable message – and he should count himself lucky to be received and supported, in however so modest a fashion, by a patron who was so magnificent.

This relationship was sustained in elections. Because Roman magistrates held office for one year only, elections were annual events, one result of which is that political campaigning was an almost constant activity. Candidates began their canvassing often more than a year in advance of standing, and it was essential for any successful campaign that a candidate demonstrate his popularity with Romans of all classes. After all, would-be magistrates had to persuade elite voters that they enjoyed the esteem of the masses (if only in order to perpetuate the deference that kept the public in line), so long as they could do so without matching the profile of a rabble-rouser. In order to beat their competitors, candidates plied voters of all classes with games, with presents, with banquets and with outright gifts of money – all in exchange for their votes but just as importantly, since the votes of the poor literally counted for less than the votes of the rich in the Roman constitution, for their attendance. Patronage and political campaigns rewarded deference, even as they inhibited the electorate from assuming a collective identity: patrons and candidates interacted with and helped *individuals* or, at most, small groups. The masses, then, were cultivated by an elite who offered them favors, designed to prompt personal gratitude, the exchange of which, by constant experience, enacted and enforced the inferiority of the people.

The people at least had the moral consolation of knowing that, in their assemblies, they were sovereign. In Rome, all offices – all honors – were dispensed by the people, and all legislation had to be passed in the assemblies. And yet in these undertakings the people were led by their magistrates and guided by the senate. No assembly could act without a magistrate's summons – as you might by now expect, grass root initiatives were not fostered in the Roman republic – nor could the senate convene on its own authority. Roman magistrates acted as military and judicial officers, and they managed the very limited government that Romans regarded as necessary to a free state. They did so without salary and at considerable personal expense. In fact, Roman senators were expected to lavish their own wealth on the community: this was the price of their superior honor. Aediles, for example, who were responsible for the celebration of public festivals and for repairing the fabric of the city, routinely reached into their own wallets to pay for whatever that the state could not or would not afford. Magistrates possessed important legal powers, but in applying them they regularly heeded the instructions of the senate, the body of ex-magistrates whose collective wisdom and authority gave direction to the whole of the republic. For its part, the senate could neither legislate nor issue executive commands. In reality, however, an advisory decree from the senate – a *senatus consultum* – was freighted with so much majesty and clout that one could by no means ignore it with impunity.

In the *res publica*, literally "the public thing," all citizens had a share, but not an equal share. One's standing was determined by the extent of one's individual contribution to the community of all Romans. Senators gave the most, so everyone agreed. Consequently, they got the most. Hence they could describe themselves as *boni*, good men, or *optimates*, *really* good men. Still, it was obligatory for them to give the people their due. The rights of the people and the sovereignty of the assemblies were essential, if frequently contested, principles, and no aristocrat could neglect them. There was even a responsibility to observe these rights and to go so far as to attend to the necessities of the ordinary populace. As Disraeli put in a different time but in a similar context, "the people have their passions and it is even the duty of public men occasionally to adopt sentiments with which they do not agree, because the people must have their leaders." Politicians who tended to endorse popular rights were often denominated *populares*, whereas champions of senatorial prestige conceived of themselves as *optimates*.

These, then, were the twin foundations of the *res publica*: the authority of the senate and the power of the people. But it would be a mistake to imagine that Roman politics were dominated by two political parties – the *populares* and the *optimates* – as if these were ancient equivalents of Democrats and Republicans. In fact, Roman politics lacked parties altogether. Individual aristocrats competed for prestige and influence in what all perceived to be a zero-sum game. In certain situations and over certain contested issues, individuals might unite, and needless to say there were always some senators who were like-minded enough to be, in effect, a power block. But this tendency toward *ad hoc* conformations, this makeshift particularity, reflects the Roman norm. These individual struggles for superiority, which were played out within the poorly defined dynamic existing between popular sovereignty and senatorial prestige, yielded in their totality the untidy reality of Rome's unwritten constitution – an amazing construction perhaps best described by filching Edward Bulwer-Lytton's formulation of the British constitution as "that deformed and abortive offspring of perennial political fornication."

The ideal senator, the ideal politician, was the man who knew how to cultivate both constituencies, the masses and the elites. A politician who wielded influence with the people had clout amongst his senatorial peers. A senator who commanded respect amongst the mighty attracted a following amongst the masses. This was the essential basis of *dignitas*, a concept that combined prestige with power. As one ancient writer put it:

> The senate must believe, on the basis of your past conduct, that you will be the guardian of its authority; the Roman knights and the prosperous classes must believe, on account of your past actions, that you will be a supporter of peace and stability; the multitudes must believe, because you have championed their interests, at least in your speeches in public meetings and in court, that you will not be hostile to their entitlements.

The Roman republic, then, was, from the aristocratic perspective at least, an arena for competition the aim of which was to excel all others in preserving the senate's prestige, domestic stability and popular rights – "there honour comes."

Let us turn, then, to the senatorial aristocracy. What did *they* want? For the best of the best – the nobility – we can find the answer in the earliest of extant Roman funerary inscriptions, the epitaphs of the great family of the Cornelii Scipiones. Two specimens, each from the second century BC, will practically speak for themselves:

> Lucius Cornelius Scipio, the son of Gnaeus.

> Lucius Cornelius Scipio Barbatus, begotten by Gnaeus his father, a brave man and an intelligent one, whose physical beauty matched his courage. He was consul, censor and aedile amongst you. He captured Taurasia and Cisauna from the Samnites. He subjugated the whole of Lucania and carried back hostages.

This man's son left behind a similar claim to fame:

> Lucius Cornelius Scipio, the son of Lucius, aedile, consul and censor.

> Everyone agrees that this man was by far the very best of all the good men at Rome. The son of Barbatus, he was consul, censor and aedile amongst you. He captured Corsica and the city of Aleria. He dedicated a temple to the Goddesses of Weather.

27

An obvious pattern emerges, and it is made fulsomely clear in a passage preserved by the elder Pliny that touches upon another noble family:

> Quintus Metellus, in the panegyric that he delivered at the funeral of his father, Lucius Metellus, who had been pontiff, consul twice, dictator, master-of-the-horse, and land-commissioner, and who had celebrated a triumph, left it in writing that his father had achieved the ten greatest objects in pursuit of which wise men devote their lives: he had made it his aim to be the best in war, the best orator, the bravest general, to be in charge of the most important undertakings of the state, to enjoy the highest office [*which also means: "to enjoy the greatest honor"*], to be supremely intelligent, to be deemed the most important member of the senate, to obtain great wealth in an honorable way, to leave many sons and to have gained the greatest glory in the state.

Now while we cannot admire Metellus's lack of neatness in constructing pigeonholes, his speech, along with the Scipionic epitaphs, make it absolutely clear that, for the aristocrat, the purpose of life was to exercise one's superior talents in the service of the state, service actualized in waging war, holding magistracies and directing the senate.

Key to the realization of these ambitions was the office of *consul*, the highest office in the republic. Obtaining the office of consul ennobled a family, and the consular families, the *nobiles*, guarded the office jealously. It was very rare for a non-noble, however well established in the senatorial aristocracy, to attain to the consulship. At the same time, it was imperative for the sons of the nobility that they overcome all obstacles in order to make the grade. Not to do so was a dismal failure and a signal disgrace. Hence the personal intensity of aristocratic politics. And hence the abundance of failure: over the course of the republic, very few families sustained their place in the nobility. Some died out. Some could not preserve the wealth required of an elite senatorial career. Many, however, simply lacked the industry and talent to match the achievement of their fathers. This is why the very few families who endured possessed such formidable prestige, families like the Metelli, the Claudii and the Aurelii Cottae. These families contrasted sharply with flashes in the pan, or with ancient houses fallen into eclipse. One such lapsed family were the Julii Caesares.

We know next to nothing of Caesar's childhood: the biographies of Suetonius and Plutarch are both of them missing their earliest chapters. But the circumstances of Caesar's boyhood are well documented. When he was 12, there occurred the first outbreak of the civil war between Gaius

Marius and Lucius Cornelius Sulla. Marius, a new man, a municipal aristocrat of inconspicuous social standing, had risen to become the greatest general in Roman history. Six times consul (ultimately seven before his death), a record no noble could dream of matching, he had, through his valor and organizational genius, saved Italy from invasion and the senate from revolution. No man was more popular with the common people of the city, all of whom, like their betters, admired military brilliance the way modern types worship stars of pop, film or sport. Sulla, on the other hand, having spent his youth in dissipation, had now, rather late in the day, arrived at the consulship and at his chance for glory. Sulla drove the Marians from Rome, then departed to fight the Mithridatic War in the east. His absence allowed Marius and his ally, Lucius Cornelius Cinna, to become masters of the city. This was the state of affairs when young Caesar emerges into the historical record, at the age of 15, shortly after the sudden death of his father.

Caesar began his career with more than one handicap. Although the records of the fifth and fourth and even third centuries were adorned by the presence of Julii, and the Julii were one of the original patrician families of Rome, the family had, in the intervening years, collapsed. In response to their decline, the Julii had preserved their patrician heritage scrupulously, leveraging their social cachet into profitable alliances with socially ambitious equestrian families. The family remained ambitious. Of Caesar's grandfather we know nothing, save that he married a Marcia, daughter of the ancient house of the Marcii Reges, allegedly descended from the kings of Rome. This marriage produced a son and a daughter, though it is just possible that the consul of 91 BC, Sextus Julius Caesar, was our Caesar's uncle. In any case this man seems to have perished very soon after holding office, and he is never in our sources associated with Caesar or with Caesar's father, who must have seemed a promising fellow. After all, he married an Aurelia, very likely the daughter of Lucius Aurelius Cotta, the consul of 119 BC. His death in 85 BC naturally put an end to his career, but, inasmuch as his praetorship came only in 92 BC, he had already fallen behind. Caesar's aunt, and here we return to the political crisis of Caesar's youth, had been married off to a rich equestrian whom her discriminating father must have realized was a good bet: Gaius Marius. Now Marius died in 86 BC, but Cinna was to remain the master of Rome for several years. Something had to be done about young Caesar, whose aunt and whose mother were too well connected to ignore.

Their solution was a surprising one, and suggestive. It was determined that Caesar should be nominated to fill the vacant priesthood of Jupiter, the office of *flamen Dialis*. Now I should say at once, though we shall deal with this more thoroughly in a subsequent chapter, that priesthoods in Rome typically went to aristocrats with political ambitions. Roman society recognized no barrier between church and state. Quite the contrary. Civic life was suffused with religious observances, and the senate functioned as the ultimate arbiter of religious controversy. Caesar himself, as we shall see, went on to become *pontifex maximus*, and that is undoubtedly the greatest political achievement of his early career. The ancient office of *flamen Dialis*, however, was a vocation of a very different order. The *flamen Dialis* had to be a patrician who was married to a patrician by way of *confarreatio*, an ancient and restrictive species of Roman marriage. Consequently, Caesar, who was engaged to a very rich equestrian named Cossutia, was obliged to break it off. He was then married to Cornelia, the daughter of Cinna. Afterwards, the elaborate process of inaugurating Caesar as *flamen Dialis* could begin. Now this was a dubious honor, to say the least.

It is true that the *flamen Dialis* was automatically entitled to sit in the senate and enjoyed considerable prestige. Never the less, unlike the other priestly offices in Rome, the *flamen* labored under numerous taboos: he could not mount a horse, he could not sleep outside the city for more than three successive nights, he could not gaze upon a corpse, he could not view an army drawn up in battle formation. In other words, he could not have a military career, a condition that was anathema to any ambitious Roman politician. Still, this post, necessary for Roman religion, also had an obvious social use: it was a natural repository for well-born losers. For example, the son of the great Scipio Africanus, the conqueror of Hannibal, was a weakling. Because he was anointed *flamen Dialis*, however, he was thereby able to sustain the family's prestige and to evade the complaint that he lacked the merits of his father. Appointments on these terms seem to have been fairly commonplace. Which raises the question: why Caesar? Modern historians tend toward two explanations: either to shield him from the dangers of these turbulent times (though it is worth noticing that the post had become vacant in the first place because its holder had committed suicide) or because, *from the very beginning*, Caesar's menace to the republic could be discerned. And as to the taboos, Gelzer's verdict is typical: "later he surely would have found a way round these obstacles." This, however, is to invoke super-Caesar, and demonstrates the peril of retrospection.

But a more obvious answer suggests itself. This must have been judged the best Caesar was likely to do. If Caesar's epilepsy had begun to manifest itself during his teenaged years, and epilepsy was a disease that frightened the Romans to the degree that a seizure at an assembly cancelled all public business for that day, his aunt and mother may have despaired of his future. One could add to this the fact that his family's track record had not been that good for centuries. And this is really the point to be emphasized: Caesar did not start out with many advantages – in terms of the aristocratic world in which politics took place. The flaminate, then, was surely seen by Cinna as a plum for his new son-in-law and more than satisfactory for Julia and Aurelia. And it could well have marked the very end of Caesar's career.

Except that Sulla returned, routed his opposition, declared himself dictator and either prevented Caesar's final inauguration or actually stripped him of his flaminate (the priesthood remained unfilled for the remainder of the Roman republic). The new dictator, who purged many of his enemies, offered young Caesar an opportunity for safety – *if* he divorced Cornelia, whose father, by then dead, remained odious to Sulla. Caesar refused, at the risk of his life and at the price of his wife's ample dowry. This, too, is important. Whatever deficiencies Caesar suffered in health, prospects and station, he possessed, and for the whole of his life displayed, abundant physical courage. Sulla had executed hundreds of senators, and thousands of equestrians, and there was no serious stigma attached to divorce in Rome. Sulla was making him an offer he couldn't refuse. None the less, he did. Why one cannot say. It was certainly not an intrinsic hostility toward Sulla, his family or his new regime. As a matter of fact, Caesar immediately placed himself under the command of Sullan officers, and, after Cornelia's death in 69 BC, he married Pompeia, Sulla's grand-daughter. What we can say is that Caesar's apparent loyalty to the cause of Cinna and, especially, to the memory of Marius was to become the vehicle that would carry him to the success so long denied his own family. But we are not there yet.

It is sometimes suggested that Caesar had to flee Rome to escape Sulla's wrath. In fact, however, he joined the military staff of Marcus Minucius Thermus, a staunch Sullan who was proconsul of Asia. At once, Caesar distinguished himself in diplomacy by representing Roman interests in the court of Nicomedes IV Philopater, the king of Bithynia. This cannot but strike us as impressive, but I should add that it was also a perfectly normal activity for a young aristocrat in service abroad, as were Caesar's robust exertions in combat. Here Caesar was a standout. In recognition of his saving the life of a fellow citizen during the final assault on Mytilene, Caesar was awarded the civic crown, a signal distinction. In 78 BC Caesar transferred to Cilicia, where he served under Publius Servilius Vatia, who had been consul in the previous year and was another Sullan ally. What we see here is fairly typical for young men of the aristocratic mold: service abroad in order to demonstrate competence in soldiering and diplomacy under the command of senior figures who, if suitably impressed, can become future supporters. And all of Caesar's activities took place under the auspices of the Sullan establishment.

When Caesar returned to Rome, he immediately tried another traditional tack to a public distinction. He prosecuted, on a charge of extortion, Gnaeus Cornelius Dolabella, consul in 81 BC and a recent *triumphator*. He lost the case, but he published his speeches against the man anyway, in the hope of advertising his rectitude (prosecutions like Caesar's were voluntary actions against corrupt public figures) and to make a lasting display of his eloquence, itself a vital source of political power in Rome. Undaunted by his failure, Caesar went on to prosecute a second noble, although again unsuccessfully. Still, public prosecutions were almost a duty for young men on the make. Not only were they proof of good citizenship, not only did they allow one to demonstrate his oratorical gifts, they also provided a legitimate social and political space in which to make enemies.

Make enemies? The necessity of making friends will be obvious to anyone with a shred of political instinct. But how do enemies fit into it? A Roman's public figure was defined by his accomplishments, his supporters (of whom he should have an abundance), his friends (not *too* many of these because you cannot be a reliable friend to too many people) and his enemies (not too many of these either because you can't hold out against too many enemies). Even today it is difficult to admire someone who has never offended anyone, and in Rome there was no fame to be attached to keeping silent or avoiding conflicts. Powerful enemies, so long as you did not have too many of them, created the impression that you, too, were powerful – what Tacitus called *ipsa inimicitiarum gloria*, the sheer glory of enmities. This mattered in a society in which vengeance was a moral obligation. Sulla's epitaph, as a single illustration, is supposed to have read, "I surpassed all men in doing kindness to my friends, and harm to my enemies." Gentle Romans.

Despite all these efforts, Caesar cannot have been doing very well in terms of public estimation. In 71 BC he reached his first elected post, the office of military tribune. Now in ancient days, the position had mattered quite a lot. By Caesar's time, however, it was useful only for small fry struggling along in the hope of making it into the senate in the first place. Even a new man like Cicero couldn't be bothered. That Caesar deemed it necessary to come before the people in order to acquire this paltry office is nothing short of astonishing.

Why was Caesar not coming along better than he was? It may well have been that his civic crown was small consolation for his failed prosecutions (the Roman public, after all, tended to assume that all aristocrats, civically crowned or not, were valorous). Or it may have been Caesar's lifestyle that others found disturbing. Roman aristocrats of a traditional ilk eschewed fancy clothes and excessive elegance, opting instead for a homelier look, replete with bushy eyebrows and conventional homespun garb – all the better to identify themselves with their unspoiled and unimpeachable ancestors. Caesar, by contrast, was fussy about his appearance. He dressed in swanky, natty clothes that many of his contemporaries found too fine, if not actually a bit effeminate. He also displayed too much care about the looks of his body, plucking hair from here and there, and he was so disturbed by his early baldness that he made it his habit to comb his hair straight down in order to get maximum coverage. He was Rome's first metrosexual. Or maybe not. It was rumored that, while in the court of Nicomedes, Caesar had entered into more than backroom negotiations with this eastern and Greekified monarch. And then there were the women. The man was already notorious as an adulterer. And he lived with this sort of abuse for the whole of his career. Years later, for instance, when Caesar had become a powerful politician, one wit once referred to Pompey as the king of Rome and Caesar as its queen. Again, in a senatorial debate, he was attacked as "every woman's man, and every man's woman." Whatever the reason for Caesar's standing for such a trifling public office as military tribune, joining the ranks of desperate men on the make, it remains all too clear that Caesar was not yet a terrific hit with the Roman public.

His standing was sufficient, however, to elevate him to his first real magistracy (and to win him his ticket into the senate) in 69 BC, when Caesar was elected quaestor at the appropriate age of 30. Given that the Romans elected twenty quaestors each year, this election, although necessary for a senatorial career, was hardly a splendid attainment in itself. The year of Caesar's quaestorhip, however, was truly consequential for the fashioning of his public image and for his subsequent rise in popularity.

It began with the death of his aunt Julia. A woman of her years and standing was entitled to a funerary procession and a public funeral oration. These events were grand affairs that attracted big crowds, which naturally turned them into opportunities to celebrate the rich history of the family whose private loss the Roman public assembled to grieve (Fig. 6). Caesar, who delivered his aunt's funeral oration and who arranged for the procession itself, seized the occasion to add a bold wrinkle to the solemnities. In addition to the trophies and death masks of the Julii, which everyone will

Figure 6 Funerary procession in a relief from Amiternum, 1st century AD. Museo Archeologico Nazionale, Aquileia, Italy. Photo: Alinari/Art Resource, NY.

have expected to see, Caesar added those of his uncle Marius. This proved to be nothing short of sensational. The people were thrilled and delighted to see their champion restored. Taking the cue, when his wife also died later in the same year, Caesar arranged to give her a public funeral as well (something less common for a woman so young, but Caesar knew he was on to a winner), during which her father, Cinna, and by extension Caesar's own association with Marius, were again objects of display and speechification.

Suddenly, Caesar stood for something – not a cause but instead something far more resonant in Roman society, a value. Caesar was emerging as an embodiment of *pietas*, loyalty to one's family, and in this instance not just any family (and not actually Caesar's own family) but *Marius's* family, a move that combined gestures toward two of the Romans' core principles, familial devotion and militarism. Perhaps this young patrician – or so an ordinary Roman, ill-versed in logic, might be forgiven for believing – carried in himself something of the great plebeian's charisma! Hence the tradition of early Marian sympathies and Sullan hostilities. For Caesar, restrospective interpretations of his career began early.

Thereafter a more popular Caesar kept himself before the people to whatever degree that he could manage. He secured the post of curator of the Via Appia, the kind of banal-sounding job that in fact allowed its holder generate lots of benefactions beloved of the people and likely to acquire widespread enthusiasm amongst voters (so Cicero tells us in a letter to his friend Atticus). Furthermore, and more important for enhancing his reputation with the electorate, as aedile Caesar spent a fortune on the public works and the festivities required of that office. Not his own fortune, mind you. He seems to have run through that. The curatorship and the aedileship, done in style, forced Caesar to borrow heavily. During his aedileship he also held, at his own expense (by which of course I mean at his creditors' expense), funeral games in honor of his father's memory, at which he displayed the most fabulous gladiatorial show Rome had yet seen. *Pietas* – and fun for the entire family (one must remember that in Rome public entertainments were free, for the audience at least). Caesar also took advantage of his aedileship to restore all the statues, inscriptions and trophies of his beloved Marius, a gesture that secured his reputation for familial loyalty and cast him as the great man's political heir. By now, Caesar enjoyed massive popularity. It was time for him to take a chance.

In 63 BC the head of public religion in Rome, the *pontifex maximus*, died. His name, by the way, was Metellus Pius, called *Pius* not for his religiosity but for his profound loyalty to his father (*pietas* again). At this point in Rome's history, the high priesthood was an elected office. There were three candidates, two of them ancient and noble ex-consuls, while the third possibility was Caesar. The novelty of Caesar's candidature has been exaggerated by scholars – there are plenty of instances of men becoming high priest before being elected consul – but its sheer boldness has not. By Roman standards his competitors were more deserving, and there was a strong senatorial sentiment that Caesar's bid was presumptuous. Which means there was elite resistance, which forced Caesar to borrow heavily, campaigning with every degree of bribery and favoritism Roman custom would allow. Naturally, he will have pushed his Marian connection very hard. But the race remained close, and it was viewed by Caesar as decisive for his future. When he left his home on the day of the election, he remarked to his mother, "I shall return as *pontifex maximus*, or not at all." He won. It was a sensational outcome and a striking demonstration of the depth of Caesar's personal popularity with Roman voters (Fig. 7).

Figure 7   Obverse of a denarius of 44 BC representing Caesar as *Pontifex Maximus* and as *Parens Patriae* (Father of his Country). British Museum, London, England. Photo: ©The Trustees of the British Museum.

Caesar's family was at once removed to the official residency of the high priest, the *Domus Publica* or People's House, located in the forum, near the Regia (the formal offices of the *pontifex maximus*), and the Atrium of Vesta, the home of the Vestal Virgins – in sum, the religious and political center of the city. Now that was a glamorous address! And with this election Caesar could well believe his future success, his elevation to the consulship, was secured. No *pontifex maximus* in Roman history had failed to gain the office when he stood for it. In this same year, Caesar was (by now unsurprisingly) swept into the praetorship. And when his creditors threatened not to allow him to leave to take up his province in Spain, his bills were paid by the richest man in Rome, Marcus Licinius Crassus, consul in 70 BC. Crassus was an extraordinarily shrewd politician, who knew a good investment when he saw it.

Let me say a little more about this. Indebtedness, in general, is not a good thing, and it especially was not a good thing in Rome. Bankruptcy in Rome meant total and permanent ruin: all of a man's property could be seized and he himself sold into slavery. Anyone who risked disaster on this

scale could only be viewed as dangerous, so desperate must he be to preserve his fortune and public standing. Which is why the accusation of
bankruptcy rubbed shoulders in Roman invective with insults like parricide
or child molester. Nothing could be more wicked. There were, however,
further political dimensions to the matter of Caesar's indebtedness. From
Crassus's perspective, by salvaging Caesar's finances, he had secured himself
a valuable political ally. He could certainly expect this support for a likely
future consul to pay off. From Caesar's point of view, on the other hand,
the sheer extent of his indebtedness to Crassus meant that Crassus must
continue to invest in Caesar's political future – if he ever wanted a proper
return on his money. Caesar was too much in Crassus's debt not to have a
certain hold over the man. Their relationship, born of opportunism, was a
lasting one, and their alliance remained a constant of republican politics
until Crassus' death in 53 BC.

Having alienated the traditionalists in the senate who found his election
as *pontifex maximus* hard to stomach, Caesar wanted to establish strong
political connections with powerful but less hostile figures. In addition to
Crassus, he cultivated the absent but overshadowing Pompey the Great. As
his name suggests, Pompey was the leading man of the day: a brilliant
general, who triumphed before he was even a senator and who was elected
consul (in the same year as Crassus) by special dispensation at an age when
he was legally too young to hold the office. He was now extending Rome's
domination of the east, and, as was regularly the case with glorious generals
in Rome, he was the people's darling. Which meant naturally that the
residue of the oligarchy resented him as much as they feared his singular
stature. Caesar was one of Pompey's earliest advocates in city politics,
despite the fact that Crassus and Pompey loathed one another and although,
by doing so, he ran the risk of offending the nobility. Caesar's speeches and
legal proposals in Pompey's behalf will not have escaped the Great Man's
notice – not least because the Great Man, who returned to Rome at the end
of the sixties, soon found that he, too, needed political allies.

The arrogant Pompey had arranged Rome's eastern affairs without
seeking any form of traditional senatorial cooperation, and he had promised pensions to his troops. He expected a compliant senate to leap to the
ratification of his requests without demur or discussion. He had not reckoned on an aristocracy that preferred to cut everyone down to size. All his
enemies insisted on a full debate of every issue, and Crassus, working
behind the scenes, found many ways to frustrate his enemy. Crassus,
however, had problems of his own. He had invested heavily, and possibly
illegally, in the operations of the tax-farmers, the rich equestrians who

collected Rome's taxes for a hefty fee (borne mostly by the taxpayers in the provinces, I should add, and not by the public in Rome and certainly not by the government). These were the *publicani*, the publicans of New Testament fame, an early example of the false economy of out-sourcing. The *publicani* had recently overbid for the taxes to be collected in the province of Asia – and they wanted a rebate. The senate, convinced that profiteering equestrians were poor candidates for public charity, refused, and the result was deep hostility between the government and the tax-farmers. For Crassus, it was a personal matter but also a political one. His reputation depended on his ability to deliver for the *publicani*.

This was the political state of affairs in 60 BC, when Caesar was to be a candidate for the consulship. Although he was an odds-on favorite to win a place, his enemies were none the less lining up against him. This became clear immediately upon Caesar's return from Spain, where he had waged unprovoked war against various local tribes, on the basis of which activities he applied to the senate for permission to celebrate a triumph. This action necessitated a further request on Caesar's part, to the effect that he be allowed to submit the formal announcement of his candidacy (what the Romans called *professio*) in absence (for technical reasons Caesar could not enter both the city and preserve his eligibility to celebrate a triumph, yet it was obligatory to make one's *professio* in the forum). This was a reasonable request on Caesar's part, but it was refused owing to the exertions of Marcus Porcius Cato.

Cato, despite his relative youth (he was five years younger than Caesar), had emerged during the sixties as the leading spokesman for the most distinguished and invidious segment of the nobility, an elite and admired group whom we sometimes refer to by the shorthand expression *optimates*, the best of men, which is certainly how they regarded themselves (though this term was nothing like so narrow in republican usage). Swaggering in his protestations of old-fashioned probity, stubborn in every dispute and unafraid of giving offense, Cato was nothing short of a moral force – within the confines of the senate. His nobility of birth and his uncomplicated exploitation of traditional principles more than compensated for his lack of intelligence or his subtle opportunism. It was he who had blocked the rebate to the *publicani*. Cato had also repulsed the friendly advances of Pompey the Great: after his return from the east, Pompey had proposed a marriage alliance uniting his family with Cato's. Cato would have none of it, and he cooperated in the senate's resistance to ratifying Pompey's eastern acts. Now it was Cato who compelled Caesar to choose between a triumph and standing for the consulship.

There was a clear purpose to Cato's obstruction. Another of the candidates for the consulship that year was Marcus Calpurnius Bibulus, who was also Cato's son-in-law. Now Bibulus and Caesar had a long history: they had been colleagues as quaestors, aediles and praetors. The two men had little affection for one another and it was especially galling to Bibulus that at every turn Caesar's magisterial performance had surpassed his own in the view of the Roman public. Which is not even to mention Caesar's unexpected rise to become *pontifex maximus*. Bibulus did not look forward to facing Caesar yet again, and the circumstances of this election were complicated by the presence of yet another candidate, Lucius Lucceius, who enjoyed the strong backing of both Caesar and Pompey the Great. This is why Cato now deployed his constitutional rectitude in the hope of tripping up Caesar. He was certain that Caesar would postpone running for consul until the next year, after he had basked in the glory of a coveted triumph, a decision that would thus remove any impediment to Bibulus' election.

Cato entirely (and not for the last time) misjudged Caesar, who abandoned his triumph in order to stand. But the senate's refusal to balk at Cato's obstructionism was enough to make it plain to Caesar that his support amongst the senators was less than enthusiastic, which can only have been worrying. In reaction to this, Caesar pressed his old friends, Crassus and Pompey, for every ounce of support they could lend to his campaign, including the traditional emoluments for winning over Roman voters (viz. bribes). This was their intention anyway. Granted they were each of them committed to Caesar on account of his past associations, their connection to him was intensified further by their desire to defeat a common adversary, Cato. Consequently they threw themselves behind the candidacies of Caesar and Lucceius. For their part, Bibulus and Cato quickly sank to any depths to win. The ever-upright Cato even countenanced spending lavishly if shamelessly on bribes in order to bring the voters to the optimate cause – anything to elect Bibulus and to keep out Caesar.

At the end of this hard-fought election, Caesar was elected consul for the year 59 BC. Thus, he had renewed the lapsed nobility of his family and he had done so at his earliest opportunity. He was an unqualified Roman success. And he had reached the top of the greasy pole by means of a calculated combination of boldness and conventionality. *Pietas* and *gloria* were hardly exceptional values, but, in Caesar's case, they gave traditional cover to his innovative exploitation of the virtues and popularity of his aunt's husband and his wife's family connections – a move that compensated for the fallen condition of his own family's reputation.

Caesar had also risen to the consulship owing to his connections to two formidable figures, Crassus and Pompey, to each of whom he remained under an obligation. These relationships were complicated, however, by the antipathy that existed between Caesar's two friends. How much more effective they could be in cooperation with one another was all too obvious to Caesar, and it is another of Caesar's real achievements that he managed to persuade Pompey and Crassus to put aside their mutual loathing and to be reconciled with one another. Caesar was able to persuade his allies that, in the teeth of inevitable optimate opposition, it was in the interests of all three of them to combine their resources. Insofar as their assets went, Caesar actually brought the least to this arrangement, but it was he who, as consul, had to be the one to supply the constitutional and executive muscle necessary to get any of their business through the senate. And it was Caesar who had to be the one to take the heat for it all. It was obvious to all three that the going would not be easy, not least because Caesar's colleague in the consulship would not be the friendly Lucceius. Instead, it was to be none other than Bibulus.

Now this state of affairs invites a comment about the gap between senatorial politics and the motivations of Roman voters. As we have seen, there was a strong personal animosity between Bibulus and Caesar, one that was exacerbated by constant association. They were different sorts of men, with quite different political affiliations. Bibulus had been the candidate of the senators who hated Caesar and hated his friends, Crassus and Pompey. It tells us a lot about Roman voters, each of whom was allowed to cast two votes for the two vacant consuships, that both Caesar and Bibulus were elected in the same year. The mechanics of Roman consular elections make it inescapable that most voters voted for both men. However strong the passions and acidities within the aristocracy, the people of Rome saw politics very differently. They, too, looked at individuals, and they cast their ballots in terms of their own requirements regarding individual merit and their own expectations of magisterial leadership. Their voting habits were not decided by the factionalism of the senatorial order. This disconnection between the perspectives of the public and the feuds obtaining within Rome's political class must never be allowed to slip from our notice.

It was the opinion of later Roman historians that the fall of the Roman republic and its replacement by the empire could be traced back to the deal cut in 60 BC, whereby Caesar, Pompey and Crassus united to become what their critics dubbed the Three-Headed Monster and what modern scholars inaccurately call the First Trimvirate. Perhaps, in a sense, that's true. But the destruction of the republic was hardly what any of the three had in mind at the time. Crassus, Pompey and Caesar, each had his own immediate agenda, which for none of them included toppling the state. The year of Caesar's consulship, each of them knew in advance, would be a struggle for high stakes, but stakes of an entirely conventional if elevated nature.

And then what? A man in Caesar's position could, if he wished it, look forward to a life that was sweet and relatively undemanding. After all, he had made it to the consulship. No more was really expected of him. Once retired from office, he could luxuriate in his prestige, speak in the senate with authority, reflect on his splendid rise or even enjoy leisure without guilt, what Cicero described as *otium cum dignitate*, honorably earned inactivity. As everybody knows, that prospect did not enter, even momentarily, into Caesar's designs. Neither Crassus nor Pompey had taken up the Roman equivalent of shuffleboard – nor was Caesar likely to lapse into obscurity if he could escape it. He had claimed the mantle of Marius, who had won seven consulships and had garnered them on the basis of his military glory. Caesar's further ambitions lay along those lines. To prove himself the equal of Marius, much less of Crassus or Pompey, he needed a war, even one that was entirely contrived for his benefit. This was exactly what Caesar manufactured – in Gaul.

Further Reading

A superb account of the history of historians writing about Caesar can be gotten at in Yavetz 1983. More recent and more exhaustive (for readers fortunate enough to be comfortable with German) is Christ 1994. The mentality of the Roman nobility is a fascinating topic best approached by way of Earl 1967 and Flower 1996. The experience of ordinary Romans is naturally harder to get at, but MacMullen 1974, Whittaker 1993 and Atkins and Osborne 2006 are good starts. The political institutions of Rome are given concise and authoritative treatment in Lintott 1999. Of the biographies referred to in this chapter, the most accessible are Balsdon 1967, Gelzer 1968, Meier 1982, and Goldsworthy 2006 – to which list one might add Kamm 2006 (designed to be entirely introductory). Each of these offers a detailed account of Caesar's early career. The remaining relevant works cited by author in this chapter are: Mommsen 1894, Ferrero 1933, Strasburger 1938 and 1968, and Scullard 1959 (Strasburger's are exclusively in German).

2

Conquests and Glories, Triumphs and Spoils: Caesar and the Ideology of Roman Imperialism

On September 19, 1893, New Zealand became the first self-governing nation in which women possessed the right to vote. The moment marked a milestone in the history of human rights. But it must also inevitably raise the question: why so late? Not even in classical Athens, the cradle of democracy, could women attend the assembly, speak their views or express their will by way of voting, a state of affairs lampooned (to various purposes) by Aristophanes in his *Thesmophoriazusae* and (more famously perhaps) in his *Lysistrata*. An immediate answer of course leaps to mind – patriarchy – the mere utterance of which, however, provides all too little insight, inasmuch as this word, like the word "imperialism," for all its many syllables, is freighted with too much abstraction and not enough sense. These are modern magic words, and the problem with magic words, as one modern historian has observed, is that their pronunciation too often conjures not history but fairy-tales. The historic subjugation of women, like the historic subjugation of peoples, has its origin, at least in part, in something far less sophisticated: the realities of ancient warfare.

The principal task of the ancient Mediterranean city-state was survival, an occupation that demanded internal stability and the capacity for self-defense. Citizenship, in its fullest sense, was reserved for those with might and wealth enough to preserve the community. Hence the regular identity, in Greek states, between what we might call the voting public and the army. Children were excluded, for reasons that even now seem sound enough, though the current condition of the world has permitted their deadly enlistment. The poor also were usually forbidden to serve – they had nothing to contribute and too small a stake in the defense of the status quo – whereas women, who might possess the requisite property, were regarded as unbellicose and unsuitable for battle. Consequently, Greek constitutions (like their European descendants) tended to be timocratic and masculine in character. But by the nineteenth century, the concept of the citizen had shifted, from soldier to ratepayer (a productive extension of the sentiment inspiring such earlier slogans as "taxation without representation is tyranny"). It was argued that because women paid taxes, or at least many of them did, they should have the right to vote in municipal elections in New Zealand. This was extended to the national level. But the martial argument has never lost its original quality: when the American voting age was lowered to 18, a central element of the case was the instance of the drafted teenager who could die for his country, but was not allowed to vote for his commander in chief.

War, then, was a central preoccupation of the ancient state. A great deal was at stake: ancient warfare could – and did – result not simply in the humiliation but in the actual annihilation of the defeated side. The literary example of Troy was enacted more than once. When we think of the Greeks, we see them habitually through Roman eyes as poets, artists and philosophers. The Greeks, however, viewed themselves as warriors. From the heroism of Homer's *Iliad* – in which epic Achaean and Trojan alike strive to be *aristos* (the best), the embodiment of *arête* (courage), a quality most dramatically realized in *aristeia* (destructive combat) – to the realities of the classical period, when Spartans and Athenians waged war throughout the Mediterranean, Greek status remained connected with valor. The Athenians were the first to appreciate the advantages of enlisting the poor in military service, one of the reflexes of radical democracy. This was an innovation that allowed the Athenians, champions of freedom from the evil empire of Persia, to create for themselves an empire of subordinated democracies (they were both willing and quite able to put to the sword those democracies that did not elect to become subordinate). The tribute of their subjects, as the Athenians unabashedly described their allies, paid the tab for the construction of the Parthenon and other Athenian monuments to liberty. No wonder the residue of Greece was delighted with their defeat at the hands of the Spartans – until, that is, they learned what the Spartans had in mind.

It should not be thought that the Greeks, even the Greeks of Homer's day, adored warfare. Quite the reverse: Ares was a hateful god, and the devastation to individuals and communities entailed by war is a familiar theme of Athenian tragedy (the same Athenians who destroyed the Melians could lament the fate of Hecuba). But war, or so it was believed by all, was simply unavoidable: courage, then, was necessary to honor, and therefore glorious. In Thucydides' account of the Peloponnesian War, composed at the end of the fifth century, no less a figure than Pericles makes this point in the bluntest and most unsentimental of terms:

> If in other respects you are enjoying good fortune and you can choose whether or not to go to war, war is enormous folly. But if you have to choose either to give way, and promptly become subject to your neighbors, or to confront the risks, it is shirking the danger rather than withstanding it that is blameworthy.

The European study of history begins with Thucydides, and it is no accident that his history is about war and the politics that shaped and were shaped by it. These remain central and necessary concerns. Thucydides, a general himself (though admittedly an incompetent one), had no illusions about the horror of war – which in his view, at least in the case of Athens and Sparta, had as its causes unlimited ambition and fear.

What a thoroughly depressing picture. And I haven't yet gotten to Rome! Nor can I offer you the consolation that Rome was the last imperial power, or that right-thinking people everywhere now join in repudiating the idea of empire. To take only a single (but distinguished) example, Niall Ferguson, past Professor of Political and Financial History at Oxford and now ensconced at Harvard as the Laurence A. Tisch Professor of History, in his fat but best-selling book *Empire: The Rise and Demise of the British World Order and the Lesson for Global Power*, devotes all his considerable learning and intelligence to making the case that the British empire was, for all our post-colonial moaning about this and that, "a good thing." Native Americans and Aboriginals and the Maori may perhaps be forgiven for taking a somewhat different view. The book goes on to urge America to do more to take up what Kipling called The White Man's Burden (Ferguson quotes the poem at some length): the USA should find in the British empire a model for, as he puts it, "impos[ing] its preferred values on less technologically advanced societies." The USA, in its recent history, seems not to have required Professor Ferguson's prompting in the matter of imposing its values, or at the very least those of its administration. The allure of conquest, however nobly expressed or even noble in its intentions, persists, with (alas) consequences that can only be described as predictable. Caesar, for his part, made himself into a great man by way of warfare. There was collateral damage.

During Caesar's consulship, in 59 BC, legislation was proposed and passed by Publius Vatinius, a tribune of the people, that established a major military command for Caesar. Instead of being allocated his province in the normal fashion and for a normal term, Caesar would exceptionally become the proconsul (the provincial governor) of Cisalpine Gaul and Illyricum for a term of five years and with an army of three legions (later raised to four and, eventually, to ten). On the motion of Pompey the Great, Transalpine Gaul, modern Provence, was added to Caesar's command, on the grounds that there were disturbances in the region and that Rome's allies, the Aedui, had come under strain. The command was a welcome refuge for Caesar, whose extremities in behalf of Crassus and Pompey – Caesar had resorted to violence and shocking enormities – had so alienated the senate and even public opinion that without it he would surely have been prosecuted in court and very likely convicted. For five years – and eventually his command was extended to ten years – he was immune (Roman proconsuls, like Roman consuls, could not be touched by the courts until they resigned their office). But, obviously, he had to accomplish something on an impressive scale to legitimate his extraordinary command.

Caesar was being sent to his province with a large army: they were not expected to sit on their hands. They were there to fight *somebody*, but whom? And why? In the end, as you know, Caesar would conquer Gaul, although clearly that was not his original intention. The process was brutal. Women and children were slaughtered, often by strategic design. Masses of captives (over a million we are told) were sold into slavery (a lucrative business). By Caesar's own reckoning, he destroyed more than a million enemy troops during his Gallic campaigns, or so he boasted in his eventual triumph. This was savage work, but it made Caesar amazingly rich and provided him with the legions that raised him to absolute power. Surprisingly, or maybe not, this episode in his life, the conquest of Gaul, has come to be regarded as his greatest achievement: generations of schoolboys and schoolgirls have plodded (and, in nations where Latin continues to be taught in the schools, continue to plod) through Caesar's tripartite Gaul, and have won extra credit by drawing charts of major battles and by building miniature replicas of Roman siege instruments. The experience seems to have been formative, since biographers, while lamenting the unpleasant reality that you can't make a good French omelet without breaking a few Gallic eggs, continue to celebrate Caesar as the founder of Europe. As it is expressed in what remains the standard university textbook for this period, H.H. Scullard's *From the Gracchi to Nero*: "The Gauls fought for freedom, but freedom for what? . . . Indeed, if Rome had not stepped in, the Germans would probably have done so; and they would have brought, not a higher civilization, but a regression to barbarism. . . . [Caesar's] conquest of Gaul represents a vital act in world history: central Europe was opened up to Mediterranean civilization, and on the Celtic foundation there grew up a peaceful Latin civilization . . . France emerged into the modern world as a Latin country. In that sense, Caesar was the founder of France." Sigh, or rather *merci beaucoup*! The Roman historian Tacitus, however, saw it all with less saccharine sentimentality. Now Tacitus very much believed in Roman conquests, but he knew exactly and without illusion what it all meant: in his biography of Agricola, a governor of Britain, a subject complains to the Romans, rightly but ineffectually, that "you have made a desolation, and call it peace."

That Rome was an imperialist state, however one defines the expression, is obvious enough. From a modest village on the Tibur, Rome expanded to become the dominant power in Italy – what handbooks and textbooks still describe as the "unification" instead of the conquest of Italy, as if the Etruscans and Samnites and Greeks who lived there were all waiting with baited breath for the privilege of being obliged to learn Latin. Thereafter, in three major wars, in one of which Rome was nearly crushed out of existence, Carthage was destroyed, by which action the Romans became masters of the western Mediterranean. In the second century BC, Rome extended her hegemony over the east, defeating most of the Hellenistic kings. Rome ostensibly fought these wars, as had been the case for the Athenians and Spartans before her, to secure the liberation of the Greeks. The actions speak for themselves.

Or do they? An ideology of imperialism, existing either as a coherent set of principles or an unorganized batch of attitudes, is never a simple or straightforward matter – despite the consistent claims to the contrary of modern scholars and public intellectuals. When a nation is a great power, or even a middling one, it is at the very least obliged to engage what we should call the question of imperialism – how forceful can and must it appear in its dealings with others? – inasmuch as said nation will inevitably be viewed by its neighbors as a potential threat (even Canadians can fret about their gentle neighbor to the south). By way of contrast, a tiny power cannot really take up the same question. Whether it is hostile or fearful or complacent is, at the end of the day, irrelevant: it is at the mercy of the mighty, and even of the middling. And Rome, it must not be forgotten, was once a very tiny and unimportant place. Did Rome even then look ahead to its domination of the Mediterranean as its manifest destiny?

Like the city-states of Greece, Rome's organization was based on its military requirements. The magistrates, the consuls and the praetors, were elected to command troops: they alone possessed the right to give orders to soldiers and to civilians, for which power *imperium* is the Latin word. These magistrates were elected on the Campus Martius, the Field of Mars, outside the *pomerium*, the sacred boundary of the city. The mental geography of this is important: the territory within the *pomerium* was described as *domi*, civilian space; that outside was *militiae*, military terrain. Once an early Roman left his city, he was, psychologically, in enemy territory. The voters were the Roman people articulated by class, the centuriate assembly, in theory, the people organized for conscription. Like other central Italian states, Rome began her year in spring, when the agricultural calendar allowed her peasants to mobilize into a citizen militia (this was later changed). Romans could then fight until autumn restored them to their lands. And so the first month of the year – March – was devoted to Mars, a month of rituals and festivals that prepared Romans for war. October, the end of the fighting season, saw similar religious occupations. And during the early years of the republic, so far as our meager and unreliable evidence can tell us, the Romans fought every year. Whether at this stage they fought wars of conquest or of self-defense, we cannot say.

We can say that later Romans believed that their predecessors had fought only defensive wars, what in Latin can be called a *bellum iustum* – a just war. This expression remains with us, in the vocabulary of human rights experts and just war theorists, where it has a different meaning than it did in antiquity. But for now let me simply describe what was necessary in early Rome to render a *bellum iustum*. The Romans experience an injury (*iniuria*) from another people. A college of priests, the *fetiales*, is then sent to the offending state, to whom they report, in legalistic and highly repetitive (i.e. ritual) language, what is owed to the Romans. The offending state is allowed 33 days to decide whether or not to meet the Romans' demand for reparation. If not, the *fetiales* give their report to the senate, where the question of war is then debated. If a motion for war is carried (in the historical period that was not always the case), the senate instructs the consuls to sacrifice to the gods for a successful outcome. The consuls then take the matter to the centuriate assembly, which alone has the power to declare war or approve peace treaties. In early Rome, the soldiers would be selected from this assembly, so their opinion naturally mattered. So far as we know, the centuriate assembly only once rejected the senate's recommendation. The *fetiales* were then instructed to return to Rome's border with the offending state, where, after the pronunciation of a ritual formula, a ritual spear was cast into the enemy's land. It will be evident, in this early process, that questions of justice indeed played a part: after all, the offending party was given a fair opportunity to agree with the Romans that it was in fact in the wrong and to make it up to them along the lines dictated by – the Romans. But the preponderate impression of all this fuss is its religious and legal correctness, its attendance to what the Romans called *ius*. All parties involved, the enemy, the gods, the magistrates, the senate and the people, have an opportunity to prevent war from taking place. However, if each party acts in accordance with the correct procedure dictated by *ius*, whether the outcome is peace or war, the matter is 'just'. Hence a *bellum iustum*, for the Romans, was as much a *correct* or *legal* war as it was a *just* one.

Now this procedure was greatly altered by events: when the Romans came into conflict with peoples who worshipped different gods from themselves, when they seized an overseas empire, much of this was simply impracticable (the *fetiales*, for instance, fell into abeyance, and it was not felt necessary to consult the people on matters of policing or distant emergencies, since communication across the Mediterranean could take months). Still, the basic pattern of religious and legal correctness remained. And, when we emerge into the historical period, we begin to have reliable accounts of the reasons expressed by Romans for going to war and for avoiding war.

But first let me explode a few myths about the Roman army: it did not succeed, despite the propaganda of its governing class, on account of its brilliant generals. The Romans lost battles, lots of them, and often on a Wagnerian scale. Brilliance in command was rather difficult to demonstrate in any case, given the simple tactics of ancient warfare and the primitive technologies that supported them. For the most part, generals were expected to deploy their troops intelligently and to lead them courageously. The common Latin word for a general is *dux*, leader, because that is what he was. Multitudes of Roman aristocrats fell in battle: no one lounged about in comfort while he ordered his men to go over the top. This courage on the part of Roman commanders was a key ingredient in the soldiers' loyalty and remained vital to Roman victories. But the real essentials to Roman success were, oddly enough, rarely mentioned by the ancient sources, perhaps because they were less than entirely glamorous from an aristocratic perspective.

In the first place, there was the striking obedience of the troops – deference and conformity once again – and the fact that the Romans refused to surrender or even to negotiate from an inferior position: this was a reality that certainly disturbed the Greeks, who could never understand it. In the second, the Romans took extraordinary pains to secure their retreat – because they knew they lost a lot and that the consequences of that reality had to be minimalized. And so they built roads, easy to march out on (that was their purpose) and easy to employ when retreat was necessary. And when on the march, Roman armies – every night – constructed a camp that was, in essence, a fortress. They spent more time building camps and roads than marching or fighting, and this goes a long way toward explaining the engineering talents of the Roman legions. The purpose of the camp was patent: it provided the Romans with a place to run away to, when the order was given that running away had suddenly become the Roman thing to do. An army on the march had much to defend: a Roman legion was part of a larger cluster that included suttlers of all sort, camp-followers who sold boots, bought captives, exchanged plunder for cash, and provided prostitutes – in short, they were the Halliburtons of antiquity. These logistical lines had to be maintained, and the greatest generals, such as Marius and Pompey, succeeded largely owing to their patience and organizational skill. And, finally, there were lots of Romans. The Athenians dominated Greece because they could regularly throw thousands of men into their wars. A single Roman legion comprised 6,000 men, and the population of the city was always teeming. When the cities of Italy became Roman subjects, it also became their duty to supplement Rome's legions as auxiliaries. This is why the Romans could tolerate the destruction of tens of thousands of men in their heavy warfare against the Carthaginians or in Spain. One is reminded of Napoleon's greatest resource: the sheer manpower of France, which he remorselessly squandered.

But naturally the Romans, and especially the aristocracy, saw matters differently. Let us return to a text we examined in the previous chapter, the eulogy of Quintus Metellus for his father. Let me print it once more, this time adding a few supplements to make its martial nature more obvious:

Q. Metellus, in the panegyric that he delivered at the funeral of his father, L. Metellus, who had been pontiff, consul (*i.e. general*) twice, dictator (*i.e. general*), master of the horse (*i.e. general*), and land-commissioner (*an official who, amongst other things, settles the pensions of veterans*), and who had celebrated a triumph (*the greatest achievement of all, celebrated by a general who has slain at least 5,000 enemy troops in battle: he gets a tickertape parade and, for a single day, is assimilated to the god Jupiter, hence the necessity for a slave to remind him that he is mortal*), left in it writing that his father had achieved the ten greatest objects in pursuit of which wise men devote their lives: he had made it his aim to be the best in war (*I think that's fairly clear*), the best orator, the bravest general (*redundant and obvious*), to be in charge (*as a magistrate*) of the most important undertakings of the state (*that would be war*), to enjoy the highest office (*that would be a consul or a dictator, who are essentially generals*), to be supremely intelligent, to be deemed the most important member of the senate (*ex-officers and generals*), to obtain great wealth in an honorable way (*there are only three honorable ways: inheritance, agriculture and the spoils of war*), to leave many sons and to have gained the greatest glory in the state (*"gloria," the word used here, means glory won in war*).

The Roman aristocrat endeavored to be the embodiment of *virtus*, which is Latin for virtue principally of the hairy-chested variety: *vir* means *man*, *virtus* is manliness, demonstrated in battle and, later, in public life, a position earned by way of military exposure. In order to stand for high office, a Roman was required to serve in ten campaigns (though by Caesar's day the number had been reduced considerably; still, we have seen how seriously he took the obligation). The reward of *virtus* is *honor*, office. These were not merely values or concepts, they were gods in the Roman public religion, worshipped together as *Honos et Virtus*, courage and the honor it deserves, for whom the Romans constructed not fewer than two temples (one of them dedicated by Gaius Marius). The pair also appear on Roman coins. It was the job of the aristocrat to win *gloria*, to bring home spoils, which he might lavish on the population, not least in public building. As in Athens, the monumental architecture of the city was evidence of the Romans' successful conquests of others.

So much for the generals. What of the ordinary slob on the Roman street? Here matters become more complicated. In the second century, it is clear that the centuriate assembly was actually more inclined to vote for war than was the senate: war brought Rome prosperity, and even the urban poor got a taste of that (the spoils of war paid for construction projects that yielded jobs, for public festivals, for a grain dole – and eventually Roman citizens were freed from most forms of taxation, owing to the revenues of the empire). At the same time, Rome never had a volunteer army: Roman soldiers were drafted, and, beginning in the second century, the term of service began to become very long indeed, usually longer than six years and perhaps as long as twenty. The Roman wars in Spain were brutal for both sides, and soldiers conscripted for duty there often failed to show, or went so far as to riot against being sent. But at least a part of this apparent contradiction can be explained fairly simply: by this time, the citizens who voted for war – the urban population – were not the citizens who were being drafted. Conscripts came from the peasants in the countryside, regarded by their officers as more robust and virtuous than their citified compatriots. Now, it is a very easy matter to send someone else off to war, as recent American history makes all too obvious. Never the less, there is no evidence of a widespread Roman aversion to going to war, so long as the cause wasn't entirely hopeless. And for many rural citizens, warfare became a means of modest social improvement, however temporary its effects.

By now the militarism of the Romans should be obvious, not that there can have been much doubt. I have dilated on these matters in order to protect you from the incomprehension that is likely to result from even the most summary exposure to modern scholarly discussions of Roman imperialism. You might be surprised to learn, if you turned the pages of eminent historians like Theodore Mommsen or Maurice Holleaux or Ernst Badian or Erich Gruen or A.N. Sherwin-White, that the Romans never fought an aggressive war in their life. Roman imperialism, we are informed, was "defensive imperialism," and Rome's conquests all came about more or less by accident. On the other hand, you might read the important but equally one-sided book by W.V. Harris, published in the 1970s, in which it is argued that the Romans were unrelentingly aggressive warmongers who, once in a while, found specious pretexts for their world domination. Now there is something to be said for each of these views, but each, on its own, is too reductive to explain the Roman attitude toward war.

Even the idea of "the Roman attitude" must be jettisoned. Different Romans had varying attitudes at various times – or even at the same time. When we have good evidence, we find that the Roman decision to go to war was almost always subject to sharp debate. Now this will have been motivated by a range of concerns: for instance, if it is *gloria* that raises a senator above his peers, then many senators will have been keen to limit their colleagues' opportunities to win it. But this is not something that could be confessed in senatorial debate: consequently, a complaint would be raised against investing too much power in the hands of a single man, a risky proposition even in dangerous times, a defiance of custom and therefore a constitutional disturbance. A pre-eminent senator might even be accused of aiming at *regnum*, supreme power, for which a military command was mere pretext. In fact, however, most of the debates about war that we can overhear regularly resort to *moral* arguments. And the argument for war invariably included an element of the argument for self-defense (however elastic the interpretation of that concept). But this can hardly be surprising.

Let us step back for a moment. It seems that everyone with even the slimmest chance of using violence to his advantage wants to do so, and is perfectly capable of finding self-satisfying reasons to do so. Contemporary human-rights discourse on justice in war, for example, derives to a large extent from the arguments of Christian theologians, traceable to Augustine by way of Aquinas, designed to put the Hebrew Bible to work as a counterweight to the pacifism of the New Testament, all in order to define the appropriate circumstances under which Christians might go to war. These arguments obviously proved compelling, inasmuch as European Christians did their fair share of conquering other peoples. Otherwise I should not be an American (we all have dirty hands). But there is a similar line of reasoning in the legal history of Islam. Even in the *Text of a Declaration by the World Islamic Front with respect to Jihad against the Jews and the Crusaders*, one of whose authors was Osama bin Laden, published in February 1998, the justification for violence anytime and anyplace – even against civilians (which diverges from traditional constructions of the *Quran*: for instance, the prophet says "do not mutilate or kill women, children or old men") – is self-defense, in this instance against the occupation of Islamic lands and the destruction of the Islamic faith. Buddhism, too, the Mike Tyson of pacifistic world-views, has, in the case of the civil war against the Tamil Tigers in Sri Lanka, discovered arguments that justify the defense of the sacred isle in defense of the *dharma*. It is an interesting fact that the Romans felt obliged to justify their wars, but that hardly renders them remarkable. Nor does it demonstrate an aversion to war.

More important is the variation of conviction that moral arguments carried amongst the Romans. The debate over the Third Punic War, for instance, was intense and lasted several years: it was in pushing for this war that the Elder Cato concluded his every speech in the senate with the words, *Carthago delenda est* ('Carthage must be destroyed'). Yet this same Cato, when the Romans were contemplating war against Rhodes, delivered a speech *against* that war, suffused with moral insistence that such a war would be the wrong war at the wrong time. These differences suggest to me that circumstances and arguments genuinely mattered: after all, today one may have very different opinions about the American war in Afghanistan and the American war in Iraq – and in fact many do. Often the Romans, even when provoked, elected not to go to war. There was no simple reflex.

Nor is it obvious that Romans loved going to war for its own sake. Cicero clearly did not. And he was not alone. The proof of this is indirect, but irrefutable. In Roman laws – for example, the Roman law against provincial extortion, passed in the second century BC and preserved on stone – it was the responsibility of private citizens either to prosecute offenders or to bring the matter to someone competent to do so (we have seen Caesar in this role). If the prosecution made its case, there were rewards for those involved. For example, a non-citizen was rewarded with Roman citizenship for himself and his descendants. If a Roman citizen was involved, he was regularly rewarded with *militiae vacatio*, release from military service. This reward clause appears in numerous inscriptions, for numerous laws, and always in the same formula, demonstrating thereby its routine nature. Now if every Roman citizen were eager for war and if every Roman citizen shared the aristocracy's insistence on its necessity, *militiae vacatio* would be, not a reward, but a punishment. Yet it was deemed to be so attractive a reward that it was the common inducement to come forward in order to do one's duty. Still, the simple fact that many Romans did not desire to go to war personally – in fact, felt fortunate if they could avoid service altogether – only complicates our perception of Roman militarism.

Why, then, have so many historians believed that Rome's was a defensive imperialism and their empire an entirely accidental attainment? The major argument for this view has always been the apparent Roman reluctance to annex conquered territory. Although annexations did eventually take place, they were very slow in coming, and this inertia has been interpreted as an unwillingness on the part of the Romans to become an imperial power. It was this pattern that led Badian to see the Romans as hegemonial imperialists and which represented, for Harris, the biggest obstacle to his model of Roman aggression. All of which was wasted effort: for the Romans, annexation was always beside the point, though this has not always been generally appreciated.

What did the Romans understand by *imperium Romanum*? The concept was not exclusively geographical. Rome's empire extended to any place and to any person who was obliged – owing to friendship or alliance or past favors – to respect and, therefore, to obey Roman instructions. This degree of deference was certainly the permanent expectation of anyone whom the Romans had defeated and to whom they had demonstrated their capacity for mercy. We can observe this mentality in operation in the fine print of Roman expressions of clemency.

When Romans went to war, however careful they were to accumulate justifications, they entered war with no sense of proportionality. Polybius, writing in the second century and a great fan of the Romans, made it plain that he had never seen anything like the ferocity of Romans in battle. And, if the Romans elected to lay waste a conquered city, they destroyed everything inside: men, women, children – even the dogs! Romans fought for total surrender on the part of their opponents – what in Latin was called *deditio in fidem*, placing oneself in the *fides*, in the confidence, of the Roman people. Rome demanded the unqualified *trust* of those whom she defeated in war. *Deditio* was extreme: it meant that the fate of the conquered was entirely in the hands of the Romans, who might take what they wished and who might exercise their right, freely given by the defeated, to destroy them root and branch.

Most of the time, though certainly not always, it was the Roman practice to restore the vanquished, satisfying themselves with an indemnity. But the legalities of the *deditio*, from the Roman point of view, reveal to us their concept of the implications of victory. This is now evident to us owing to the publication, in 1984, of an inscription from Spain that records the only extant *deditio*, offered by an otherwise unknown people to an otherwise unknown Roman general. Here is the relevant portion in English translation:

> During the consulship of Gaius Marius [*yes, that Gaius Marius*] and Gaius Flavius [*i.e. 104 BC*], the Seanoci put themselves and their possessions in the *fides* of Lucius Caesius the son of Gaius Caesius, conquering general, and of the Roman people. After he accepted them into his *fides*, Lucius Caesius consulted his advisors about their views concerning what commands he should give. On the basis of their advice, he commanded that they [*i.e. the Seanoci*] should surrender any weapons, deserters, captives and horses they had captured. They did so. Then Lucius Caesius, the son of Gaius Caesius, conquering general, ordered them to be free, and he restored to them all the lands and buildings and laws and everything else which they had previously put into his *fides* – all so long as the Roman people and the senate should wish it so [*dum populus senatusque Romanus vellet*].

This last expression is a good Latin restrictive clause, and it is of immense importance for understanding Roman imperialism: once conquered, always conquered, and the condition of the vanquished was always subject to revision – *from the Roman side*. Annexation was utterly unnecessary: wherever the Romans marched, in a very real sense, they never left. Peace with the Romans, then, always came at a cost. For us, the word peace is so resonant with harmony, serenity, tranquility, and goodwill that, at its very mention, we want to get cozy, smoke a joint, join hands and launch into endless choruses of *Kumbaya*. By contrast, for the Romans, *pax* implied conquest: the beating down of their enemies, who capitulated when the jackboot was on their throat. The only word for "peaceful" in Latin that I know of is *pacatus*, which actually means "subdued." Any other posture, from the Roman perspective, was arrogance.

54

Victory in war had made the Romans great, so the Romans believed. They were masters of the world, so they regularly said, incorrectly as they knew, but it suited them to say it. In his *Aeneid*, Virgil has Jupiter granting the Romans *imperium sine fine* – boundless empire – by means of which it is their mission to spare the humbled and to crush the proud. Humility and pride were the only alternatives when confronted by Rome. Equality was out. Republican inscriptions make it clear that they believed the gods favored their domination of others, and by the time of the late republic, Stoic philosophers had sweetened the Romans' pot: they argued, and the Romans quite naturally agreed, that Roman rule was good for you; the Romans' superior morality brought justice and peace to peoples who, whatever their virtues, needed this guiding hand. Here we see the original version of the White Man's Burden. Even Cicero, who disliked war, cherished victory. In an intellectual essay, not for common consumption, he describes Rome as deserving of her citizens' love because she is, in the whole of the world, the sole home of *virtus*, of *imperium*, of *dignitas*.

When Caesar took up his province, it was his intention to wage war – in Illyricum, against the Getae and their ambitious king Burebista. But his situation was complicated by unrest in Gaul: the Romans' allies, the Aedui, were being pressed by the Helvetii, in one of the many migrations that occupied continental tribes. In 60 BC the senate had sent an embassy to Gaul to investigate matters. His enemies will have hoped that it was beyond Caesar's capacities to deal with both matters at the same time – after all, there was no proof at this time that Caesar was anything more than an adequate general. In the event, it was Gaul that drew his attention: Illyricum would have to wait for Augustus.

The first year of Caesar's campaigning in Gaul was all stimulus and response. In that sense, I suppose, one could describe the Gallic conquest as an accident. The Helvetii sought his permission to pass through Transalpine Gaul. Caesar properly refused – migrations are messy and dangerous matters – but he amplified his refusal by observing that, in the Cimbric war (the war ultimately won by Marius), the Tigurini (a Helvetian clan) had inflicted an unavenged defeat on the Romans. Thus they were already enemies – and Caesar was fully in the right to strike at them if he so elected. When the Helvetii attempted to force their way never the less, Caesar repulsed them, and, owing to serendipity (or, Caesar suggests, the will of the gods), he himself confronted the Tigurini, whom he destroyed. So far, so just. This victory led some Gallic tribes to seek his assistance in repelling the German Ariovistus, an official friend of the Roman people, who had been invited into the conflicts amongst the Gallic tribes, but had now become too influential for any of them to handle. It was obviously the intention of the Gauls to exploit Caesar similarly – let's not pretend that the ultimate victims were naïve or simple (I can assure you that Caesar didn't). It is doubtful that Caesar believed the intelligence he was given by his Gallic allies, but it served his purpose to believe that Ariovistus posed a gathering threat, and a profession of loyal support for Roman allies provided sufficient cover for a confrontation with the German, who naturally refused to back down. The issue was settled in combat – a war of liberation – in which, again, the Romans were victorious.

But before the war against Ariovistus could begin, Caesar's legions came close to mutiny. According to Caesar's account, the motive was fear, but not the variety of fear that conventional wisdom insists was a spur to Roman conquest. Now Romans, it must be conceded, had a natural fear of Gauls – and of Germans (when they could tell them apart, the Romans being less than accomplished anthropologists). For one thing, the Gauls had once sacked Rome – in 390 BC – and the catastrophe was never forgotten. For another, Gauls and Germans were *big*. Romans were not. To make matters worse, Gauls and Germans painted their bodies strange colors, leapt suddenly out of the forests, and killed Romans in serious quantities: it was an important part of Marius's glory that he had subdued such mighty foes. As Caesar's legions put it, "the very expression on their faces and the fierce glance of their eyes were more than men could endure." Cassius Dio, however, preserves another version: the troops had come to believe that Caesar was willing to put their lives at risk in order to pursue a private war for spoil and for glory. They were willing to fight, but not yet to fight for Caesar. Caesar's invocation of Marius and the perpetual danger of Teutonic hordes will have been for his legions' benefit. The men had to be properly motivated. And so they must be led to believe that a pre-emptive strike was in the national interest.

I should say a word about Caesar the general. In his *Gallic Wars*, unsurprisingly, Caesar always gets it right. When there is a reversal, it can be attributed conveniently to a subordinate. Closer analysis reveals that Caesar was often lucky and that his grasp of the situation in Gaul was very often shaky. But his hold on his men was impressive. Suetonius tells us that Caesar was lax about rules of the camp, gave his soldiers latitude when they were at rest, was generous in getting them booty (he also raised their regular pay) – but absolutely insistent that they obey him without question in battle. He was a commander who knew what was important, and what was not. And his men came to respect that. More than once he exposed himself to danger in order to rally his soldiers: in combat with the Nervii, for example, when the Twelfth Legion was suffering frightening casualties and in one cohort every centurion had fallen, Caesar grabbed a soldier's shield and rushed into the foremost, crying out at the remaining centurions – by name. His personal courage reversed the battle. By the end of the Gallic Wars, his men adored him.

The conclusion of Caesar's first season went more or less unnoticed in Rome. But by now it had become his intention to conquer the region, for which purpose he could rely on contentiousness amongst the Gauls themselves – it was their lack of unity that made them vulnerable to Roman arms. Gallic fractiousness allowed him to deploy his alliances to justify his occupation and the continuation of warfare. And, in the end, as the Gauls began to realize what was in store for them, their very resistance to Roman domination became justification enough for their reduction. By Roman standards, they had become ungrateful – and arrogant. No one, after all, either citizen or stranger, was permitted to deny the *maiestas* of the Roman people (it was in fact a crime for a citizen to do so). *Maiestas* does not mean majesty, or even greatness: it means, literally, the "greater-ness" of the Roman people. Interestingly, in his *Gallic Wars*, Caesar never demonizes his enemies. In fact, he openly admits that they were struggling for their *libertas*, their freedom. But what had begun as a war of liberation was now a war of self-defense, Roman-style. The Romans were fighting to defend the domination that had been established by their earlier victories: their message to the Gauls – *start liking it.*

One cannot say that the campaign was intelligent. Caesar ripped through Gaul like an undergraduate through a case of cheap beer. And having done so, he declared victory, without consolidation. Subsequent rebellions required further warfare, after which, again, victory was declared. In 55 BC, during which year his command was extended for another five years, Caesar extended Roman arms into Britain and across the Rhine into Germany proper. In neither case was there any real provocation, but by then Caesar was uninterested in niceties. The *maiestas* of the Roman people required these demonstrations of Roman superiority. How else could Romans feel safe in their possession of empire? Nonetheless, in 52 BC it all nearly came to an end: Vercingetorix led an uprising of nearly the whole of Gaul in which the Romans suffered reversal after reversal. It was only the hard-fought, but ultimately successful siege of Alesia that resulted in the Gauls' capitulation, a moment immortalized with a vengeance in Royer's familiar painting (Fig. 8). This was the end. The region remained pacified for the remainder of Caesar's life.

Figure 8 Lionel Royer's *Vercingetorix throws his arms at the feet of Caesar*. Musée Croziater, Le Puy-en-Velay, France. Photo: Bridgeman-Giraudon/Art Resource, NY.

The citizens of Rome were impressed, in multiple ways. Caesar's victories were honored with offerings to the gods, with epic poems, with panegyrics from the lips of orators like Cicero. The conqueror of Gaul was now Pompey's equal in glory – and in wealth. The subjugation of Gaul was a profitable business: Caesar's troops prospered, as did his officers. In fact, nearly every young aristocrat on the make sought a place with Caesar during the latter years of the war, and, in Book Thirteen of Cicero's correspondence *Ad Familiares* ("To his Associates"), we have a collection of some of Cicero's letters of recommendation in behalf of candidates for posts in Gaul. Each of them wanted Caesar's friendship – he was now a great man – and each wanted his share of the plunder. No one did better than Caesar himself, of course. He was now rich enough to buy influence as Crassus had once done: he even lent money to Cicero, a favor Cicero later came to regret. His wealth and his influence and his glory made him popular with the people and with the prosperous classes: amongst the nobility, however, he (predictably) became an object of envy and a potentially menacing figure.

His enemies identified Caesar as a war criminal. The younger Cato insisted that Caesar had no legitimate reason to attack the Germans across the Rhine and proposed in the senate that he be handed over to them for punishment. It would be a mistake to view this purely as political opportunism: Roman morality, as I remarked earlier, had become, for those with a philosophical education at least, an important basis for Roman domination. Roman rule was supposed to be good for you. That could hardly be said for Caesar's treatment of the Gauls: more than once he sold entire peoples into slavery – or put them to death. In the last piece of serious fighting in Gaul, the suppression of a few thousand men at Uxellodunum, Caesar gave the order that every captured fighter have his hands chopped off, all the better "to be living evidence of the fact that punishment is visited on crime," in this instance on the crime of seeking freedom from Roman rule. But Cato's complaints counted for little next to the adulation of the crowd and the profits rolling in from the north. Even Cicero found it all irresistible.

It was as the thunderbolt of war that Caesar made himself one of the two most formidable men in Rome. And it was as a warrior that he would sweep away the forces of the republic, in battles in Greece, in Egypt, in Africa and in Spain. *Veni, vidi, vici* are his most famous words – and they became his complete obsession. In Caesar, the complex ideology of Roman imperialism collapses into a frightening will-to-power. After the civil war, when he was dictator for life and sole ruler of the Roman world, Caesar had one further ambition: to invade Parthia, to conquer the east, to return to Rome in triumph, having turned their myth of world mastery into a reality. His subjects – the citizens of Rome – were willing to follow him anywhere. But the aristocracy, the men for whom *gloria* meant everything, were not. How did he not see it? In his *Gallic Wars*, Caesar demonstrates his acute understanding of the psychology of his enemies – unlike the British or the Americans, Caesar could grasp his opponents' passion for dignity and freedom and power. There is no more eloquent account of the Gauls' love of liberty than Caesar's own. The animosities of his equals, however, he did not divine. When his assassins struck him down, their cry was simple: freedom.

Further Reading

Although Roman militarism is a fairly straightforward matter, the nature of Roman imperialism remains remarkably controversial. Useful and learned treatments of the topic include Badian 1968, Harris 1979 and 1984, and Champion 2004. An authoritative treatment of the Roman army in our period is Goldsworthy 1996. For a detailed account of Caesar's Gallic conquests the reader can hardly do better than the relevant chapters in Goldsworthy 2006. The complex cultural ramifications of Gaul's annexation by Rome are the subject of Woolf 1998.

3

Pontifex Maximus: Caesar and the Manipulation of Civic Religion

That we wholly and constantly have attached the highest importance to reverence of the gods one can estimate from the goodwill we have experienced on this account from the supreme deity. Not only that, but for many other reasons we are convinced that our own high respect for the divine has been made obvious to everyone.

So wrote Marcus Valerius Messalla, praetor in 192 BC, to the citizens of Teos, on behalf of the tribunes and the senate of Rome, in a letter which the Teans carved into stone and erected in their own Temple of Dionysus – because it guaranteed the political independence of their city in the aftermath of Rome's victory in the Second Macedonian War. This inscription, like many others that might be adduced, displays much that is intriguing about Roman religion. In the first place, it will be obvious that the Romans (and for that matter the Greeks) suffered far less anxiety than do moderns over the proper barriers between religion and government. What is perhaps less obvious is the Romans' pride not specifically in their own brand of religion, but in their religiosity. "If we wish to compare our culture with that of foreign peoples," claims Cicero in his treatise, *On the Nature of the Gods*, "we shall discover that in some respects we are no better and sometimes even worse. However, with respect to religion – by which I mean the worship of the gods – we are superior by far." What is unmistakable in this letter is the intimate connection between religion and power – in this instance, the power exercised by Rome over the Teans, who evidently felt obliged to display to their own gods this evidence of the Romans' superior piety. This crucial link between the success of the *res publica* and the proper cultivation of the gods fell well within the perceptions of the Romans themselves: "Jupiter is called Greatest and Best," observes Cicero, "not because he makes us just or sober or wise, but because he makes us healthy and rich and prosperous."

Do ut des – I give so that you will give – was the sentiment dominating the Roman's confrontation with the divine, a bargain the Romans conceptualized as the *pax deorum*, the peace treaty with the gods. In their every action, the Romans took pains to demonstrate their respect for the gods' superiority. Not because Jupiter was in the business of washing away his worshippers' sins, nor because the devoted life inspired warm feelings of brotherly (or, for that matter, sisterly) love. Instead, religion was a practical necessity, because the gods were stronger than the Romans, as a consequence of which their accommodation was vital for Roman successes in this world. The Romans *feared* the gods, or at the very least they suffered enormous anxieties about discovering the best methods for keeping them content.

This is not to say that their gods were anything like a mighty fortress offering the Romans refuge in times of crisis. Jupiter was not invoked or propitiated so that he might right the Romans' wrongs or fight the Romans' battles like a cuirass-clad Lord of Hosts. The Romans were quite capable of fighting their own battles and solving their own problems, thank you very much – so long as the gods did not intervene *against them*. Naturally, Rome always hoped for divine allies, and, as Messalla's letter indicates, the Romans certainly believed that the gods had opted for their success. But because Rome was content with the gods' neutrality, she strove to avoid their hostility. For this reason, the gods were frequently consulted, by carefully prescribed methods.

For example, Roman armies never took action without consulting the sacred chickens: if, when offered food, they ate greedily – the chickens, that is, not the Romans – that signified that Jupiter did not object to the Romans' fighting on that day. But if they did not eat, the warning could not be ignored. Once, during the Punic Wars, a Roman admiral, frustrated because despite many attempts he could not get the sacred chickens to eat, lifted their cage into the air crying, "if they won't eat, then let them drink!" But no sooner had the sacred chickens glubbed their last glub than a great storm arose, wrecking the fleet. And for this misdeed, the admiral was tried – not, however, for a religious crime (unlike the Athenians or the British, the Romans did not make blasphemy or impiety a crime), but rather for treason.

This wariness regarding the gods suffices to identify the alien quality of Roman religion. In America, for instance, religion, for all its psalm singing in celebration of the splendors of the afterlife, is never the less routinely and intimately associated with this-worldly success. It is all too common for winning sports teams to praise and to thank the Lord for their victories. But this equation is entirely one-sided. I can assure you that you will never hear an American basketball player, if he should wind up on the losing side, complain that Jesus keeps stripping the ball when he's in the key or keeps blocking his lay-ups. Jocks (at least American jocks) don't *blame* Jesus when they lose. Christianity, and here Christianity is not alone, tends not to construct God as a troublemaker. The Romans, when they lifted their eyes unto the hills, preferred to play it safe.

Consequently, they endeavored to preserve the *pax deorum* with a scrupulousness that marked their religiosity out from that of other ancient peoples. The Greeks were astonished by it all. One of the keenest Greek observers was Polybius, a historian and statesman of the second century BC who for many years lived in Rome, where he became intimate with numerous senatorial families. In the Sixth Book of his monumental history of Rome, Polybius attempted to describe the Romans' constitution, which, in his view, was the basis of their remarkably stable republic and their irresistible domination of the Mediterranean world. He concludes this book with the following observation:

> The quality in which the Roman constitution is most conspicuously superior is, in my opinion, the nature of their religiosity. It strikes me that very thing which amongst other peoples gives reason for reproach – I mean their fear of the gods (*deisidaimonia*) – is what actually sustains Roman affairs. My opinion is that they have designed this feature of their constitution for the sake of the common people. Perhaps this approach would not have been necessary had it been possible to form a state composed of wise men. But every multitude is fickle, full of lawless desires, irrational passion and violent anger: it must be held by invisible terrors and pageantry of that sort. If you ask me, the ancients acted sensibly when they familiarized the multitudes with vulgar notions about the gods and beliefs about the terrors of the underworld. It is we moderns who are rash in banishing such beliefs. The result is that nowadays, amongst the Greeks, to cite a single example, men in public service, if they are entrusted with no more than a talent, though they have ten copyists and as many seals and twice as many witnesses, still cannot be trusted, whereas, amongst the Romans, the magistrates and legates who routinely deal with large sums of money conduct themselves correctly just because they have sworn an oath to the gods to do so.

Here Polybius invokes the "religion as crowd control" hypothesis, already popular amongst Greek philosophers then and, of course, current in the present day. But his own illustration reveals its inappropriate application to the Roman situation. The men whose fear of the divine prohibited their violation of oaths were, on his own evidence, not the slobs on the street so detested by Greek intellectuals, but instead representatives of the Roman aristocracy, who filled the ranks of magistrates and legates. In Rome, the elite really believed this stuff, or at least they really conformed to this stuff – a degree of conviction Polybius found impressive and significant even while he found it a trifle embarrassing.

Caesar, according to the ancient sources, was a different man altogether. As his biographer Suetonius put it: "not even religious scruple frightened him away from any enterprise – or even gave him pause." In other words, no *deisidaimonia* for Caesar. But that is far from the whole of the story. The elder Pliny, in a long discussion of magical charms, reports that Caesar, after having suffered a serious spill, never seated himself in any vehicle without first reciting three times a spell designed to guarantee a safe journey – "something which most people do nowadays," he goes on to observe. Caesar, then, was no stranger to vulgar superstition, even if he was perhaps more afraid of traffic than of divine wrath. Furthermore, Caesar was *pontifex maximus*, the official head of Roman civic religion, itself designed to preserve the *pax deorum*. In his actual career, though it was not to Suetonius's purpose to say so, Caesar will have presided over numerous public religious ceremonies – as praetor and as consul as well as in his role as chief pontiff. Furthermore, as a general in the field, it was essential that he observe the religious practices of the armies – and of the navies. In this he often showed himself astute to the religious sensibilities of others: at the time of his invasion of Africa, during the civil war, as he disembarked from his boat when landing, he fell spreadeagled onto the beach, a graceless move and an obvious bad omen. The troops were stunned, but Caesar saved the day by shouting, *teneo te, Africa* – "Africa, I embrace you and hold you fast." This was a traditional and very proper reinterpretation of an omen, and his soldiers legitimately foresaw victory.

It is never held against Caesar that he had no apparent religious beliefs (though, as we have seen, the evidence on this point is somewhat weaker than modern scholars tend to admit), and in any case it is perhaps worth recollecting that Cicero's definition of *religio*, cited above, said nothing about *belief* anyway. Nor was Caesar much criticized for his lack of religiosity, despite this remark in Suetonius. This will have been because, most of the time, Caesar conformed to the obligations of his rank and office. But not *always* – or at least not always without controversy. And here we must attend to a consequential episode from Caesar's consulship, one the importance of which Suetonius failed to appreciate. Furthermore, at the end of his career, Caesar generated another lasting religious controversy. This was not owing to Caesar's rejection of the gods, but instead to the danger that he might actually join their own number. And in fact, he *did* join their number, though not exactly according to his own design.

The study of Roman religion, like the study of religion generally, is beset by multiple impediments. We have just now drawn serious conclusions from our examination of Polybius, but Polybius is only a single informant, and a foreigner at that. We may legitimately wonder to what degree he got it right. The construction and deconstruction of an alien religion, after all, is by no means a simple matter. It is all too easy to bring to bear the wrong assumptions, and to be distracted by differences the perception of which depends almost wholly on those assumptions. Polybius's informants will have been elites, after all, who, like Valerius Massalla, took extraordinary pride in their own religiosity – not least for its value in sustaining Roman security and extending Roman domination. But Polybius, owing to his philosophical education, could only understand that in terms of the Greek intellectual debate about the nature and purpose of religion. Hence the bad fit of his appropriation.

Polybius is hardly alone in such misinterpretation. It is, after all, not immediately obvious what is meant by *religion* – or, for that matter, what was meant by *religio* (notice that Cicero felt obliged to provide a definition: it is "the worship of the gods"). Let us take as an illustration a modern difficulty. It was once quite common for occidental students of Buddhism to concentrate on the Buddhism of canonical and philosophical texts to the exclusion of the actual practices of living Buddhists in south and east Asia – Buddhism "on the ground," as it were – hence (for example) the regular assertion in religion textbooks that "there are no gods in Buddhism." This habit of mind, a product of the largely Protestant outlook of the former colonizers of Buddhist lands and of Buddhist study, effectually banished from the ranks of Buddhism a majority of its practitioners, as David Lopez demonstrated only so recently as the 1990s. This raises the question of what actually constitutes Buddhism. Is Buddhism something out there, a Platonic form in which some participate more properly than others, or is it the collection of actions and attitudes on the part of its professed practitioners? Or even those of its *unprofessed* practitioners?

The impediments to recovering Roman religion are especially formidable. We know depressingly little about the "shapeless profusion of polytheism," as Ramsey MacMullen has described it. The biggest problem is that we are not dealing with a living religion: there is no paganism "on the ground" to amplify and correct the perspective of our extant sources. By the way, it is because these religionists are all dead that we can continue to employ so derogatory term as "pagan" – which means something like "redneck" – in the first place. After all, spiritualists are no longer called primitives, although Wiccans, admittedly, are still called crazy. Our sources for Roman religion fall into one of three categories. First and most important are the literary productions of the elite (of which Polybius and Cicero are by now familiar examples). Secondly, and we have already seen the value of this, are non-literary written sources, such as inscriptions. And the third source, often the most difficult to interpret, consists in data of a purely archeological quality. All of these are limited in multiple ways. And rarely do they cooperate with one another. It is often as if one were assembling not pieces of an immense jigsaw puzzle but pieces of several immense jigsaw puzzles, without a clue as to how many pictures one has to do with – and with the very real possibility that one's instructions are for an altogether different game.

To take problems only of the most obvious order, the religious experiences of women and the religious experiences of the lower classes are now lost to view. We get tantalizing glimpses of each. Cicero, for instance, tells us that only the vulgar continued to practice divination by lots at the Temple of Fortuna at Praeneste. Why did they persist when their betters left off? And why did their betters leave off in the first place? Not because no one at the top believed in divination, as Cicero's dialogue *On Divination* proves clearly enough (this work is a debate amongst elites on the efficacy of divination, the conclusion of which is left undecided).

It was only in the late republic that the Romans, by way of the influence of Greek philosophy, developed a discourse for discussing religion as an object of intellectual analysis and reflection, a reality that itself requires us to scrutinize these writings for their importation of Greek premises. Elite Greeks and elite Romans agreed that ordinary people were "crude, untaught yokels to whom it is not even granted to understand citizen affairs, much less to discuss matters pertaining to the gods," and so naturally Cicero can include in one of his essays the sneering insistence that no educated person believed in fables of punishment after death. But we have precious little evidence that ordinary Romans of Cicero's day had any serious ideas about the continuation of life after death at all. By far the most common Roman tombstone for lower-class persons in Rome, so common it becomes a simple abbreviation, is the sentiment "I was not, I was, I am not, I don't care." It appears as if Cicero is here simply regurgitating a recurrent observation of Greek philosophizing, indifferent to the realities of life amongst Rome's urban poor. Not, then, a very useful informant – in this instance anyway.

Humble Romans seem, in fact, to have pestered the gods with *this-worldly* concerns. The most commonly expressed reason for making even the most modest offering to the gods, including the mighty Jupiter, was the restoration of one's health, unsurprising in a world lacking anything even nominally deserving the word medicine. No other prayer is attested nearly so often. And Cicero distinguishes *religio* from *superstitio* by referring to the distasteful habit of those persons, not all from the lower classes, "who spent whole days in prayer and sacrifice to ensure that their children should outlive them." To pray without ceasing, from Cicero's perspective, betrays a selfish, unproductive and un-Roman habit of mind.

And perhaps a feminine one as well. During his exile, Cicero composed a letter to his wife, Terentia, in which he complained that "neither the gods, whom you have worshipped so religiously, nor mankind, whom I have always served, have kept their side of the bargain." Was this distribution of labor normal? Was Terentia responsible for her household's relationship with the gods? Years later, Cicero reported to his wife that his morbid anxiety had been relieved when, during the night, he had vomited bile: "I was so relieved that it seemed to me that one of the gods must have doctored me. So do please pay our debt to this god, with piety and purity, as is your habit." To what extent was family religion the work of women? Our sources simply let us down.

But we must now direct our attention to one important slice of Roman religion: the civic religion, the religion that preserved the *pax deorum* and consequently sustained the *res publica*. This was practiced by all Romans, though in varying ways. Members of the elite presided over the ceremonies of civic religion. The populace, for its part, participated by observing. In order to supervise the mechanics of civic religion, the Romans employed three colleges of priests, each of which possessed its own area of expertise. The most distinguished were the augurs, who were obliged to know and interpret the augural law that determined the appropriate means by which Jupiter expressed his approval or disapproval of public actions, such as elections. Along with them were the pontiffs, the priests, whose knowledge extended to consecrations and the *sacra* of the state and of families. The third were the Fifteen Men for Observing the Sacrifices, who consulted the Sibylline Oracles and Etruscan soothsayers. The head of this apparatus was the *pontifex maximus*, the office occupied by Julius Caesar. Elected magistrates (as we shall see presently) also played important roles in civic religion. And they were all of them subordinate to the senate, which had the final say in matters pertaining to the *pax deorum*. The priestly colleges acted in many respects like special committees, to whom the senate referred religious problems and whose advice the senate was not obliged to accept.

Roman priests were not clergy; they had no special powers, such as the sacraments, nor did they possess a unique personal sanctity. What they had, once they were appointed, was access to specialized information, the accumulation of the Romans' religious observations, not revealed truth. The Romans regarded their religious practices as the product of centuries of empirical research and induction. For them, the will of the gods was a complicated actuality, the correct apprehension of which was frequently possible (especially where the central issues of civic life were concerned) on the basis of past and present evidence. Some mysteries remained, to be sure, and fresh indications of the gods' displeasure (a novel omen, say, or an unpredicted ritual outcome) were unmistakable markers of mortal ignorance that prompted continued investigation. Religion, then, was a sort of science: it had to be gotten right to get the right results. We might compare contemporary economics. Although we know quite a lot about reading and reacting to economic signals, we have not yet arrived at a stage where honest and passionate economic debate is superfluous. Nor have we gotten past our legitimate anxieties when it comes to managing our modern economies, even with expert guidance. The dismal science remains a work in progress. Likewise *religio*: it was an ongoing dimension of life, one in which the Romans were constantly feeling their way. Roman religion acknowledged no prophet who had delivered the whole truth in one cosmic communication. This is why so many religious problems could arise in Roman society and why their solution could prove contentious.

The *pax deorum*, because it was fragile, was a constant concern. All meetings of the senate took place in a temple, in a space inaugurated in conformity with the augural law. The first item of business was necessarily religious affairs. All assemblies were preceded by religious observations. This could only be done by a magistrate, whose election and subsequent inauguration invested him both with *imperium*, the power of command, and with *auspicium*, the power to consult the gods on behalf of the *res publica*. Even after these observations, an assembly could still be disturbed by an unexpected and untoward omen – but only if the presiding magistrate accepted the report of this omen, the sole exception being a report by an augur, who, by pronouncing the formula *alio die* – on another day –

could postpone any public transaction. It is often and wrongly claimed that the Romans could not distinguish religion from politics, and this insinuation of religious observance into the instruments of government in Rome is the first item of evidence. But Romans grasped the difference between a bad omen – which did not imply that the proposal before the assembly was bad, only that it could not be dealt with at that moment – and a sound argument for or against a proposal. They could certainly distinguish *auspicium* from *imperium*.

Nor was civic religion an entirely somber matter. The *pax deorum* was also maintained by sacrifice, festivals and games – which could involve dramatic contests, acrobats, chariot racing or – eventually – gladiatorial combats. There was certainly a sacred meal, which was lavish at the major and official sacrifices. Almost every major sacred precinct included dining rooms, and we know from later authors how pleasurable holy banquets could be. "No visit," writes Plutarch, a pious intellectual of the late first century of our era (admittedly a Greek but also a responsible Roman citizen), "gladdens us more than a visit to a shrine, no season more than a festival, nothing done or said more than what we see and do in regard to the gods, whether we are present at secret rites, or at dancing, sacrificing or initiations." What inspired such delight? Again Plutarch: "It is not the abundance of wine or the roasting of meat that makes the joy of festivals, but the good hope and the belief that the god is present in his kindness and graciously accepts what is offered." Insistence like this can only mean that in fact it *was* the abundance of wine and the roasting of meat that made the joy – at least for some attendants. In fact, one notices how often cult members are instructed not to carve their initials on the walls of the temple's banquet hall and most certainly not to spit up their wine. Roman civic religion, then, was essential to the continuation of the state – and it was also *fun*. And classicists have not liked it very much.

It is not merely because Roman religion could be fun that scholars have disliked it. In the nineteenth and most of the twentieth centuries, it was owing to its emphasis on ritual – rituals practiced by the likes of Cicero and Caesar, who never once offer anything like a sincere confession of genuine faith – that classicists became suspicious. Like Buddhism, the study of Roman religion has been very much influenced by Christianity, and especially by Protestant categories of analysis. Indeed, the historical and comparative study of religion in Europe was to a large extent a concern of Protestant scholars, reflecting Protestant notions about the discovery of authentic religious kernels in the midst of historically accumulated husks. And so naturally there was an obsession with true belief as the hallmark of religious vitality. For instance, Warde Fowler, in his magnificent but now thoroughly outdated *The Religious Experience of the Roman People*, first published in 1911, could say of Roman religion by the second century BC that "worship has become meaningless – the outward form of the cults may be maintained in such particulars as most closely concern the public life of the community; but as a religious system expressing human experience, we have done with these things." Similarly, Kurt Latte, in what was long the standard German *Handbuch*, entitled his chapter covering the same period "the collapse of Roman religion." Now these seem odd conclusions to draw in the teeth of Cicero's insistence of the superiority of Roman *religio*: the problem, for these scholars, was that Cicero's heart was not strangely moved as he penned his insistence.

Nowadays classicists, even the ones who are atheists doomed to perdition, endeavor to be more self-conscious when it comes to the potential distorting effects of modern religious frames of reference. We have finally begun to catch up with our colleagues in anthropology. Belief, while central to Christianity, can and does occupy other positions in other religions. As Wilfred Cantwell Smith expressed it, "the peculiarity of place given to belief in Christian history is a monumental matter, whose importance and relative uniqueness must be appreciated. So characteristic has it been that unsuspecting Westerners have been liable to ask about a religious group other than their own, 'what do they believe?' as though this were the primary question, and certainly a legitimate one." Modern classicists, fully apprised of the centrality of ritual in many traditional societies, have at least shrugged off their previous obsession with authenticity of belief. But in doing so, they may have swung too far in the opposite direction.

In my opinion, "what did they believe?" remains a legitimate question to ask of the Romans, so long as it is not blown out of proportion. I take this view because the Romans of the late republic spent so much time discussing their beliefs and the variety of their beliefs in philosophical essays. And, despite the narrowness of Cicero's definition of *religio*, this brand of philosophizing was clearly a part of Roman religion, just as mythology or theology is today a part of certain religious traditions. One does not understand another culture simply by accepting it entirely on its own terms: this would be like limiting one's understanding of ancient tragedy to the prescriptions of Aristotle's *Poetics*. *Its* terms must be translated (with the requisite sensitivity needless to say) into *our* terms. And, in any event, Romans other than Cicero did include philosophizing in their conception of *religio*. When the first century Epicurean poet Lucretius attacks the mentality he associates with *religio*, he includes in that attack his criticisms of Roman *philosophical* interpretations of traditional practices and myths. He did not distinguish between sacrifice, of which he disapproved, and academic ruminations on the symbolism or significations of sacrifice, of which he also and clearly disapproved. Never the less, dogma was remarkably unimportant in Roman religion: what was central to the preservation of the *pax deorum* was punctilious ritual performance. Ritual, as Clifford Geertz has taught us, is what there was. And the philosopher Seneca could complain that in religious observances "the greater part of the people do not know why they do what they do." But, as we shall see, ritual can be a locus for contesting the meaningfulness and the meaninglessness of religious actions and attitudes. Some Romans, at least, believed that they knew what they were doing and whether or not it mattered.

It was a controversy over ritual correctness that deeply marred Caesar's first consulship in 59 BC, leaving him forever hateful (and frightening) to the conservative nobility who dominated senatorial politics. Now in what follows, I must be a bit technical, and for that I apologize. But it will give you a flavor of what it meant to be Roman – and to be political and religious in Rome. And if you find yourself somewhat confused by it all, don't worry: so did they.

Caesar began his consulship graciously. He displayed deference to the senate and to his detested colleague, Calpurnius Bibulus. When he proposed an agrarian law, to meet the needs of Pompey's veterans, it included stipulations and safeguards that ought to have satisfied everyone. Caesar discussed his bill in the senate, and offered to amend its details. None of this, however, placated Bibulus – or the many in the senate who simply could not abide the idea of the state's buying and distributing land to veterans and to the poor. When Cato obstructed discussion of the bill by filibuster, Caesar lost patience and ordered him removed. But Cato was accompanied by the bulk of the body's members, including Marcus Petreius, who famously remarked that he should prefer to be in prison with Cato than in the senate with Caesar. The fact that Petreius was a close and faithful friend of Pompey – and a likely supporter of any agrarian law in Pompey's interests –indicates how objectionable Caesar's conduct was deemed to be.

Caesar then blanked the senate and turned directly to the people (an action which was also objectionable): at public assemblies, he invited Bibulus, Pompey, and Crassus to speak about the law. Pompey and Crassus were united in its support, and each intimated that opposition would be answered by violence. Undeterred, Bibulus blazed that however much the people may desire Caesar's law, they would never have it during *his* consulship. Bibulus had tribunes enough to veto the measure, but Caesar had a champion in the tribune Publius Vatinius, an unattractive but valiant new man, who, it was soon realized, would run roughshod over any colleague who tried to block Caesar's law.

Consequently, Bibulus turned to a new tactic: consuls, praetors and tribunes had the authority to observe the heavens for ill-omens (*spectio*), the report of which (*obnuntiatio*) required the postponement of any legislative or electoral assembly. Bibulus solemnly announced that on every night preceding an assembly, he would watch the sky. Now ordinarily the mere announcement of an observation was sufficient to cancel an assembly, though technically it was the report itself that actually enacted the effects of an omen, a distinction that was in practice lost on most Romans and evaded even most members of the senate. At the same time, it was unnatural for a magistrate to employ *spectio* in order to paralyse government for an entire year (remember that Bibulus had declared in public that the people would not have this agrarian law during his consulship). Enormity begat enormity. Ignoring Bibulus, Caesar set a date for a vote on his bill. The Forum was packed with Pompey's veterans, into which company Bibulus and his entourage, which included Cato and three tribunes, forced their way. The consul was heaped with excrement (put less delicately, somebody dumped a bucket of shit on his head). Still, the persistent Bibulus succeeded in reaching the platform where he intended to announce the omens. This, however, he was prevented from doing by violence: a riot – and injuries – ensued. Bibulus and his followers were ejected, after which Caesar's bill was passed into law. The following day angry crowds intimidated the senate when it considered invalidating the law – religious vitiation was a legal basis for abrogating a law – and Vatinius ordered Bibulus imprisoned when he attempted to address the public. Caesar then demanded that all senators take an oath of obedience to his agrarian law: in the end, even Cato capitulated.

The senate was shaken. Bibulus, and the three tribunes who supported him, retired from public life. They continued to observe the heavens and to announce unfavorable omens by edict, a practice that was intended to put in doubt the legality of all the legislation of the year and certainly emphasized the violent nature of Caesar's consulship. These gestures were not pointless: over the course of the year, the shamelessness of the triumvirs became offensive to the Roman people, who did not hesitate to express themselves with public hissing and booing, and the senate simmered in its resentment at Caesar's outrageous methods. Caesar, Pompey, and Crassus, it could be complained, held both the gods and the senate in contempt.

For years after this event, it was maintained by Caesar's enemies, and by many who were neutral in this contest, that Caesar's laws were all passed in violation of the omens and could – and should – be abrogated. This is remarkable, because we know that according to the technical requirements of augural law it was necessary for any magistrate observing the heavens to be present and to report the omen on the spot. Bibulus's non-stop and long-distance *obnuntiatio* had no basis in the strict rules of Roman ritual. Nor was Caesar – technically – in the wrong for ignoring Bibulus's original announcement – because Bibulus never got to make it. It is irrelevant that he was prevented from doing so by violence: the announcement must actually be made to be valid. If Jupiter had *wanted* the announcement to be made, after all, it was his responsibility to make that happen, gods being mightier than men. Since Bibulus and his supporters had to have known this, their actions must have been nothing more than a misleading political show. That, at least, is the verdict of a majority of Roman historians.

But this ignores the extent and the intensity of the controversy, in which many augurs, when questioned in public, publicly took Bibulus's part by expressing the view that Caesar's acts, because they ignored Bibulus's observation (his *spectio* not his *obuntiatio*), were invalid (admittedly these were unofficial opinions, because the senate never referred this matter to the college for a formal judgment). There can be little question but that public opinion was impressed by Caesar's violence – Bibulus's rights as consul had been denied him by force – and I have no doubt that that reality led some to look for reasons to undo Caesar's actions. But I also suspect that, by the first century, in the minds of most Romans of all classes, the relationship between *spectio* and *obnuntiatio* had been confounded. Never before, so far as we know, had an announcement been prevented by violence. Which means that the ritual pattern had always been either the declaration of an observation (*spectio*), after which there was no assembly at all, or a declaration followed the next morning by a peaceful and formal announcement (*obnuntiatio*). Over time, many will have believed that *spectio* was sufficient to cancel an assembly. Cicero, who was an augur, remarks in another context that in the secret books of the augurs one finds that it is forbidden to hold an assembly after a *spectio* has been declared, though he has not been credited on this point. To try to settle this issue along doctrinal lines is, in my opinion, to miss the point. The controversy was real, however political its implications, because even among the elite there could be controversy over what exactly constituted the punctilious performance of a ritual. Ritual is what there was, all right, and it was more than enough to be getting on with. It was by no means a simple service: more than one voice could be raised and raised legitimately. This ritual was not an empty show, nor was it so narrowly perceived that every participant invested it with meaning in the same way.

Here Roman historians would do well once more to consult their colleagues in anthropology. The recognition that expectations respecting religious practices can differ amongst individuals and groups in response to changing contexts and new personalities hardly represents a return to Christianizing assumptions about beliefs. On the contrary, contemporary anthropological research has made it clear that, even in traditional societies, the differences between individuals and groups can over time establish new interpretations for hereditary practices, "new senses of the meaningfulness – or meaninglessness" in rituals, as Sherry Ortner has put it. Rituals are not "out there" and therefore determinative: they are cultural forms that are constantly recreated by new individuals, who can and do employ them to discover "new meanings that are already there." In the cultural space between the agents of a ritual and the form they are enacting, the struggle over meaning can and does take place. In the religious struggle between Caesar and Bibulus, we find an instantiation of just that struggle. Ironically, Caesar was the traditionalist. And he was ultimately the winner. But that was, to a large extent, owing to a law passed during the subsequent year by his ally Clodius Pulcher, that redefined, in strict and clear terms, how observations and announcements must thereafter be managed. In 59 BC, however, it was neither logic nor religion but political violence that dominated affairs. Caesar's enormities were not forgotten, and he knew it: this is why he feared prosecution and conviction at the termination of his proconsulship.

That, of course, never happened. The civil war intervened, and soon Caesar was the master of Rome. And he may well have become more than that. He may have become – a god. The great scholar Terentius Varro dedicated his *Antiquities of Roman Religion* to the victorious Caesar and in it urged him to reform and to restore traditional civic religious practices (he might have begun by appointing a *flamen Dialis*, as the post had remained empty since his abortive nomination in the eighties). Rome's new master had other plans: although already a pontiff, he had himself made an augur as well – an exceptionable accumulation of sacred offices. He increased the number of all the important priesthoods, so that he could install his allies. Only his reform of the calendar – in Rome as elsewhere the calendar was first and foremost a religious matter and by the mid-first century it was a disaster – can have satisfied Varro's expectations. Instead, Caesar was offered and accepted honor after honor, each more impressive than the last, until finally his status began to take on superhuman, even divine, proportions. On the current condition of our evidence we cannot be certain, but it is at very least a possibility that, during his dictatorship, Caesar became a god incarnate.

Modern scholars have difficulty wrapping their heads around this idea. And to normal sensibilities it remains a bit absurd. "And this man / is now become a god," complains Shakespeare's Cassius, immediately after commenting critically on Caesar's limited swimming talents,

> . . . and Cassius is
> A wretched creature, and must bend his body
> If Caesar carelessly but nod on him.
> He had a fever when he was in Spain,
> And when the fit was on him, I did mark
> How he did shake: 'tis true, this god did shake.

But divine honors for mortal men were scarcely unheard of in the Greco-Roman world. Founders of cities, though mortal, received divine honors as part of civic religion. And heroes, like Heracles, could, by accomplishing mighty deeds for the benefit of mankind, transform themselves into gods. It was along the lines of this model, presumably, that Alexander the Great could demand veneration from the Greeks, however unconvinced the Greeks' obedient response (The Spartans famous reply was, "if Alexander wants to be a god, so let him be a god already"). More relevant to the Roman experience was the divine status of Hellenistic kings, the very kings whom the Romans defeated in expanding their empire. Hellenistic monarchs each assumed a unique divinity, taking on the attributes of conquering and civilizing gods like Dionysus and the Dioscuri and Heracles. They confirmed their divine status by delivering justice to their subjects and defeat to their enemies. Incompetent monarchs, however, could not take refuge in their sanctity: in Caesar's own lifetime, the King of Egypt, Cleopatra's father, Ptolemy XII, known to us as Auletes (the flute-player) but to his subjects as Theos Philopator Philadelphos Neos Dionysos – Ptolemy the God, Loyal to his Father, Loyal to his Brother, the New Dionysus – had more than once been driven from Alexandria by angry mobs.

75

Romans, too, had enjoyed divine honors in the east. After the Second Macedonian War, the victorious Roman general, Titus Quinctius Flamininus, declared, at the Isthmian Games, that Greece had been liberated from Macedon and that the Romans were going home: hereafter, all Greeks would forever be free. In response, the Greek cities competed with one another in heaping praise on Flamininus: he was declared *soter*, savior, and honored in prayers alongside Heracles and Apollo in some places, alongside Zeus in others. A cult in his honor was established, and priesthoods that existed well into the empire. His image appeared on coins, and statues portrayed him as a hero and as a god. The Greeks, one can see, had a knack for embracing liberators. This set the pattern for subsequent provincial governors in the east, when the Romans changed their mind about the freedom of the Greeks. These men received temples and priests and cult. It was remarkable to refuse them, as did Cicero's little brother, who governed Asia, and Cicero himself when he was proconsul of Cilicia. When it came to divine honors for men in power, the Romans knew all about it. But it was all rather foreign. Or at least it had been.

But after Caesar's victory at Thapsus (in April of 46 BC) and after his final victory at Munda (in March of 45 BC), the senate began to heap honors of a sacred or divine nature upon Caesar; whether at his instigation or owing to the natural spanieling instincts of inferior men we cannot say. Now Caesar already possessed certain pretensions to divinity. The Julii claimed to be descended from Venus, by way of Iulus, the son of Aeneas. Other families made similar claims: for instance, it was accepted that the Antonii stemmed from Hercules. Caesar intended to emphasize his claim to divine ancestry by constructing a temple to *Venus Genetrix*, Venus the mother of the Romans (owing to their descent from Aeneas), but also Venus the mother of the Julian house. Still, this was small beer. After Thapsus, the senate decreed a bronze statue of Caesar that represented him as a world conqueror: the statue was situated on the Capitol and bore an inscription, later erased on Caesar's instructions, that identified him as a divinity (our Greek source prohibits our being more specific than that). After Munda, Caesar was honored as a second founder of Rome, his image was carried in the procession of the gods, and his statue was placed in the temple of Quirinus (the divine manifestation of Romulus, the original founder of the city). A temple and cult to a new god, *Clementia Caesaris*, the Mercy of Caesar, was established. After this, a new house for Caesar was decreed, equipped with the architectural features of a temple. There were further distinctions: a golden chair, a privilege of the gods, and Caesar's symbols were to be placed amongst the sacred couches of the gods. Finally, and here matters are murkiest, a *flamen Caesaris*, who was to be Mark Antony, the appointment of which ought to imply the elevation of Caesar to *Divus Iulius*, Caesar the God.

We must unfortunately remain uncertain about all this. Caesar, between Munda and his assassination, was clearly in a rush to march east to Parthia in order to continue his world conquest, whatever his cosmic status. None of our sources for his religious policies or aspirations is unproblematic: most are late and Greek and all are contaminated by the effects of the Caesar legend and of the emperor worship that became an imperial habit. Old-fashioned scholars simply could not believe that the Romans – the genuine Romans of the free republic – could succumb to the fawning practices of the Hellenistic Greeks, whereas more recent scholars seem determined to prove that, on the contrary, they did – a view they embrace not least because this runs counter to the intuitions of old-fashioned scholars.

Let us assume that the senate did indeed elevate Caesar to divine status. Let us further assume that it was Caesar who insisted on it. How degrading then for his aristocratic contemporaries, who could not fail to appreciate the full significance of it all. The senate of Rome was reduced to the condition of its Greekling subjects. Roman power was now unmistakably in Caesar's hands: the senators were become Alexandrians or Asians or Cilicians. That would be the inevitable state of things, given our assumptions at the beginning of this train of thought. What is nothing short of stunning is that, given all the senatorial grievances about Caesar's dictatorship, they don't seem to have complained much about his godlike pretensions – if, in fact, he had any. In Cicero's enormous correspondence, his dissatisfaction with Caesar is patent. And in the historical record of Caesar's time at the helm of state, we can detect plain indications of resistance to his autocracy. His religious honors never really enter into it. Senators were mainly obsessed with whether Caesar would be a temporary dictator, like Sulla, or become a king, and it is Caesar's attitude toward monarchy that dominates our record of his brief tenure in power. That uncertainly was removed when he was appointed dictator for life. Caesar the god was entirely beside the point, so far as the senate was concerned. And, after his death, although a degree of embarrassment about some of Caesar's divine honors is detectable on the part of some senators, it was either as a tyrant or as a friend that Caesar was chiefly remembered by the aristocracy – not as a god amongst them.

On the streets of Rome, it was a different story. On the site of Caesar's funeral rites, the mob erected an altar and a column, spontaneous gestures of their willingness to worship their dead master as a god. This cult was sustained by the energies of a certain Amatius, who claimed to be a grandson of Gaius Marius. Public disruptions were associated with the cult, and Antony won commendation from the senate by executing Amatius and suppressing the cult. But the people restored it almost immediately. Antony also refused to become Caesar's *flamen*, and resisted the implementation of other sacred honors that had been voted to the dictator. But in this he was plainly out of step with the public mood. During the summer of this same year, at the games celebrated in honor of Caesar's victories, a comet appeared in the night sky, which was immediately hailed, by the masses, as Caesar's star, the *sidus Iulium*. In the popular mind there was no question but that *Divus Iulius* was a god. Newly arrived in Rome, young Octavian, the dictator's heir and the future Augustus, began to describe himself as *divi filius*, the son of god. This would soon prove to be an advantageous political slogan in his looming contest with Antony.

It was not only in the mean streets of Rome that Caesar's divinity was asserted: in municipal Italy we find inscriptions, at least some of which must be from Caesar's lifetime, in which he is indicated as a god. For example, "to Marcus Salvius Venustus, the son of Quintus, decurion owing to the kindness of the god Caesar," and, really quite interesting, a dedication to Caesar's wife, Calpurnia, by one of her clients that reads in part, "my patron, the wife of the magnificent Caesar, the god." Ordinary men in the Italian municipalities, like the ordinary citizens in the streets of Rome, had no difficulty in finding in Caesar a god, a god not obviously different from any other god: *Divus Iulius*, as we have seen, even had his martyrs. The religious sensibilities of these men – I hesitate to speak of their beliefs – were of an entirely different order from those of the senatorial aristocracy.

In the end, that would perforce change. At the Battle of Actium, the *divi filius* would lead the forces of Italy against the shameful oriental pantheon commanded by Cleopatra and the *new* New Dionysus, Antony. On one side, in Virgil's representation of the cosmic forces at work, Apollo and Mars the Avenger and Divus Iulius – sound western divinities – on the other, barking Anubis from Egypt and other monstrosities of comparable eastern ilk. Jihad, or a crusade? Certainly politics. But thereafter, when Augustus had become the new master of the world, there was a thorough and detailed and costly religious reform – of the sort dreamed of by Varro. Temples were restored, old cults were dusted off, the priesthoods were filled and properly subsidized. The civil war, according to the ideology of the Augustan age, descended upon Rome when she violated the *pax deorum*. As the poet Horace put it in the last of his Roman odes:

> You will continue to pay for the sins of your fathers, O Roman, until you restore the crumbling temples and shrines of the gods, and their statues filthy with black smoke.

Roman religion would henceforth be observed with the same scrupulosity that had intimidated Polybius and had made the republic great. And there could be no exceptions. Not even when there arose in the east a new god incarnate. But that of course is another story.

Further Reading

Roman religion quickly becomes technical. Still, there are useful introductions, such as Dowden 1992, North 2000, and Warrior 2006, that will quickly and accurately situate any newcomer to this difficult territory. Beard, North and Price 1998 is a wide-ranging yet thoroughly accessible textbook. Readers will also profit from Liebeschuetz 1979, MacMullen 1981 and Wardman 1982. Feeney 1998 profitably combines the investigation of Roman religious sensibilities with literary inquiry. Emperor cult, its Hellenistic background and Caesar's place within it, all remain controversial and have been extensively studied. Taylor 1931 remains a classic. A penetrating account of the practice is provided by Price 1984. A recent and important (and therefore also controversial) contribution is Gradel 2002. Caesar's religious program is examined in learned detail in another controversial book, Weinstock 1971.

4

The Stones of Rome: Caesar and the Sociology of Roman Public Building

For the modern visitor to Rome, it is a special treat to lounge at a café in the Piazza della Rotunda, while savoring the languid summer air, sipping an iced vermouth, and gazing at the Pantheon, perhaps the most beautiful extant specimen of classical Roman public building and unquestionably the most influential of all Roman buildings in the European and American architectural traditions. Although it is the unsurpassed interior space, covered by what was until 1958 the largest concrete dome in existence, that endures as the Pantheon's most celebrated feature, there never the less remains an exquisite pleasure in studying the structure's deceptive and cosmopolitan classical porch, the pediment of which is supported on Corinthian columns with shafts of Egyptian granite and capitals and bases of Pentelic marble.

But all of this is just eye candy, at least so far as senatorial sensibilities were concerned, and a distraction from the temple's essential feature: the inscription set in the entablature. For any right-thinking Roman aristocrat, it was this bit of the building that first and foremost made its claim on the gaze of the truly serious observer of public architecture. The Pantheon's inscription is as concise as it is steeped in significance. Here it is:

M. AGRIPPA L. F. COS. TERTIVM FECIT
(Marcus Agrippa, the son of Lucius, when consul for the third time, built this)

Now this inscription is interesting for many reasons, the most striking of which is that it is entirely false. Marcus Agrippa did not build the Pantheon in Rome: the emperor Hadrian did. In fact, Agrippa did not even build the temple this building replaced, the Pantheon constructed by Domitian, which was struck by lightning and burned in AD 110. It was the original Pantheon, nothing at all like the third in this trinity, that Agrippa erected (that building was destroyed in the great fire of AD 80). Which must raise the question in anyone's mind, what is the point of this false advertising?

Now in all fairness Hadrian's inscription on the Pantheon was not intended chiefly to cater to the requirements of architectural historians or enthusiasts of a conservative bent. The emperor was, in what may to us seem a roundabout style of boasting, making a point about his own imperial virtue. By way of contrast, and in order to clarify Hadrian's strategy here, let us consider the Pantheon of Domitian. It is as certain as these things can be that Domitian's temple preserved no mention whatsoever of its predecessor. Suetonius tells us that

> Domitian restored many splendid buildings that had been destroyed by fire, including the Capitolium, which had been burned yet again. But all of them he restored with only his name on the inscription, without any recollection at all of the original builder.

This observation is intended by its author as a criticism: when Domitian obliterated the names of builders of the past, who, as we shall see, were invariably senators of the highest distinction in traditional terms, he behaved like a very bad emperor indeed.

The correct imperial style was set by Augustus. We can read about it in his immodestly entitled *The Achievements of the Divine Augustus by which he Brought the World Under the Empire of the Roman People and of the Expenses Which he Bore for the Republic and for the People of Rome* (in the spirit of justice I should point out that Augustus didn't include the "divine" bit), itself an inscription, which was inscribed and displayed not only in Rome but throughout the empire (lest anyone anywhere fail to be impressed by it). There Augustus informs us that, amongst his many construction projects:

> I built the portico at the Flaminian Circus, the Octavian Portico, which I allowed to continue to be known by the name of the man who had originally built it.

Likewise:

> I restored the Capitolium and the Theater of Pompey at great personal expense – without inscribing my name on either one of them.

81

Augustus, as always, eats his cake and has it too. He erects an inscription in which he takes full credit for the restoration of these great monuments from the past, but he also claims credit for *not* taking full credit: after all, he restored not only the buildings but also their inscriptions – features that were the most important elements in the message of these buildings in the first place. The politics of inscriptions, these passages alone suffice to demonstrate beyond any doubt, were important in the empire – and they were also important in the late republic.

But allow me to dilate for a moment on the full significance of these inscriptions, which, like other features of Roman public life, at once displayed and exposed to invidious scrutiny the reputation, the *dignitas*, of every public benefactor. As I have just observed, they were not meant to be informative in any modern sense. They were, instead, written instructions for the appropriate appreciation of the structure under view. When Agrippa or Augustus writes "I built," he in effect eliminates the contribution of architect and artist, surveyor and contractor, even realtor and solicitor. "I built" means "I paid for and took responsibility for the construction of." This contrasts plainly and remarkably with our own practices of building and commemoration (our foundation stones routinely convey detailed information about multiple and frankly boring aspects of a building's genesis, construction, and dedication – which is perhaps why we regularly ignore them). Roman habits also clash with the architectural conventions of the Greeks, who tend to record the names of the architects and artists employed to do the work, but leave unmentioned the political movers and shakers whose initiative made the structure possible in the first place. But from the perspective of Roman public building, funding and management were what mattered, and the subjects of the verb "built" – men like Agrippa and not the government – got the credit (and the blame) for public projects. Much could be at stake, not least in the smallest of details, even for a great man.

In 52 BC Pompey the Great dedicated the Temple to *Venus Victrix*, Venus the Conqueror, which constituted a part of his great theater complex (we shall have more to say about this project presently). In that year, Pompey was consul for the third (and, in the event, the last) time in his career. And so he needed (and of course very much wanted) to make this clear in the inscription. Now it was a very rare thing to be consul more than once, much less consul for a third time, and it was even rarer to build anything so grand as the Theater of Pompey (in fact, the edifice was in all respects unprecedented in Roman public architecture). But Pompey's attentions were concentrated on his inscription, and he was uncertain of the correct Latin formulation for describing his unusual status. This was not because he had been a substandard student in school but rather because it was one of those instances where distinguished stylists took different views on what constituted best usage. Think of the split infinitive in English: is it to be avoided or accepted? The issue has been known to generate passion. In the original edition of Fowler's *Modern English Usage*, for instance, the author denounces writers who condemn splitting infinitives as "bogy-haunted creatures" even as he despises all those reckless enough to enthusiastically embrace the habit, dismissing them as "deliberately rejecting the trammels of convention." Best of all, naturally, is the stylist who knows when and when not to split an infinitive, discernment that reflects an author's taste as much as his good sense. Who knew so much could be at stake? Fortunately for the likes of you and me, there are Fowlers aplenty to consult. The Romans, on the other hand, had not yet descended to prescriptive grammars. Which, of course, raised the stakes considerably.

The dilemma for Pompey was whether "consul for the third time" ought to be *consul tertium* or *consul tertio*. The epic poet Ennius, he knew well enough, would have selected *tertium*. So, too, the scholarly Varro. But different senators put it differently in ordinary (but cultivated) speech, a practice that lasted till well into the empire, and from the many learned men whose opinion he sought, he had received varying opinions. The great man was frustrated, and timid of looking like an unlettered trammeller of convention, much less something along the lines of a bogy-haunted creature. Finally, and sensibly, he turned to Cicero, who, so his freedman Tiro later reported in a letter, "was reluctant to pass any judgment on men known for their erudition, lest he might seem to have censured the men themselves in criticizing their opinion." Consequently, Cicero advised Pompey to write neither *tertium* nor (or is it *or*?) *tertio*, but instead to inscribe simply TERT. – the first four letters only. That way everyone could amplify the abbreviation to his own satisfaction. When Augustus restored the theater, he replaced Pompey's TERT. with the Roman numeral III, perhaps owing to the same discretion – or anxiety. I don't need to unpack this story any further: it will be obvious how much hesitation even a figure of Pompey's eminence could have about the framing of a simple inscription. Nor will it elude anyone that Cicero was, for different but not entirely alien reasons, similarly fretful. This monument, by which I mean the temple's written instructions, mattered enormously – because it was the crucial bit of the entire complex.

This story supplies us with the context in which to view Agrippa's original inscription on the Pantheon. Marcus Vipsanius Agrippa was Augustus's greatest general and was soon second only to Augustus in wealth, influence, and ambition – to the extent that Gaius Maecenas eventually advised Augustus that either he must make Agrippa his son-in-law – or put him to death. He chose the former. But Agrippa, like Gaius Marius, had come from the provinces, and his name, Vipsanius, rang in Roman ears rather like Huckleberry Hound Dog might do in ours. Snobbery on the Romans' part must under no circumstances be discounted. Cicero's drunkard son, himself by definition nobly born (though his father was of course a new-comer like Marius or like Agrippa), openly despised Agrippa as vulgar, and once threw a drink in his face. The contempt of the aristocracy for the likes of Agrippa, then, was, to put it mildly, unmistakable. He knew how to push back.

Now Agrippa's inscription, you will notice, suppresses his family name. In so doing, however, he is not hiding it but is instead aping a fashion of the very nobility who resented him. By the late republic and into the early empire, it was common for Romans with the best family names, like Appius Claudius Pulcher or Quintus Caecilius Metellus, simply to drop their actual family name for, say, Quintus Metellus, that sort of thing, in complete confidence that nobody could conceivably fail to supply the glamorous missing ingredient. Agrippa's self-fashioning, motivated no doubt by a certain degree of social embarrassment, makes him look like a noble. And you will notice that his inscription boldly and proudly reads TERTIVM – the full word, no half-measure. This contrast with the nervous Latinity of the republican elite was meant to be noticed, especially by the nobility, who had been replaced by the likes of Agrippa.

Caesar understood the politics of inscriptions and early on attempted to ingratiate himself with Pompey by that very means. The Temple of *Jupiter Optimus Maximus*, Jupiter Greatest and Best, on the Capitoline Hill, was conceived by the Roman king Tarquinius Priscus, carried forward by his son Superbus and dedicated in the republic after Junius Brutus had thrown out the Tarquins. After its destruction by fire in 83 BC, it was rebuilt by Sulla. But it was dedicated, in 69 BC, by Quintus Lutatius Catulus, the Catulus whom Caesar defeated for the position of *pontifex maximus*. Red-edications, as we have seen, enjoyed all the prestige of original dedications, and this achievement contributed mightily to Catulus's public stature. However, although the temple had been rededicated, and Catulus's achieve-ment had been memorialized, the actual building had not yet been com-pleted (perhaps owing to the expense or to the complexity of its gilded bronze roof). Inept administration on this scale left Catulus exposed to criticism – and worse.

On the very first day of his praetorship, in 62 BC, Caesar promulgated a bill that would have required Catulus to render an account of his expenses for the project (*where* was Sulla's money going?) and would have transferred responsibility for its completion (along with an opportunity for a new inscription) to Pompey. In other words, Catulus's part would be rubbed out, quite literally. The consuls of that year, along with the bulk of the aristocracy, resisted Caesar's proposition so urgently that he immediately dropped it (which fact alone demonstrates the force of the opposition to it, Caesar being no push-over). Never the less, he will have gotten credit where he wanted it – with the people, who were losing patience with Catulus's dawdling, and with Pompey, who no doubt regarded himself as a more appropriate successor to Sulla than Catulus in this or any other matter. Caesar's action was as offensive to Catulus's friends as it was attractive to his enemies. But the rule that lay behind Caesar's bill (and made it so volatile) was simply this: the last restorer gets the credit. Augustus's practice had not yet been established.

The mechanisms of public building in Rome were complex and several. In each of them, the role of personal initiative and personal wealth was paramount. To be sure, the treasury of Rome often funded repairs and major projects for the public good. But it was always the individual in charge, be he censor or consul or aedile, who regularly took the credit (or, if things went poorly, the blame). There was no bureau of public works in Rome, no city planning, no vision for the future. All civic construction resulted from a stimulus–response mentality that relied on individual initiative and private contractors. Only in the imperial period would something like a civil service develop in Rome. But, during the republic, Roman magistrates who initiated large-scale projects, always with private building firms, were soon merely private citizens themselves (though admittedly well-connected ones who could hope to persuade a praetor or consul to back them up). They possessed no executive power with which to coerce big companies to complete big or complex buildings. Hence an expansive opportunity for unfinished or leaky temples, with little opportunity of redress available. Nor, to illustrate the limitations faced by would-be city planners, did the *res publica* enjoy any right of eminent domain: private property was sacred, and no one could be expected to part with his land for the sake of public construction, however salutary the likely result. For instance, the censors of 179 BC, in an attempt to solve the problem of Rome's water supply, sought and received permission from the senate to construct a new aqueduct. Unfortunately for Rome, because a single individual refused to sell one of his farms, the entire enterprise collapsed. Even

Caesar, during his dictatorship, had difficulties with recalcitrant landowners, and the irregular shape of the plan of the Forum of Augustus is the result of the refusal of one man to yield to his emperor's blandishments. All of which, by the way, is why the delay in completing the Capitolium may not have been owing to Catulus's corruption or incompetence. He may in actuality have been the frustrated victim of a sleazy building firm. Advocates of outsourcing, like advocates of small government, would do well to look at the Roman republic, which was replete with the effects of both ideas.

The most glamorous form of public building was what modern scholars call manubial construction: public building *ex manubiis*, out of the profits of war. In any campaign, its commander was responsible for the distribution of booty, to his troops and to his officers – and to himself. The legal technicalities that governed a general's disposition of the spoils (i.e., what was his and what was the republic's) are currently a matter of scholarly review, but they need not detain us. A great deal of the loot certainly became the generals' personal property, and the remainder, it was generally conceded, could and should be used in accordance with his designs. There was a moral obligation to devote a sizeable portion of the funds of each variety to the public good. This could take the form of public games, or simply a healthy deposit in the treasury – or these profits could pay for public construction, a visible and enduring symbol of the commander's success. The degree of that success will have gone a long distance in determining the choices available to any Roman general. A modest campaign, after all, will hardly have delivered the plunder necessary for public construction on a respectable scale, whereas a brilliant victory over a mighty (and so by definition wealthy) enemy might allow a Roman to perform all of the above, as Pompey did when he returned from the Mithridatic War in 61 BC.

The decision to build something spectacular carried the greatest prestige and won the most acclaim. There were obvious, practical reasons for this. These projects – the construction of temples and basilicas and aqueducts – were laudable in themselves. They improved the lives of the people even as they adorned the city. And they enriched equestrian contractors even while they provided necessary employment for the common people. And the result, a concrete expression of a senator's greatness, could be expected to last forever. This not simply because there was a big inscription on a big building: this edifice was understood to symbolize not an individual's but rather a family's glory. Roman public building was dynastic.

Here is the typical pattern. During a military campaign, a Roman general vows a temple to a god. Or, in the aftermath of a successful war, he elects to adorn his city with a suitable monument. A general with resources of this order will ordinarily have done well enough to have merited a triumph. But for this he needs the consent of his peers: the senate must concede his triumph. The senate also has the final say on how any general may spend his manubial funds and on the construction of any public works. And so the triumphant general must again seek the permission of his peers to engage in public building. These consents, it hardly needs saying, were by no means automatic: the natural jealousies obtaining in any oligarchy meant that it was every senator's natural instinct to resist awarding triumphs and licenses to erect monuments in their memory. At the same time, public welfare and religiosity – senatorial deliberations will regularly have included consultation with the priestly colleges – remained genuine and inescapable senatorial concerns, and in any case some victories were simply so glorious that all of Roman society insisted on their celebration and memorialization. Consequently, amongst other things, the erection of a public building demonstrated the extent of a senator's clout within his own class. This is why Cicero can describe public buildings with adjectives like *gratissimus*, evidence for and signifiers of influence, and, more commonly, *gloriosissimus*. When, in the case of a sacred structure, it was time to perform the ritual dedication, the builder had again to come to the senate – no private person could dedicate, nor could any dedication take place without the explicit permission of the senate or the people – at which time, again after consulting the appropriate priests, a senatorial decree would help to make the necessary technical arrangements.

Take the case of the Temple to *Venus Erycina* that was constructed by Quintus Fabius Maximus Verrucosus: Fabius sought permission to dedicate in 216 BC. The senate, after the obligatory examinations, passed a decree instructing the consul-designate, immediately upon entering office, to hold an assembly at which Fabius (along with someone else, probably a kinsman in line with the regular custom) would be elected a *duovir aedis dedicandi*, one of two men elected for dedicating a temple. It sometimes happened that, between the start and the completion of a project, its author died. In that circumstance, it was normal practice to allow his son (or, failing that, a suitable heir, since this is something one would assign in one's will) to dedicate – because the aristocracy conceded the dynastic implications of the project. The completed and dedicated building, it was recognized by all, was now a monument. The Temple of *Honos et Virtus* that Marius constructed, for example, and this was typical, was regularly referred to as the *monumentum Mari*, Marius's monument, his inscription having become more important to the building's reputation than the gods it housed. Once a monument had been finished and dedicated, it was thereafter a family duty to maintain it, preserving its utility and defending it fiercely if any outsider should attempt to offer too much assistance in this regard (because the final restoration trumps earlier benefactors, it must remain within the family, in which context it is a good thing for later generations to surpass earlier ones). In this way the Temple to Bellona became a museum celebrating the Claudii Pulchri, while the Basilica Aemilia, better known today as the Basilica Paulli, originally constructed in 179 BC by the censors Marcus Fulvius Nobilior and Marcus Aemilius Lepidus (and apparently known as the Fulvian Basilica), was maintained into the empire by the Aemilii, who were not too shy to borrow millions from Caesar in 55 BC in order to refurbish the portico on a monumental scale (it too was adorned with the history of this splendid family). Finally, the enduring political success of the Metelli, it has been observed, owed not a little to the building projects of Quintus Caecilius Metellus Macedonicus, who celebrated his conquest of Macedonia by erecting two temples and a portico on the Campus Martius. These monuments to martial success, to *virtus*, implied by their perpetuation the continuation of that very aspect of greatness in the descendants of a *triumphator*, whose own fame, at the time of his project's completion, was enhanced by the tremendous popularity that was naturally associated with public benefactions on so grand a scale.

Perhaps I should say a word or two to describe Roman public buildings: they were *big*. For the Romans, size mattered, and so far as I can tell it was the chief thing that mattered. When the elder Pliny looked back on the monuments of the past, he was impressed by their bulk and their cost (though he took a moralist's sniffy view of it all). The residue of the Romans looked at architecture the way most Americans look at cars and vans and trucks: the bigger the better. A Roman would have positively relished the excesses of a Hummer – especially the ones stretched out to limousine length. This was true of Rome from the start: the original temple to Jupiter Greatest and Best, constructed when Rome remained an unimportant town, was in its day the biggest in Italy. Probably the ugliest too, but who cared? Certainly not the Romans.

From the perspective of the masses, the scale and even limited splendor of their public buildings contrasted starkly with the crowded and squalid conditions in which they lived. It must not be forgotten that Rome was a third world city: its streets were open sewers, the majority of its inhabitants squeezed into rickety tenement slums or makeshift shantytowns. The complete absence of sanitation – Romans had to run home at night amid a hailstorm of fumbled chamber pots dropped from above – and the lack of decent housing actually added to the mass appeal of Rome's temples and porticoes (which is the effect even today of such amazing complexes as the Red Fort in the otherwise mostly repellent environment of old Delhi). This explains the imperial attraction of Roman baths, which could be constructed on a mountainous scale and yet offered the poor somewhat more than a basilica in the way of practical benefits. Though even here we should not overestimate the splendor of Roman baths: the elder Pliny tells us that baths were the natural breeding places of cockroaches (the Latin for which, by the way, is *blatta*, which is exactly what a roach should be called).

The most celebrated builder of the late republic was Pompey the Great. When he returned to Rome in 61 BC to celebrate his third triumph, a two-day affair that celebrated what were then Rome's most extensive and lucrative conquests, Pompey could (and did) boast that by his victories he had more than doubled the revenues of the republic, added an astonishing deposit of silver and gold to the treasury, received the surrender of more than 12 million people, eradicated piracy and extended the dominion of the Roman people to the limits of the world. He dedicated his spoils to the goddess Minerva, at a shrine constructed by him in her honor. Now Pompey could not have dedicated this shrine in this year if he had not already begun the preparations during the actual conduct of his war. But his eastern mission was so successful so early that there could not be any doubt as to its ultimate result, which will have emboldened Pompey to secure the property and permission to proceed with Minerva's sanctuary. He then immediately began to build, on the Campus Martius, an immense complex that included a temple to *Venus Victrix*, a temple to *Honos et Virtus*, a temple to *Felicitas* and a temple to a divinity whose name began with a V, possibly *Victoria*. There was also a senate house, the *Curia Pompeia*, in which Caesar would be assassinated (this too was a *templum*), and there was a sumptuous portico, mention of which is made in the love poetry of Catullus and of Propertius. And, finally, there was a theater, the first permanent stone theater in Rome's history – and this remained Rome's principal theater thereafter, a lasting monument of the complex's boldness. Near enough to the complex to be deemed a part of it was Pompey's new mansion, which was remarkably modest, thereby establishing a contrast between the Great Man's public munificence and his avoidance of private luxury. The theater and some of the temples were dedicated in 55 BC, ceremonies attended by the most lavish games Cicero, for one, had ever seen. All this took place in the year of Pompey's second consulship: the temple to Venus, which capped the theater, was as we have seen not dedicated until 52 BC, during Pompey's third consulship.

Now it is regularly asserted by cultural historians that constructions such as these fabricate their author's public image, a process described nowadays as *self-fashioning*. And there is much truth to this claim. But by 55 BC Pompey was already pretty great and pretty famous. It was in reality *his* personal glory that lent luster to, and prescribed the proper interpretation of, his theater complex. This is how it was that Roman tradition could be shattered by the introduction of a permanent theater, an urban feature that had been more or less explicitly banned by custom. This was because Romans did not like to see ordinary people sitting in public, a habit of mind that has outlasted the empire. Nowadays one must pay for the privilege (hence the double pricing of drinks enjoyed while seated in Italian cafés and bars). In antiquity, the privilege was simply denied. Sitting around, at least when done by common types, was deemed dangerous and immoral, like theater itself. Pompey's reputation, however, was more than sufficient to dissolve such moralizing prejudices. He certainly did not have to *disguise* his theater as the approach to a temple, as one reads again and again in handbooks, a subterfuge so obvious that it could have fooled no one.

While the significance of *Honos et Virtus* is unmistakable, this complex is very much an embrace of the goddess Venus. *Felicitas* – especially good luck in war – was an attribute of *Venus Victrix*, as was victory. For students of mythology, it may not be immediately obvious how it is that Venus could have anything to do with war, but this is owing to the dangerous tendency to confuse Roman religion with Greek mythology. The ecumenical outlook of the Greeks, combined with their inability to understand foreign languages, led to the religious phenomenon we describe as syncretism, whereby Aphrodite could serve as the name for near-eastern goddesses whose personalities combined fertility with violence. One such divinity, probably Phoenician in origin, was worshipped as Aphrodite in Sicily, at Eryx (modern San Giuliano). In fact, this was one of the most famous sanctuaries in Sicily in the third century, when the Romans battled the Carthaginians for possession of the island. The Romans came to believe that their final victory was owed to this goddess, whose cult soon came to be regarded as a foundation of Aeneas and who, by 215 BC, was worshipped on the Capitol in Rome – for the excellent reason that she delivered victory in war.

An inscription describes her, in the dative case, as *faustae felicitate veneri victrici* ("to felicitous, fortunate Venus Victrix"). She received a second temple in the second century, and made her share of appearances on Roman coinage. The dictator Sulla was devoted to her – his Greek nickname was *Epaphroditus* and he named his son Faustus and his daughter Fausta in the god's honor. Pompey's complex, financed by his great victories, naturally honored this divine symbol of victory. In so doing, he co-opted the heritage both of Marius – note the temple to *Honos et Virtus* – and of Sulla. This second connection was even commemorated on coins issued by Sulla's son, in 56 BC, which depicted Venus and referred to the triumph of 61 BC (by then Faustus was Pompey's son-in-law).

In 54 BC, the year after the dedication of Pompey's theater complex, Caesar began to buy land near the Forum and in the Campus Martius. By then, or so he believed at the time, victory in Gaul was a certainty. In fact, Caesar spent much of the year occupied in his invasion of Britain. Consequently, the specific chores involved in purchasing the real estate were left to his equestrian ally Gaius Oppius and to Cicero. And the going was not easy (what follows comes from a letter from Cicero to Atticus):

> Oppius and I deemed it trifling to spend sixty million sesterces on that signal construction project that you used to praise so highly: we shall widen the Forum and extend it as far as the Hall of Freedom. It was impossible to come to terms with the property owners for less money. We shall also accomplish something exceedingly glorious. In the Campus Martius we are going to construct marble enclosures for the tribal assembly and these we shall surround with a lofty portico.

The marble Saepta, the new voting enclosure on the Campus Martius, was ultimately constructed by Agrippa. Still, its intended political message is obvious enough: the conquest of Gaul was in the service of and lent luster to the people's sovereignty (little wonder then that, once dictator, Caesar lost interest in this project). More ambitious was Caesar's plan, not fully realized at the time of his death, to improve the city's center. An expansion of the congested Forum Romanum was desperately needed. In typical Roman fashion, however, it remained for private initiative and the profits of war to solve the difficulty. In the event, Caesar did more than expand the Roman Forum: he fabricated a new and adjacent one, the first of the imperial *fora*, the *Forum Iulium*. It was big: in fact, only one later forum in the whole of Roman history, that of Vespasian, is larger than Caesar's. The land alone, by the project's completion, cost over 100 million sesterces.

Today, alas, this forum is visually the least impressive of them all, owing to the effect of Mussolini's Via dell'Impero, the modern Via dei Fori Imperiali.

Caesar's schemes for public building developed during the course of the civil war and his dictatorship, the abbreviated nature of which meant that many of his ideas were left to his successor to undertake or to abandon. In 54 BC, however, there can be no doubt that Caesar regarded his real estate purchases as preliminary to manubial construction in the republican tradition. The new benchmark was Pompey's theater complex, and it is obvious that Caesar hoped to make a similarly strong symbolic statement regarding his own measure of fame. It would be a mistake, however, at this stage, to represent Caesar's investment in terms that are too suggestive of the future rift between the two dynasts (as if it was already in Caesar's mind to eclipse his famous friend). In 54 BC Pompey was still Caesar's son-in-law. And Julia, Caesar's daughter, was pregnant with Pompey's child. In virile Roman fashion, Pompey already had adult sons who could bask in the reflected glory of their father's brilliant monuments. But Caesar, to the extent that his thinking was at all dynastic – Julia, it should be remembered, was his only child – had to have given thought to the son she was expected to bear (such are the prepossessions of men in patriarchal societies), who would be heir to Rome's dominant conquerors. The Theater of Pompey and the Julian Forum would testify to this child's inherited *virtus* and ensure the future condition of both houses.

Julia died in childbirth, however, and her baby (which was a boy) soon afterwards, and by 49 BC Pompey and Caesar were at war. Caesar won the civil war but did not live to complete his forum. At least he was able to dedicate its chief architectural element: the Temple to *Venus Genetrix* (which, ironically in view of his treatment of Catulus, remained uncompleted at the time of its dedication). This he did after the celebration of his quadruple triumph over Gaul, over Egypt, over Pharanaces of Pontus (the occasion of his famous placard reading *veni, vidi, vici*), and over Africa – foreign foes all, naturally, inasmuch as it goes without saying that Romans didn't celebrate triumphs for civil wars. Catulus's name, by the way, was finally excised from the Temple of Jupiter on the Capitoline, to be replaced not by Pompey's but by Caesar's, behavior that foreshadows Domitian more than it does Augustus.

The Temple to *Venus Genetrix* was richly decorated with expensive Greek art – and with kitsch: Caesar dedicated a breastplate composed entirely of pearls removed from Britain, which should tell us something about the quality of Roman tastes. Their political instincts were keener than their esthetics, however, and this temple's situation in its new, if incomplete forum was an unmistakable advertisement for the unparalleled glory of Rome's new master. Although *Venus Genetrix* and *Venus Victrix* were divinities readily identified and understood by Romans of all persuasions, the events of the civil war had made equally clear to everyone just who in Rome was the goddess' favorite. All Romans descended from Venus, but Julians claimed the purest and most direct descent. Caesar's fortune in war, his *felicitas*, now made his family's case indisputable, whereas Pompey's divine favor had obviously evaporated when he broke his friendship with Caesar. Once again it is the reputation of the dedicator that determines the proper significance of his monument. No one in 46 BC could doubt who was boss. And so no one could fail to recognize in Caesar's temple and Caesar's forum the winning entries in the competition in manubial construction.

But Caesar's forum raised the stakes: the Forum Iulium, which was intended for meetings of the senate and for the operation of the courts, threatened to shift the focus of the *res publica* from its traditional space into a new location, one dominated, not by the relics of Rome's past greatness, but by the current constructions of one man. Indeed, this forum, and the Temple of *Venus Genetrix*, became the scene of Caesar's most bitterly resented action (and introduces once again the politics of sitting and standing). As Suetonius describes it:

> The whole of the senate brought Caesar many decrees passed in his honor. Caesar received them before the Temple of *Venus Genetrix* – but he remained seated. Some believe that when he attempted to rise, he was held back by Cornelius Balbus. Others, that he made no attempt at all and instead went so far as to glare at Gaius Trebatius when he pointed out that he should rise. This action of his seemed intolerable.

Whatever the original political significance of Caesar's building schemes, by the time of his autocracy it was obvious that, while the tokens of the manubial game had not changed, the opportunity to play it had been removed from all save one.

Political significations of sharper specificity and keener sophistication have been detected in Caesar's forum by modern scholars, some of which are even plausible. Now it was generally accepted in antiquity that Pompey the Great – who was regarded by his contemporaries as surpassingly handsome – resembled Alexander. This resemblance owed itself to the style of his representation in the plastic arts, not least in his hairstyle, which duplicated Alexander's bangs (as, later, did Augustus's). As Plutarch puts it:

> The slight upturn of his hair and the mobility of the features around his eyes made his face resemble that of King Alexander, as it is portrayed in statues, although this resemblance was not so much an obvious reality as it was something people alleged. Still, the notion of Pompey's resemblance led to his commonly being called by the name "Alexander".

The Curia Pompeia was dominated by an enormous statue of Pompey in his characteristic portrayal. In Caesar's forum, facing the Temple of *Venus Genetrix*, was placed a statue of the dictator's horse, the hooves of which resembled human feet, physiognomy that recalled Bucephalus, Alexander's famous steed. This identification was assisted by a statue of Caesar, situated beside the horse, that was in fact a re-cycled statue of Alexander (only the head was replaced) in the familiar Lysippan pose. Here, then, was Caesar as the new Alexander, or as the new Pompey – in any case, Caesar as the current world conqueror.

This much is credible, at least to me. But I remain wary of unprovoked theorization when too much subtlety is asked of me – or of the Romans. For instance, Caesar decorated his temple with paintings (one unfinished) by Timomachus of Byzantium, who by Caesar's day was something of an old master. One was a painting of Medea contemplating the murder of her children, the other of Ajax meditating on suicide. What was the message in these? When the elder Pliny, who is our sole source for this, mentions these works of art, his attention is grabbed by their cost: *almost two million sesterces!* Modern scholars have endeavored to prove themselves less philistine. For them, these must be political allegories.

The most recent extensive publication on the Forum Iulium approaches the Ajax painting in this way. In Plutarch's *Life of Pompey*, the hero's confusion at Pharsalus is explicitly compared with that of Ajax, when in Homer's *Iliad* lofty-throned Zeus struck fear into the son of Telamon. Appian's narrative of the battle includes the same comparison, and it has been suggested that each got it from a common source, perhaps the historian Asinius Pollio (a contemporary of Caesar). On this speculative literary basis, then, it is concluded that the painting of Ajax represents an "in-your-face" indictment of Pompey's failure at Pharsalus. I find this – not impossible – but simply incredible. Even *if* this literary conceit can be traced back to Pollio, I wonder how many visitors to the Forum Iulium will have read it. An interpretation along these lines can only have been accessible to a tiny elite. And, in any case, an interpretation along these lines obliges that tiny elite to overlook the elegant tribute to Pompey's heroic stature that is clearly being paid by the original author of this conceit and by the later historians who repeat it.

Paintings, especially paintings removed from their original context, are remarkably unstable in their significations anyway. Consider the case of Porcia, the daughter of Cato and the wife of Brutus. When, after the assassination of Caesar, her husband departed for the east, this distressed woman, alone and lonely in Rome, spied a painting of Hector parting from Andromache (the picture showed Andromache taking their son from Hector, all the while fixing her gaze on her husband). As Plutarch tells it:

> As Porcia looked at it, the image of her own sorrow that it conjured up made her burst into tears, and she went to see this picture time after time each day, and wept before it.

Paintings, like pop songs, are too susceptible of personal meanings to be reliable propaganda – unless they make their meaning blatant. Whatever Medea and Ajax might have meant to various observers in the Temple of *Venus Genetrix*, my own supposition is that they were introduced by Caesar to induce a gasp at the taste, the resources, and the generosity of the temple's builder. This is the same Caesar, bear in mind, who proudly displayed a breastplate studded with expensive British pearls. Pliny, I think, got it right.

Of course, all this politicism was there to be ignored or subverted anyway. In a later generation, in composing *The Art of Love*, his racy poem giving advice on how to seduce women, Ovid introduces the Temple of *Venus Genetrix* in its official role as the setting for public trials. For him, however, it is a very different Venus from the martial goddess who inhabits Caesar's temple. It will help you to get Ovid's point if you remember that, in the *Art of Love*, one conventionally falls in love with a courtesan (viz. a high-priced hooker):

> Where beneath Venus's marble temple the Appian nymph strikes the air with her spurting water, there many a lawyer is captured by love. He is a man who took care of others, but now he cannot take care of himself. Words fail him, though he is eloquent. A different case is advanced, and now he must plead his own cause. From her temple, Venus mocks him. He who was once a patron, now desires to become a client.

This, it is safe to say, is not what Caesar had in mind. Nor Augustus, his heir. No surprise, then, that the bon vivant Ovid was exiled to the Black Sea. That autocrats like to control their own press is hardly an innovation of the modern world.

Caesar, it must in all fairness be observed, appears to have had bigger and better plans for the improvement of Rome. The capital of the world could not yet rival, for beauty or for safety or for salubriousness, the great cities of the east. But the republic, as we have seen, lacked any institutional means for changing that state of affairs. However, because he had no limitations – because he no longer had any real peers – Caesar was free to remodel the city according to its needs and (of course and inseparably) according to his own desire.

Caesar's character determined the public reception of all aspects of his public building. It is interesting in this regard to compare the dreams by means of which Pompey and Caesar gave psychological representation to their respective wills-to-power. Caesar, early in his career, dreamed that he raped his mother, a nocturnal experience that soothsayers perhaps charitably interpreted as evidence that he was destined to rule the world. Pompey, on the other hand, on the eve of the Battle of Pharsalus, dreamed that he was dedicating his temple to *Venus Victrix*, adorning it with the spoils of war and receiving the adoring applause of the crowd. Neither dream will strike us as appealing, but from the Romans' perspective, one was wholesome, the other diseased. An Oedipus complex was sick. But an edifice complex (sorry about that) was admirably well balanced, even noble, by Roman standards.

The vocabulary of public building in Rome, designed to convey the sentiments of glory and influence and family honor, served a public good only by accident. Although it provided jobs, it did next to nothing to cure the ills of Roman society or to improve the fabric of the city. It was, in objective and not moralizing terms, vainglorious waste. But the Romans themselves never viewed manubial building as a misapplication of their resources: the institution was simply so deeply ingrained that they could not imagine an alternative system. With the coming of permanent autocracy – the age of Augustus – traditional manubial construction was eliminated from aristocratic society, a transformation that pressured senators to devote their wealth to the cities of Italy or to more practical public benefactions.

Augustan autocracy also saw the rise of something like a bureaucracy that could efficiently maintain the condition of Rome's public works. But this was not because Augustus failed to appreciate the glory of public building for the aristocracy. Quite the reverse: in his *Achievements*, cited at the beginning of this chapter, Augustus catalogued (at considerable length) his own monuments:

> I built the Senate House and the Chalcidicum next to it, the Temple of Apollo on the Palatine as well as its porticoes, the Temple of the Divine Julius, the Lupercal, a viewing stand at the Circus Maximus, the temples on the Capital of Jupiter Feretrius and Jupiter Tonans, the Temple of Quirinus, the temples of Minerva and Juno Regina and Jupiter Libertas on the Aventine, the Temple of the Lares at the top of the sacred way (*and so forth*).

The list continues for paragraphs. Appropriately, Augustus's building program is sandwiched between the record of his conquests and the catalogue of his spoils, which he used to pay for innumerable public games. Augustus, in his own accounting of himself, becomes the greatest builder of them all, because he is the greatest general of them all – a reality made inescapable when, after 19 BC, he limited the privilege of a triumph to himself and to members of the imperial family.

This monopoly on victory created a monopoly on manubial building. Hereafter, only the emperor could be Rome's greatest general. And only the emperor could be Rome's greatest benefactor. A good emperor was always gracious enough to repair and restore the monuments of celebrated republican families. He would not eradicate their memory, nor deprive them of their prestige. But they were eclipsed never the less. When *gloria* became the property of one man, the sociology of public building in Roman society was transformed. Augustus was able to find a balance between the requirements of senatorial sensibilities and his own pre-eminence. Caesar could not. Caesar complained that Pompey could not endure an equal. Caesar certainly could not. And that reality cost him his life, when he was stabbed to death, at the foot of Pompey's statue, in the senate house that Pompey had erected when he constructed his monumental theater complex. Pompey's building program had been perfected, its message unmistakable but well within the limits of what was recognizable as aristocratic competition. Caesar, however – owing to his terrible rush to annihilate all rivals in every category of aristocratic competitiveness – left his work incomplete.

Further Reading

Useful introductions to Roman public building include Sear 1982 and Barton 1989. An excellent, if more specialized treatment of the topic, including good discussions of Pompey's theater complex and Caesar's forum, can be gotten in Stamper 2005. One can also consult Ulrich 1994 for another recent discussion of Caesar's forum. Fuller treatments of the administrative as well as the political dimensions of manubial construction tend to be technical in nature, for instance Strong 1968 and Morgan 1971 and 1973. The deployment of art and architecture to advance the political agenda of Augustus is given masterly treatment in Zanker 1988.

5

My True and Honourable Wife: Cornelia and Pompeia, Calpurnia and Cleopatra

"I owe all to women." With this concise remark, Benjamin Disraeli, near the end of his life, assessed his own sensational success, by way of a sentiment the boldness of which will have been more apparent to his Victorian contemporaries than it can remain within our own sensibilities. It was an honest appraisal from a man whose feline charm, not merely with the ladies, contrasted almost grotesquely with the pertinacious bulldog sermonizing of his Liberal opposite Gladstone, who spent his nights converting prostitutes to nobler, if less venerable professions and his days exasperating Queen Victoria. Had the Romans been at all inclined to attribute their accomplishments to anyone other than to themselves (or to the gods), this is a statement that might have come well from Caesar. Not because he was helped to the dictatorship by his notorious amatory adventures – even if, at his quadruple triumph, his soldiers chanted "lock up your wives, citizens of Rome: we are bringing back the bald adulterer" – but rather because his early rise was made possible and given shape by the women in his life. Caesar begins his career as the dutiful son, nephew and husband: at its end, he is linked to dissolute Roman youths and to the scandalous queen of Egypt, thereby and conveniently satisfying our own prejudices regarding the inevitable decadence of empire.

It was not simply that Caesar lost his father when he was a teenager: he had no uncle, no elder brother, no cousin to provide paternal guidance and political inspiration. Consequently, it was left to the women in his life to look after young Caesar. Hence the significance of his aunt Julia, Marius's widow, whose political connection led to his marriage to Cornelia, the daughter of Cinna, and the near miss with the office of *flamen Dialis*. And hence the importance of his mother, Aurelia, daughter of a consul, granddaughter of a consul, and cousin to three brothers destined to be consuls (in 75 BC, 74 BC, and 65 BC). In the first chapter of this book, it was argued that Caesar exploited his relationship, through Julia, to Marius in order to appropriate his uncle's *gloria*, which far excelled anything in his own Julian heritage, even while he represented himself as a paragon of *pietas*, familial loyalty. In his funeral oration for his aunt, Caesar paraded before the Romans the splendor of her birth in his opening sentence:

> My aunt Julia was descended on her mother's side from kings, on her father's from the gods. Her mother was a Marcia, and the Marcii Reges go back to Ancus Marcius [*a king of Rome*]. Our own family, the Julii, traces its descent from Venus. She combined, therefore, the sanctity of kings with the holiness of the gods.

The boast of regal origins was buttressed by the monumental Marcian Aqueduct, Rome's finest, which had been constructed by Quintus Marcius Rex, who was praetor in 144 BC and who was, quite possibly, Marcia's father. Tradition ascribed the origins of this aqueduct to Ancus Marcius and pretended that Marcius Rex had in actuality restored and adorned his ancestor's benefaction to the city. But it was concrete accomplishments that won Caesar popularity, not mythology – and most of all it was the display of the trophies of the formerly flesh and bone Marius at this funeral, stimulating the people's fond recollection of that dazzling general who was seven times consul.

He was also admired for his marriage to Cornelia, Cinna's daughter. Again, this was a Marian connection. And a binding one. Although (as we shall see presently) divorce in Rome was for the most part an unproblematic affair, Caesar had been wed to Cornelia by an ancient rite, limited to patricians, called *confarreatio*. Marriage in this fashion was a prerequisite for the holy office of *flamen Dialis*, whose wife became the *flaminica Dialis*, herself subject to religious obligations and responsibilities essential to the preservation of traditional civic religion. *Confarreatio* was sacred. Its dissolution, by means of a complex ceremony known as *diffarreatio*, was an innovation to Roman society that can have been introduced no earlier than the late third century BC and which remained rare owing to the solemnity associated with *confarreatio*. For the *flamen Dialis*, however, only the death of his wife could put asunder what Jupiter and the religion of the republic had joined together: divorce was impossible.

Which is why it was not forgotten – indeed, Caesar advertised the fact – that when Sulla made his irreligious demand that Caesar divorce Cornelia, the young patrician refused stoutly. Even after Sulla had stripped Caesar and Cornelia of their sacred office, thereby opening the door to *diffarreatio*, Caesar remained true to the spirit of his marriage. It was an early – and courageous – act of *pietas*, to the legacy of Marius, to the integrity of Roman family customs and to the prescriptions of the divine order. Only a raging Sullan could pretend to find a fault in it, and it cannot have helped Sulla's position that no priestly replacements to Caesar and Cornelia could be found. No wonder, then, that the Vestal Virgins (women once again) intervened with Sulla on Caesar's behalf. The gods favored his cause.

Now Caesar's boldness relied on something more substantial than the Romans' notorious fretting about religious correctness. He was protected by the resources of his mother and her family, whose clout carried more practical implications than any Julian descent from the gods. To the exculpations of the Vestals was added political pressure from Gaius Aurelius Cotta, the future consul of 75 BC, and Mamercus Aemilius Lepidus Livianus, destined to be consul in 77 BC and an Aurelian connection (Chart 2). These men were staunch and valued Sullan lieutenants, of conspicuous nobility, and far too influential to be disregarded or refused. Caesar's rescue, at the mortal level at least, owed itself to the exertions of Aurelia.

Caesar's probity in his conflict with Sulla was no mere posture. Aurelia was remembered by Tacitus as one of the grand, traditional mothers of the Roman republic: dutiful, devoted – and very strict with her children. This strictness was extended into Caesar's youth. It is easy to forget that Caesar's first marriage was consummated when he was in his teens – almost a decade ahead of the normal schedule for a Roman. Young men in Rome, by way of a double standard that attaches itself to all patriarchal societies, ancient and modern, were permitted a few flings before they settled down into the serious business of family life. Roman love poetry, Roman comedies, even speeches from the crusty environment of the Roman courts, all reveal what wild oats Caesar missed out on sowing – in the normal fashion at least. That Caesar had a strict and restrained upbringing and youth should never be forgotten, especially by those who believe that severity in childrearing yields upright citizens. But here our focus must be on Aurelia's devotion to her son. Her unimpeachable traditionalism lent Caesar an aura of soundness – at least at the commencement of his career. Aurelia lived into the year 54 BC. One wonders what she thought of her son's maturity, not least what she thought of his first consulship.

We are not yet done with Caesar's debt to his mother's station and to her efforts on his behalf. Caesar's popularity, along with his lavish donatives to the people, elevated him to the position of *pontifex maximus*, as we have seen, the success that launched him into the political elite of Rome. But his election was possible only because he was already a *pontifex* in the first place: he was co-opted into that college in 74 BC, when he took the place, not of a Julian, but of the very Aurelius Cotta who had saved him from Sulla. This was clearly the work, once again, of Aurelia and her family. Caesar prospered, then, and more than prospered, not owing to the greatness of his paternal line, but instead because, as Julia's nephew, he could stake a claim to Marian greatness and because, as Aurelia's son, he could benefit from the deep and noble resources of that powerful family.

What of Cornelia, his wife? Caesar's loyalty to her cannot be equated automatically with devotion – or even with love. Their union, it will be remembered, had its origin in political convenience: Cinna needed a *flamen Dialis*, Caesar's relations needed a place to install their charge. Caesar remained her husband until her death in 69 BC, when he honored her with an extraordinary funeral oration which will unquestionably have made much of Caesar's having made so very *very* much of Cornelia (Marius once again, along with a large dose of religiosity and *pietas*) – but then funerals and funerary oratory are regularly more concentrated on the living than on the departed. To the very end, then, and even beyond that, Cornelia remained the perfect trophy wife, in a political sense. She was also the mother of the only child of Caesar that reached adulthood, his daughter Julia. Not many obvious cracks, then, in this marriage. Still, for large portions of the period of Caesar's first marriage, he was away from Rome, and out of his military and diplomatic service in the east came gross insinuations about Caesar's personal morality. Wild oats? Caesar was a momma's boy (he even dreamed, once, of raping his mother): did his wife, one wonders, have to suffer for it?

It is regrettable that we can know so little about the lives of women, even women of the elite classes, in republican Rome. This is not to say that we are uninformed about their clothing or hairstyles or habits or careers. But all of this information, or very nearly all of it, comes to us from a single perspective, that of Roman men (and for the most part that of elite Roman men). With precious few exceptions, Latin literature and Latin inscriptions were composed by men – and *for men*. Which means, of course, that we have next to no window into the interior lives of Roman women. Even when we possess a text that appears to give us at least some access to that dimension of ancient life, such moments usually represent what elite men believed *other* elite men wanted to hear about the interior lives and feelings of women. And so, unless we rate the sensibilities of Roman men very highly, we must confess that we remain closed off from anything like the authentic experience of Roman women. After all, it will probably not be necessary for me to convince the women who read this that, most of the time, guys haven't a clue. Some men will accept this reality. Others will carry on in self-delusion – until the day they make the mistake of purchasing a vacuum cleaner or a food processor as an anniversary gift. Never the less, if we cannot any longer hear the woman's voice in republican society, we can at least say something about their circumstances, and their capacity to control their circumstances – at least amongst their peers.

The Roman conception of Woman did not involve any notion of inherent wickedness or some exaggerated share in the blame to be suffered for Original Sin. It was an accepted fact of life in ancient Mediterranean societies that women could not serve in the military: consequently, they could neither vote, where voting was a possibility, nor hold magistracies, which meant that they were excluded from all the formalities and most of the realities of political life, a state of affairs that tended to concentrate the energies of women in domestic attainments. In fact, the ideal woman is always represented as a wife and mother. She should be prudent, beautiful and fertile.

Women in Rome were in certain respects inferior to men in the eyes of the law, but these disadvantages were negligible in practice. Nor was it naturally assumed that all women were inferior to all men. Elite women commonly acted as patrons to non-elite men, who were in every respect their subordinates. Women were commonly landlords for non-elite men, and counted men amongst the tenants on their land. Even men of substance from the municipalities had to wait anxiously for the attentions and the assistance of wealthy women in the aristocracy of the city. And, because their husbands were so often away from the city in their service to the republic, the wives of many Roman senators routinely served as their husband's representative in city dealings. To be sure, these women are always celebrated primarily for their successes as wives and mothers – just as in modern society it remains crucial for professional women to be not merely more than usually competent at their jobs, but at the same time to be (or at least to seem to be) fantastic homemakers – amazing cooks, wonderful housekeepers, nurturing parents and spouses, tireless and creative lovers. But despite the conventional emphasis on family life, women were expected to rise to multifarious occasions, and Roman men were not too shy to commemorate famous women for their *virtus*, their *manliness*.

Prudence, beauty, and fertility constituted the minimum of expectations for the ideal woman of the aristocratic variety. From an abundance of evidence, let me introduce a single passage, the historian Sallust's hostile portrayal of Sempronia, a supporter of the Catilinarian conspiracy of 63 BC. Sempronia was the wife of Decimus Junius Brutus, a man of consular rank, and she was the mother, or stepmother, of Decimus Brutus, one of the leaders amongst the assassins of Caesar and, later, a formidable opponent of Mark Antony. Sallust's depiction blends compliment and insult, each useful to our present purpose: he begins favorably, diverts to caustic abuse, but reverts to positive commentary, a literary conceit that was once known as an Oxford sandwich:

> In birth and in beauty, in her husband also and children, she was abundantly favored by fortune; she was well read in Greek and Latin literature. She was able to play the lyre and to dance [*so far so good – but*] but more skillfully than is appropriate for a respectable woman. And she had many other accomplishments that minister to lasciviousness. There was nothing she held so cheap as her modesty and chastity; you could not easily tell whether she was less sparing of her money or her reputation. Her desires were so ardent that she approached men more often than she was approached by them. Even before the conspiracy she had frequently broken her word, repudiated her debts and been privy to murder. Never the less, she was a woman of no mean endowments [*back to the good stuff*]: she could write poetry, tell a joke, and use language that was modest or tender or wanton as the situation required it. In sum, she possessed a high degree of wit and charm.

For Sallust, Sempronia is the ideal aristocratic woman gone bad, just as Catiline is the ideal patrician gone bad. If we concentrate our attention on her positive features, we get the Romans' dream-girl. You will notice how immediately birth, looks and fertility enter the picture. It might be less expected, in a martial patriarchal state like Rome, that Romans liked it best when their *babes* were learned in both languages and commanded fine literary and social sensibilities. And they were expected to be erotic beings: it is wrong for Sempronia to approach men, but there is nothing wrong with her knowing how to be a bit wanton – under the proper circumstances.

I would be giving you a false impression, however, if I let you believe that Roman men were entirely comfortable with talented or formidable women. Rome was an unregenerate patriarchal society, after all, and one of the reasons Sallust even bothered to introduce Sempronia to his narrative – she seems in fact to have played no part at all in the actual conspiracy – was to stimulate what for Roman men was their normal masculine anxiety regarding impressive and imposing women. This Roman tendency becomes clearer in the literature of the empire, when the wives and daughters of the emperors, if they emerged from the palace with personalities of their own, became regular targets of historians' smears owing to their very superiority not merely over ordinary Romans but (and this is the worry) over *aristocratic* men. This was the great bind for imperial women: convention required that such women have talents and put them to use on behalf of their family, but, when that family became the *supreme* family, imperial women were deficient if they retired from ordinary aristocratic behavior yet were tyrannical and un-feminine if they followed custom. One can compare the unhappy situation of the First Lady in the American White House. By convention, the First Family must enact the values of the American middle class, which is the dominant class in American society (this is why rich candidates for the presidency must pretend to like eating at greasy spoons and getting photographed going duck hunting). But, whenever the First Lady actually behaves like her middle-class sisters (that is, whenever she takes an active role in advising her husband about his job or his opinions), she becomes a virago. This is why the Nancy Reagans and Hillary Clintons are always unpopular with middle-class American men, whereas Stepford-wife-type First Ladies who busy themselves with adoring, if vacant gazes enjoy astronomical approval ratings. Roman aristocrats didn't want vacant gazes – that seems to be a Texas thing. Never the less, Roman women, to an even greater degree than their modern counterparts, had to know how to disguise their clout within the parameters of their roles as wives and mothers.

Which brings us to the topic of Roman marriage and its expectations. Men typically married, for the first time anyway, in their late twenties. Women, for the first time, in their late teens. Consequently, if it was a first marriage for both, there was an age difference of at least a decade. Of course, Romans usually married more than once, and a first-time bride might find herself marrying a man in his thirties or in his forties or – *oh my god!* Cicero's second marriage, for instance, which took place when he was in his sixties, was to a blushing teenager (he was marrying her, by the way, for her money, in a reversal of a not unknown modern phenomenon). Originally, Roman men had enormous legal power over their wives, designated by the Latin word *manus*, which literally means *hand* (no doubt a reference to the reality that a husband could, when necessary, put the smack down on his woman to keep her suitably un-Sempronian). By the time of the late republic, however, that was all in the past. Wives in Roman marriages, from a legal perspective at least, preserved their independence to a far greater extent than is the case in the USA today. There was, for instance, no community property in Rome. A wife kept what was her own, and, although a Roman husband had control of his wife's dowry, it reverted to her in the event of the marriage's dissolution. And wives could initiate divorce (which was for the most part a no-fault affair in Rome) as easily as could men.

Marriages were arranged. They united not simply two individuals, but two families. We have seen one example of this in Caesar's marriage to Cornelia. We have also seen an instance of this in Julia's marriage to Pompey the Great, a tie that confirmed and publicized the friendship between the two men. In fact, the Romans could not imagine a bond of friendship closer than that between father-in-law and son-in-law. Which is why Caesar was so upset when, after Julia's death, Pompey was unwilling to find his way to a new marriage alliance. But we must beware of thinking of arranged marriages as being purely political or purely economical in their implications. After all, Pompey and Julia were famously infatuated with one another.

Still, arranged marriages could also be very unpleasant, as Cicero knew all too well. The orator's closest friend was the rich and influential knight Titus Pomponius Atticus. To unite their fortunes and friendship, they arranged for Atticus's sister, Pomponia, to marry Cicero's younger brother, Quintus. Unfortunately, the couple hated each other. We get glimpses of this from Cicero's correspondence. For instance, just before the two brothers set out for Cilicia in 51 BC, they traveled to Quintus's villa at Arcae (near modern Rocca d'Arce). Without consulting his wife, and this was evidently a big deal, Quintus sent a freedman ahead to arrange for the meal. Since it was a festival day, Quintus suggested to Pomponia that she entertain the women, he the men. "Both his manner and his intention," Cicero writes, "were perfectly pleasant." But Pomponia, loudly and coldly, responded, "but I'm just a guest here." And stormed off. "There!" Quintus complained to Marcus, "This is the sort of thing I have to put up with every day." When the banquet began, there was no sign of its hostess. So Quintus had Pomponia's meal sent to her in her room. She sent it back untouched, and that night they slept separately. This unhappy marriage lasted for more than twenty years. Finally, in 45 BC, they divorced. Quintus never again remarried, observing to his brother that life offered no greater happiness than a single man's bed.

Quintus's marriage was a calamity, not least because it was loveless. Now Romans did not approve of marriage solely on the basis of romantic love, but they very much approved of loving marriages. The Roman expression *affectio maritalis*, marital affection, was at once a legal concept and a psychological insight. In Roman law, a marriage existed only when there was *affectio maritalis*, the desire to live together as husband and wife. Once that desire vanished, so did the marriage: no legal proceedings were necessary, though there were inevitable complications attending the restoration of dowry. Thus its legal employment. Now it must be admitted that it stands to the Romans' credit that they recognized that there exists a very real difference between the desire to be somebody's lover and the desire to be somebody's husband or wife. Still, *affectio maritalis* hardly excludes passion or love. A married couple, in the Roman view, should be partners, should enjoy one another's company and conversation, and should be loving. This is evidenced more in the conventions of funerary inscriptions than in literary sources, but it very much matters that these were the conventions.

Romans, like us, had contradictory expectations of marriage. The ideal marriage was eternal, yet, in the reality of Roman society, death and divorce made multiple marriages the normal practice. And, so far as we can tell, most Romans were able to cope with divorce quite easily: there is hardly a hint of the modern emotional collapse. Divorce was very easy – from a legal perspective you simply stopped wanting to be married – and there was no social stigma attached to divorce. Unless, that is, it was generally believed that one party in the marriage was being shabbily treated. For instance, Plutarch, more than once, relates the following anecdote:

A Roman who had divorced his wife was being reproached by his friends. "Isn't she well born?" they said, "Isn't she beautiful? Isn't she fertile?" [*In other words, they regarded the divorce as capricious and so unfair.*] But the man held out his sandal and replied, "Isn't it well made? Isn't it brand new? But none of you can know where on my foot it rubs a blister."

We are best able to see the expressions of a happy marriage when it has been destroyed by death – on elaborate and funerary inscriptions. Admittedly, these are for public consumption and so are hardly artless or unvarnished. But at the very least they can show us the emotional pitch many Romans hoped for in a marriage.

Here lies my wife, full of modesty, at Rome my companion and my partner in business. I have no hope of living without such a wife.

Laughter and luxury I always delighted in, in the company of my dear friends. But such a life after the death of my chaste lady Valeria I did not find. While I could, I had an enjoyable life with my wife.

And so it goes, with sentiments that certainly demonstrate the degree of affection and devotion that Romans *believed* made for the perfect marriage.

We should not have expected Roman family life to be any less complicated than our own, and plainly it was not. What *was* remarkably less complicated, however, was the role of the state in regulating family life. Marriage, as I have already remarked, was mostly a private matter: there was no license, no document. Roman law set limits on what *constituted* a legal marriage. A citizen could not, for example, marry a non-citizen – not, that is, if he wanted that marriage to enjoy the benefits afforded by Roman law and custom (there was no legal obstacle to the pair's cohabiting). The dowry agreement was a legal and actionable document, but it was a social and not a legal necessity to have one. And, again as I have said, the state did not regulate divorce, except that a husband might make claims on a dowry for child support if the divorce were motivated by a wife's adultery. Roman law forbade a man's having sexual intercourse with a fellow citizen, if said citizen was a man, with a fellow citizen's unmarried daughter or with a fellow citizen's wife. This last offense was adultery. The first two constituted what Roman law denominated as *stuprum* (illicit sex). You will perhaps have noticed that nothing prevents a man from having intercourse with foreigners, with prostitutes, and with slaves, of whatever gender. In fact, in his moralizing satires, the Augustan poet Horace recommends raping a slave as the best means of preserving one's chastity. Women did not enjoy similar latitude. For a married woman, the scope of her sex life extended only to her husband. Punishments for adultery were determined privately, within the family. It was not a crime against society. All this would change, however, when Augustus became emperor: his ambitious moral legislation, his concentration on enforcing family values, introduced the state into the bedroom long before the impositions of the church – where it has remained for more than two thousand years.

The death of Cornelia resulted in Caesar's funeral oration. The marriage had proved successful, even in the face of considerable opposition. They were betrothed as teenagers. Caesar was a man of thirty when he lost his first wife. His second wife was Pompeia, whom he married after serving as quaestor in Spain. Her father, Quintus Pompeius Rufus, had been consul in 88 BC, and she was a grand-daughter of Sulla. It cannot have passed unnoticed by his contemporaries that Caesar's new wife had Sullan ties. A hint of respectability then, and of course she will have been very rich (vital for her husband inasmuch as Caesar was in those days living well beyond his means, and it is during this period that he was at his most prodigal when it came to political expenditures). And she must have had other attractive qualities, less susceptible of documentation. This emerges in the circumstances of their divorce.

In December of 62 BC, the nocturnal rites of the *Bona Dea*, the Good Goddess, forbidden to men and therefore irresistible to masculine fantasies, were celebrated in Caesar's house, the official residence of the *pontifex maximus*. A young patrician, Publius Clodius Pulcher, dressed in drag and sneaked into the ceremonies, where he had arranged an assignation with Pompeia (or so it was later believed). In the event, he was discovered and ejected, and a great scandal ensued, one that dominated Roman politics for months. It was hugely embarrassing for Caesar, who took Clodius's side (Clodius's family, the Claudii Pulchri, was too powerful to offend, and the two would go on to be political allies in the fifties). Caesar also divorced his wife, on the regularly misquoted grounds that "the wife of the *pontifex maximus* must be above suspicion." Public probity once more, and a healthy display of religious propriety. Caesar's problem with Pompeia, it would seem, lay not in her proclivities or in her sex appeal, but in the fact that she had gotten caught – and had consequently hurt him politically. The year had not gone well for Caesar: he had been suspended briefly from his magistracy (he was praetor) and his debts were spiraling out of control. Further public disgrace was the last thing he needed. No wife could be worth that.

After his divorce, Caesar was away from Rome, again in Spain. When he returned he won the consulship for 59 BC and launched the first triumvirate. By then, of course, he was a man to be courted as a valuable son-in-law. Again, Caesar was not slow to re-marry: his new bride was Calpurnia, his true and honorable wife, the daughter of the distinguished noble Lucius Calpurnius Piso, who would himself be consul in 58 BC. Calpurnia remained Caesar's wife until his death, without a hint of scandal or unhappiness. For most of their married life, of course, they were separated, he in Gaul, she in Rome, where she will have played her part in looking after his interests, political and otherwise. She is most famous for her disturbing premonitions about the Ides of March and, after Caesar's murder, it was she who dutifully handed her husband's papers over to Mark Antony, then Rome's sole consul and Caesar's closest political associate.

This was certainly an improvement over Pompeia. Third time the charm? A help meet for him at last? Perhaps, but what cannot go unremarked is the fact that, after Julia's death in 54 BC, it was Caesar who proposed to

Pompey that he marry the great man's daughter in his attempt to preserve their friendship, a relationship on which he obviously set higher value than his marriage to Calpurnia. Politics trumped Calpurnia, and Caesar appears a quite different husband from the man who risked so much for his loyalty to Cornelia. Or was that also a specimen of political calculation? In the event, Pompey declined, and Caesar's marriage subsisted. One cannot help but wonder whether Calpurnia felt relieved or disappointed. Whatever she felt, she remained in the marriage. She didn't have to. Loyalty to her father perhaps? Or perhaps she was in love with her husband, who by then was the fabulously rich and glorious proconsul of Gaul, adored by the Roman public.

Her husband's political opportunism will not have been Calpurnia's sorest trial. "That he was unbridled and extravagant in his love affairs is the general opinion," writes Suetonius in his gossipy biography of Caesar. The Roman biographer even gives us a catalogue – marked as incomplete – of Caesar's adulteries: "there was Postumia, the wife of Servius Sulpicius, Lollia, wife of Aulus Gabinius, Tertulla, wife of Marcus Crassus and even Gnaeus Pompey's third wife Mucia." It has not been overlooked that this list of cuckolded men includes Caesar's closest political associates. Which means that we must remain skeptical (these specifics are likely to derive from his enemies' abuse). But the pattern is well established and it persisted as an integral element of Caesar's popular image.

What follows in Suetonius's account is more interesting, not least because it appears to be true: "Beyond all others Caesar was enamored of Servilia, the mother of Marcus Brutus, for whom, in his first consulship, he bought a pearl costing six million sesterces." Servilia came from noble stock, the Servilii Caepiones, and was half-sister to Marcus Porcius Cato, Caesar's long-standing enemy. By her first husband, Marcus Junius Brutus, she was the mother of that Marcus Brutus who was the noblest Roman of them all. When Pompey executed Junius Brutus in the first civil war (between Marius and Sulla), Servilia wed Decimus Junius Silanus, who became consul in 62 BC and by whom she had three daughters, each of whom married well. Two married future consuls, and the third married Gaius Cassius Longinus, the one with the lean and hungry look.

Servilia was an extraordinary woman. She was bold enough to insist that her love letters be delivered to Caesar even when he was in the midst of senatorial debate. More revealing is her conduct after Caesar's assassination, which Cicero documents in his letters. In the summer after the Ides of March, Brutus and Cassius, her son and son-in-law, met at Servilia's estate to decide whether they should accept the insulting commissions they had been offered by the senate, at that moment dominated my Mark Antony. Cassius's wife, and Brutus's as well, were also there, as was Cicero, an esteemed friend of the family. Cicero tells us that Cassius was the embodiment of Mars, but it was Servilia who ran the meeting. When Cicero was in the midst of a long address rehearsing their missed opportunities, Servilia simply interrupted him by saying – to Cicero the senior consular – that she had never heard anyone speaking such rubbish. She was not there to waste time, and Cicero knew well enough to bite his tongue, which can only have been an odd experience for him. Cassius insisted that the commissions could not be accepted. Servilia then assured them all that *she* would see to it that the senate's decree was rescinded. Which she did. As Cicero put it, in a very different context, Servilia was gifted with both brains and energy, not unlike her lover. After Brutus's death at Philippi, Antony was careful to ensure that her son's ashes were restored to her, testimony to the esteem in which she was held on all sides. Servilia had survived her husbands and her lover – *and* now her son, with no exhibition of collapse or failure of resolution. She shared with Caesar a remarkable capacity for *reality*.

It was alleged in later antiquity, and the view persists in certain quarters, that they shared something more: Marcus Brutus. That Brutus was a favorite of Caesar, even when he was on the Pompeian side, is a fact. This can be compounded with the dictator's passion for Brutus's mother at least to raise the possibility. And of course, as everyone knows, for Caesar, the unkindest cut of all came at the hands of the noblest Roman of them all, to whom he directed his final words – *et tu, Brute* – which is Shakespeare's Latin rendering of Caesar's *actual* last words, which were Greek: *kai su, teknon* ("you too, child")? This is, of course, too wonderful to be true – an element of Greek tragedy rather than Roman history. Brutus was born in 85 BC, when Caesar was 15 years old. Servilia was a close coeval, but by then she was married and packed off. Each was on the wrong side of the Sullan civil war, and each was at the time scrambling for security and not for one another's arms.

Perhaps we should have a closer look at Caesar's parting utterance. The first thing to be said about these words is that it is by no means certain that Caesar said them at all. In antiquity there were two versions of the dictator's demise, and the preferred one was that he perished emitting nothing more coherent than a pathetic moan, which, under the circumstances, seems perfectly plausible. Never the less, the alternative account, which attributed to Caesar his famous final query, remained irresistible: it *had* to be recorded, if only because *ben trovato* – and, because the sentiment was strong amongst the Romans that the manner of each man's death, punctuated with a last line as its lasting caption, defined his authentic character, this version gave Caesar a suitable exit.

But does it? Not if you ask me. After all, as ordinarily parsed, Caesar's final words can hardly be described as masterful or truculent. Where is the will-to-power? Where is the rage? In this telling of the story we get such a poor excuse for a Caesar that, face to face with the favorite who betrayed him, the best he can do is to sound peevish and (worse) sentimental. It is possible, however, that this disappointing construction of the dying dictator can be repaired if we come at Caesar's little Greek sentence by way of a less saccharine interpretation. Or such is the recommendation of the archeologist James Russell, who, in an often-overlooked paper published more than 25 years ago, called attention to the Mediterranean habit, extending from the Orontes to the Tiber, of employing the expression *kai su* ("you too") as an apotropaic formula not merely to ward off evil but actually to destroy it with a curse, *kai su* being a briefer version of *kai su erre* ("as for you, perish!"). The imprecation will have been a natural and convenient form of abuse, understood everywhere and by everyone as something along the lines of "go to hell." As for the word *teknon* ("child"), there is no good reason, outside the literary confines of Attic tragedy, for any of us to react by collapsing into maudlin emotionalism. In other contexts, *kid* just means *kid*, which is sometimes a put-down. And that, suggests Russell, is the signification of the word here, in view of Caesar's seniority and Brutus' relative youth. In other words, instead of whining something along the lines of "it breaks my heart, Brutus, that you, whom I have so cherished and protected, should join with these perfidious villains and deliver me into the next world," perhaps, just perhaps, Caesar died with a curse on his lips: see you in hell, punk! Now *that* is a Caesar I feel more comfortable with – the indomitable scrapper who ruthlessly made himself master of Rome, and who died without a Roman son.

It is time to turn to Cleopatra. Just as Servilia was the most glamorous of his Roman lovers, so, of the many queens seduced by Caesar (the conscientious Suetonius does not fail to supply a list of these as well), none has achieved more fame, or more infamy, than Cleopatra VII. She is almost universally regarded as the most fascinating woman in western history, which means that here we encounter a legend that exceeds that of Caesar himself and has certainly proved more enduring. Roman historians, when the topic turns to Cleopatra, cannot help but resort to Shakespeare. But the legend of Cleopatra finds its origin in her own lifetime, when Octavian, hoping to blacken the reputation of his daunting enemy Antony, who was also his brother-in-law, directed his propaganda toward Cleopatra, the wicked queen who had enchanted and corrupted the Roman general.

Two forms of bigotry worked in Octavian's favor. The first was what we should now call *orientalism*, the western prejudice, evident already in Herodotus, that easterners did not merely embody luxury and moral weakness and so tend toward the feminine, which was naturally bad enough, but that they also displayed a strong predilection for totalitarian states: the east is always the location of evil empires. The second prejudice, amplified by the first, was our old friend, Roman anxiety about dominant women. In Augustan propaganda, then, Cleopatra represented the most appalling specimen of foreign enemy. She did not simply defeat her enemies, she unsexed them – just look at Antony. In Augustan literature, she is a monster of epic proportions, even in lyric poetry. She is the Egyptian whore, a drunkard, mistress of eunuchs, dominatrix of Antony, and antagonist of the gods of Rome. This depiction of Cleopatra, as the instantiation of everything lurid, licentious and vile – an abomination who is dangerous because she is also irresistibly alluring – persists. It was of course untrue, which is not the same thing as saying that Cleopatra and Antony were simply a charming but misunderstood couple. The point is rather that their affair, and also its pertinence to Rome, were distorted entirely by Octavian's negative campaigning and by the ideology of the Augustan age. Never the less, as we all know, it makes for a great story. And this story has, unfortunately for the biographer of Caesar, been retrojected, giving us the romantic legend of Caesar's passion for Cleopatra.

Ptolemy XII died in 51 BC, leaving his kingdom to his eldest son and daughter, Ptolemy XIII, who was ten, and Cleopatra VII, who was 17 or 18 Ptolemy shrewdly entrusted his children into the guardianship of the senate and people of Rome. According to Egyptian custom, the two married, and, in step with Ptolemaic habits, they and their parties were soon locked in armed conflict. This was the situation when Pompey, looking for new resources after his defeat at the Battle of Pharsalus, arrived in Egypt, where he expected the support of the king, whose father Pompey had favored, and of the troops, most of whom had once been Roman soldiers. Instead, Ptolemy arranged for Pompey's assassination, for which crime Dante placed him in hell, where he rubs barbequed shoulders with the likes of Cain and Judas.

Caesar soon followed. His description of the Romans who had undertaken military service in Alexandria makes it clear that he, like the later

Romans who swallowed Augustus's propaganda, viewed Egypt in conventional orientalizing terms:

> There were 20,000 men under arms. These were Gabinius's soldiers, who had by then become accustomed to a profligate Alexandrian lifestyle and had abandoned the name and the discipline of the Roman people.

He goes on to make the extent of their corruption unmistakable to his readers:

> They had taken wives by whom most of them had children.

What could be more disgusting, or more debilitating to Roman masculinity and *virtus*, than to marry an Egyptian foreigner and to breed illegitimate un-Roman offspring? This, let me remind you, is Caesar, writing to the educated classes of the time in his *Civil War*, one purpose of which was to persuade his fellow aristocrats that it was he and not the Pompeians who represented what was best for the future of Rome.

Temporarily stranded in Alexandria, and with relatively few forces at his disposal, Caesar elected to adjudicate the quarrel between Ptolemy XIII and his sister. This was Rome's right, indeed its obligation, under the terms of Ptolemy XII's will. But before matters could be settled, Ptolemy and his generals launched an attack, in which Caesar soon found himself in a vulnerable and almost untenable position. In the end, however, Caesar emerged victorious, whereas Ptolemy perished in the struggle (he conveniently drowned in the Nile). Caesar then accepted Egypt's surrender and on that basis he designated, as queen of Egypt, Cleopatra, who presumably had been the one to offer Egypt's formal surrender to Rome. Caesar then ordered the queen to marry Ptolemy XIV, her remaining younger brother.

This decision Caesar would have made regardless of Cleopatra's notorious attractions. It was the obvious one. Cleopatra had not attacked the Romans. She was the legitimate heir. And we know enough of Egypt in this period to know that she had already invested heavily in the construction and restoration of Egyptian temples, public benefactions that even Romans understood were expected of Alexandrian monarchs. Which meant that the queen was likely to inspire public confidence amongst her subjects, thereby preserving Egyptian stability (itself necessary to the smooth operation of the all-important Mediterranean grain trade). The fact of the matter,

however, and a bit of a bonus for Caesar, is that Cleopatra *was* striking –
and fascinating – a reality that penetrates through the tissues of invention
and romance and invective. As Plutarch describes her,

> Her beauty, so our sources tell us, was not in itself absolutely beyond compare,
> nor was it the type that dazzled anyone who caught sight of her. But her
> company possessed an irresistible charm, and her physical presence in com-
> bination with her highly agreeable conversation as well as with her personal-
> ity, which suffused her every exchange with others, was all rather sexy. The
> timbre of her voice was pleasure itself. And her tongue, like an instrument
> of many strings, she easily deployed in whatever language she pleased. She
> very rarely required an interpreter for her interviews with barbarians. Instead,
> she replied to them entirely on her own, whether they were Ethiopians,
> Troglodytes, Hebrews, Arabs, Syrians, Medes, or Parthians. She is said to
> have learned the languages of many other peoples besides these, whereas her
> predecessors on the throne had not even bothered to learn to speak Egyptian
> – and some even abandoned their Macedonian dialect.

Now this account is not true in every particular. It is demonstrably not the
case that *everyone* fell under her spell. Cicero for one says that he hated her
– but then he would. But, for the rest of us, the portrait is of a powerful
intellect attired in elegance and gracefulness, all possessed by a woman of
formidable rank and wealth. For a man imbued with authentic confidence,
drawn to capable women – and Caesar was unquestionably a man of this
brand – the appeal is obvious.

I should like to add an observation on this passage, because modern
handbooks so frequently misinterpret it – a habit I attribute to academic
bitchiness: we classicists are jealous even of the long dead! By no means
does Plutarch describe Cleopatra as physically unattractive, or even
plain. In his view, she was simply not a stunner, which is hardly the same
thing. The historian Cassius Dio, by way of contrast, emphasizes her beauty.
Not that either man ever saw her. Attention is regularly drawn by modern
students to her representations in sculpture and especially in coinage, in
which she is either fairly plain or, in the case of the coins she minted when
joined with Antony, disturbingly ugly (Fig. 9). But this is to misunderstand
the evidence. It is not simply that different ages and places have varying
notions of feminine beauty, a fact all too familiar to aficionados of the
paintings of Rubens. It is that the iconography of Hellenistic monarchs –
and Cleopatra was a Hellenistic monarch – was never intended to be real-
istic. There is a concern for individuation, which conveys the idea of a single

Figure 9   Obverse and reverse of a denarius of 32 BC. The obverse depicts Mark Antony, the reverse Cleopatra. British Museum, London, England. Photo: ©The Trustees of the British Museum.

personality. But these images were far from being publicity photos. Their object was to convey the monarch's power and legitimacy, by varying methods. Augustus, for instance, was always represented as a man in his twenties, even when he was quite old. In Cleopatra's case, her earlier coinage, designed for Alexandrian subjects, assimilates her appearance to that of earlier Ptolemaic queens, thereby proclaiming her legitimacy as monarch. In her later coins, she is masculine and hard, in the veristic Roman fashion, which makes her appear, for a wider eastern audience, a suitable client-queen, loyal to Rome and loyal to Antony. These redesigns could go a long way: within Egypt, for her Egyptian subjects, Cleopatra was sometimes represented *as a man*, as a masculine Pharaoh, itself an image with historical implications for her subjects. Pascal ruminated that, had Cleopatra's nose been shorter, the whole aspect of the world would have changed. But it was her brains, and not Cleopatra's beauty, that made her fascinating. None the less, there is no point in calling her homely, against the grain of the evidence. Give a girl a break.

Did she and Caesar fall in love? Did they sail down the Nile together? Did she bear him a son and follow him to Rome, only to flee after the Ides of March? Or is it all romantic fiction? In view of Caesar's character and the queen's vulnerability – and accessibility – there seems little point in denying that she must have joined the list of Caesar's sexual conquests. The Nile cruise, alas, we must jettison. There simply wasn't time to squeeze it

116

in (Caesar had a civil war to win), and it appears to be a fabrication. But there can be no doubting that Cleopatra was in Rome for Caesar's quadruple triumph and that she resided in Caesar's own property in Trastevere. She came with husband and baby in tow.

We know at least one reason for Cleopatra's presence in Rome. Egypt had just been conquered by the Romans – one of Caesar's four triumphs celebrated the Alexandrian War – and it was vital for Cleopatra to obtain Rome's endorsement of her own position and of Egypt's current status. In the event, the senate enrolled Cleopatra and her husband amongst the friends of the Roman people. It was not in the least extraordinary that Caesar offered his hospitality to the Egyptian monarchs. When her father had come to Rome, to beseech the senate to restore him to his throne, he had been the guest of Pompey the Great. Roman aristocrats enjoyed displaying their royal connections, and, in view of Caesar's position, it was his responsibility to see to the needs of the Egyptian dignitaries.

But Cleopatra evidently remained in Rome for a long time: 18 months, during which period Caesar was mostly away, campaigning in Spain. This is a problem, and it has recently been proposed that Cleopatra was sent back to Egypt only to return after the Battle of Munda. But this reconstruction rests on strained Latinity and a misapprehension of the political circumstances in Rome and in Egypt. Caesar had further business with Cleopatra, and I am not talking about monkey business: her father, Ptolemy XII, had left enormous debts to a range of Roman investors, amongst them Caesar and Caesar's friends. Payments had to be negotiated and scheduled, and the matter could hardly be an uncomplicated one. For Cleopatra, this was a deal that had to be cut without offending Caesar and without ruining her kingdom. As for that, Egypt's stability was guaranteed by the Roman garrison installed there by Caesar. Her future, for the moment, depended on Roman finances and politics. And she must have known that the outcome of the Spanish campaign was by no means certain (in fact, Caesar very nearly perished at Munda). What if great Caesar fell? She needed to be on the spot. A love affair, then, need hardly be postulated.

Two items of evidence remain to be dealt with, a statue and a boy. A statue of Cleopatra was placed in the Temple of *Venus Genetrix* (Fig. 10). It was still there in the second century of our era for the historian Appian to see. Much has been made of this statue and its situation. Cultural historians love it. Maria Wyke, for instance, in her important book, *The Roman Mistress*, observes that, "Julius Caesar . . . placed her gilded statue in the Temple of *Venus Genetrix* at Rome – thus juxtaposing the Egyptian queen with the mother and founder of the Julian clan." In so doing, "Caesar

Figure 10   Portrait of Cleopatra, probably (in large degree) a replica of Cleopatra's statue in the Temple of *Venus Genetrix*. Antikensammlung, Staatliche Museen zu Berlin, Berlin, Germany. Photo: Bilderarchiv Preussischer Kulturbesitz/Art Resource, NY.

displayed Cleopatra in Rome neither as his unlawful wife nor as his *meretrix*, but as a divine mother-figure." This is an odd conclusion to draw. If this had been a religious dedication, it is astonishing that this bizarre un-Roman gesture received no commentary whatsoever, not least since such a dedication required senatorial or popular authorization. In other words, it could hardly have been carried out in secret or even without formal and official sanction. Was Caesar so inflamed by passion that he must elevate his eastern lover to the status of amorous god and of amorous mother (remember the incestuous dream . . .)? But *Venus Genetrix*, as we learned in an earlier chapter, was a goddess of war and of conquest, not of love, and it would have been an error of Ovidian proportions to try to screw around with *that* symbolism. It is far more likely, if disappointingly

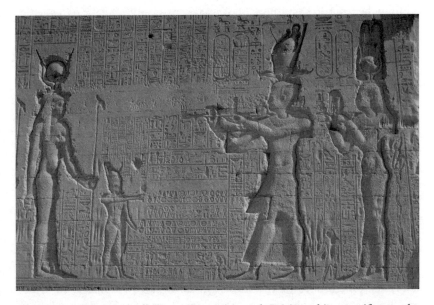

Figure 11   Cleopatra and Caesarion as Isis and Osiris making sacrifice to the goddess Hathor. South wall of the Temple of Hathor, Dendera, Egypt. Photo: Erich Lessing/Art Resource, NY.

straightforward, that this statue was simply a token of victory, a sign of Rome's conquest of Egypt, a gesture no doubt welcomed by Cleopatra herself inasmuch as her kingdom's surrender was an established fact and was the actual basis for her present diplomatic negotiations (remember the Roman distinction between humbled and insolent foreign powers). This is why Augustus elected to leave the statue in the temple even after the Battle of Actium. It continued to celebrate Roman victory.

We turn now to Caesarion, whom Cleopatra claimed was Caesar's son. This assertion will have empowered the boy in Alexandria, and, his mother may have hoped, it would render him more attractive to the Romans as the future king of Egypt (Fig. 11). Caesar did not acknowledge Caesarion or include him in his will, but this can settle nothing: Caesar's remarks on the Roman soldiers of Alexandria illustrate the correct Roman attitude toward such connections. Apparently, Caesar did not wish to challenge those conventional prejudices. Admittedly, there was some curiosity about Caesarion. In a letter to Atticus, Cicero writes that he "would like to know the truth about the queen and especially about *that* Caesar." Eventually

Antony became a champion of Caesar's paternity. Octavian denied it bitterly. But that was all part of an argument, carried out by way of propaganda, about *Octavian's* legitimacy as the son of Caesar. Which is why, in the aftermath of Actium, Caesarion was put to death by the new regime, because, as it was put at the time, too many Caesars are not a good thing.

Cleopatra's residence in Rome went remarkably unremarked by Caesar's contemporaries, who, it must be admitted, had more pressing concerns. Only later, and only in the baleful afterglow of her grand passion with Antony, did Cleopatra's association become, by way of retrospection, a love affair instead of a one-night stand. But by then Cleopatra had been exploded into a figure so lurid and sensual that only Elizabeth Taylor could play her. She *must* have captivated Caesar. How not?

As for Caesar, although he commenced his career as a paragon of *pietas* – the beloved nephew, the adoring son and the loyal husband – he soon became notorious for a quite different attitude toward women. He was a master practitioner of the most cynical brand of dynastic marriage, and he was a serial philanderer. As he rose to power, his close associates were mostly men like himself – Clodius Pulcher, Caelius Rufus, Cornelius Dolabella, Mark Antony – talented, ambitious, and dissolute in private life. This is not intended as a bit of posthumous scolding. It would after all be the worst sort of moralizing to blame the fall of the Roman republic on the personal decadence of some of its leading politicians, as if there were a necessary link between personal probity and statesmanship. Not everyone, for instance, would prefer to see the White House occupied by the faithful George W. Bush instead of, say, Bill Clinton, a sleazy woman-izer, or John F. Kennedy, a perhaps less sleazy womanizer. In the case of Caesar, his personal immorality seems to be entirely unconnected with his politics or with his ultimate tyranny. It was in fact fairly customary in antiquity for tyrants to attract allegations of rape and seduction. Even Augustus accumulated such accusations. Caesar the dictator did not. His affairs were always with capable women who knew what they were about. There were no victims, at least not by the standards of his day. But if we have by now gone this far in plumbing this aspect of the man's life, we can perhaps no longer help but wonder if, with someone and at some time, Caesar found even a spark of that wonderful seasoning of all enjoyments, the protection and greeting of two solitudes, the all-ennobling experience of . . . *love*. Perhaps he did, if only by accident. Or perhaps, child and favorite of Venus though he was, it was not love that Caesar was after.

Further Reading

Our understanding of the Roman family and of women in Roman society has been advanced dramatically in the past twenty years. A helpful introduction is D'Ambra 2007. Dixon 1992 is a superb yet very accessible account of the Roman family. The nature of our evidence, alas, more or less requires that women be studied in the aggregate rather than as individuals. Still, much can be learned of the opportunities and limitations of women by combining literary, legal and historical sources. Two authoritative studies along these lines are Gardner 1986 and Treggiari 1991. The impediments, theoretical and practical alike, to such research are examined by Dixon 2001. The intellectual lives of upper-class women receive lively and informative treatment in Hemelrijk 1999. Cleopatra resists aggregate treatment. Recent accounts of her career and its significance include Burstein 2004, Kleiner 2005, Jones 2006a and Ashton 2007. The evidence for Cleopatra is assembled in translation in Jones 2006b. Elegantly written if outdated (and in some respects unattractive to modern sensibilities), Balsdon 1963 should not be overlooked. The possibility that Caesar's last words were anything but sentimental is the proposition of Russell 1980.

6

Great Men and Impersonal Groundswells: The Civil War

In his great book, *The Age of Revolution*, first published in 1962, the eminent historian Eric Hobsbawm *dispenses* with Great Men, indeed, with men and women full stop, who become, to a remarkable degree, merely accidental to the deeper reality of historical necessity. In his masterly representation of the late eighteenth and early nineteenth centuries, he insists that, in order to understand – in meaningful terms – the Industrial Revolution and the French Revolution, as well as their implications for the formation of modern European society, one must ponder, as he put it, "the impersonal groundswell of history on which the more obvious men and events of [the] period were borne." Hobsbawm's emphasis is itself the result of what were then recent tendencies in historiography, not all of them implicated in the author's thorough-going Marxism, but each enjoined by a similar predilection for exhuming historical causation from geographical circumstances, economic constraints, contending ideologies, and social institutions – historical forces that could be explained and comprehended (such was the current faith) like physical laws.

The *origin* of Hobsbawm's distinction between what we might call proximate and ultimate historical causes can never the less be traced back to Thucydides, an author we have encountered before. In his *History of the Peloponnesian War*, Thucydides rejected the idea that specific and particular actions on the part of the Athenians or the Corinthians constituted the source of the terrible war between Athens and Sparta. He did not deny that they were *amongst* the war's causes, but, in his view, the "truest cause" of the war was the expansion of Athenian power, amplified by the natural and aggressive energies unleashed by radical democracy, and the Spartans' congenital fear in reaction to it: national character, then, another abstraction, made the war inevitable.

This concept of historical necessity reveals itself in just such formulations: in *The Age of Revolution*, the words *irresistible* and *inevitable* occur on almost every page, sometimes making multiple appearances on a single page. Whereas Thucydides remained in an age still capable of appreciating the importance of individuals for ill and for good – if only, Thucydides observes ruefully, the Athenians had adhered to Pericles's policies – the modern age, for reasons all too obvious in the aftermath of the mid-twentieth century, has tended to minimize the contributions of individuals, at least in political contexts, even as it continues to misconstrue what is patently intended by the expression *great man*. We have, fairly enough, become frightened of the great men who once, it had been alleged, embodied the *Zeitgeist*. But for some modern historians, the rejection of "great men" in favor of historical necessity has led to the conviction that this thing, historical necessity, determines events by means of a predestination that borders on a kind of secular Presbyterianism. The *particularities* of events simply stop mattering. Again, in Hobsbawm's formulation with respect to the revolutions of the eighteenth century, these details "can clearly explain at most the occasion and timing of the great breakthrough and not its fundamental cause"; or, again, "it was clearly inevitable that changes – whatever their precise institutional character – could not long be delayed," as if such details were trivial. Individuals, actual people, may struggle to control events, but, if in retrospect they were on the wrong side, then the inevitable verdict is that "history was against them." It is perhaps more than a little ironic, then, that Hobsbawm lived to write an autobiography.

The chief job of the historian, after she or he has recovered the facts of the past, is to render them meaningful to the present. For the political historian, this necessarily enjoins grappling with historical causation, an endeavor that is regularly caricatured by the way in which history is taught in the schools, where pupils are regularly hectored with instructions along the lines of "please name the three causes of the Second World War" (historical causes, in common with the persons of the Christian god and the parts of Gaul, like threesomes). But there are always multiple causes for significant events (and, for that matter, for insignificant ones), and it is not enough simply to adduce them: one is obliged to assess their relative importance. And, in my opinion, in history the *personnel* matter. Not perhaps if you take the long view, but the long view is surely the least gratifying perspective from which to study the past (or to contemplate the present). This is true whether one is studying elites or history from the ground up. And I suspect that most of us believe this, not least because it is the justification for biography, a genre that stretches back to antiquity and shows no sign of abating amongst our contemporaries. We believe this because we are well aware, on the basis of our own existence, how profound a difference individuals actually make – *now* and so, presumably, *then*. How different would the world be now if Al Gore and not George W. Bush had become president of the United States? And, grand affairs notwithstanding, if you have ever interviewed for a job, or asked someone for a date, then you know just how crucial a single decision made by one person can be – perhaps for the residue of your life. This is not to deny the obvious significance of social structures and ideological (and other) parameters for the conditioning and configuration of historical outcomes. But, simply put, lots of things enter into it. The means by which you make your own life meaningful to yourself, and perhaps to others, are not so very different from the best means by which we recover the essential qualities of the past – even the civil war.

First the facts, to the extent they can be recovered with any degree of accuracy (little in what follows is entirely uncontroversial). Explaining the civil war of 49 BC requires, at the very least, a hasty review of the complicated political history of the fifties. Unfortunately, it also involves certain constitutional technicalities and too many Latin terms. It's a nuisance, I know, but there's nothing to be done about it. In real life, the particularities, even the hard ones, really are important.

By the mid-fifties, as the term of Caesar's proconsulship was reaching its conclusion, his enemies were mobilizing themselves: a tribune attempted to recall Caesar for trial, while Lucius Domitius Ahenobarbus, a candidate for the consulship of 55 BC, declared his intention to terminate Caesar's command as soon as possible. There were other stresses, none of which need detain us here, in the arrangement between Caesar, Pompey, and Crassus. Simply put, the oligarchy had reasserted itself and, as the establishment tends to do, it was winning: consequently, a renewal of the three men's mutual commitment was necessitated. The principal goal of this new coalition was a second consulship for Crassus and Pompey, which they secured for the year 55 BC, by means of constitutional chicanery and by violence. The new consuls saw to it that each of them received a special command. Crassus got Syria, from which base he intended an invasion of Parthia (modern Iraq and Iran, amongst other bits), whence he anticipated glory and treasure to match his colleague and Caesar. Pompey was assigned the Spanish provinces. Because he was also at this time in charge of Rome's grain supply, Pompey decided to manage Spain by means of his legates, which meant that in the next year Pompey would possess an accumulation of promagistracies, one of which allowed him to command legions in a distant province while he remained in the vicinity of Rome, a situation that anticipated the mechanics of the government of the future emperor Augustus. Pompey's stature, now quite simply incomparable, was dramatically punctuated when he dedicated, with sensational games, his splendid theater complex.

Caesar's requirements were not ignored. His tenure in Gaul was extended, by way of a law advanced by Pompey and Crassus in combination, for another five years. Now inasmuch as this law will become crucial to the outbreak of the civil war, let me dwell on it for a moment. After 52 BC the central conflict between Caesar and his enemies would be over when, precisely, Caesar's command could legally be brought to its end. This issue did not die with the Romans, not least because the specifics of this law are as poorly understood as they have been copiously debated by modern scholars. Never the less, it now seems clear that this law did not stipulate an exact date for the termination of Caesar's extraordinary proconsulship.

Generally speaking, a governor's provincial command, owing to primitive conditions of ancient transportation and communication, as well as to the Romans' native pragmatism in reaction to that fact of life, lasted until his successor was determined and until said successor arrived in the province. The procedure for making and filling provincial appointments was itself unhurried: typically, the senate decided in March which provinces should be allocated to the consuls of the subsequent year, who would normally spend the bulk of their consular year in administering the city before setting off for their provincial assignments. This meant that in practice a provincial governor would know months in advance whether or not he was to be replaced or whether for some reason his term was to be extended. In Caesar's case, the grant of a new five-year command in Gaul meant that his province would not be discussed in the provincial deliberations of 55 BC (which concerned the provinces to be allocated to magistrates holding office in 54 BC) or in the deliberations of the following four years. The issue of his succession could only be taken up in 50 BC, presumably but not explicitly in March of that year. He is unlikely, then, to have expected this replacement to arrive until sometime in 49 BC. The question of his term in Gaul, then, was entirely uncontroversial – in 55 BC. It was a clear win for Caesar – and for his partners. A jealous oligarchy simmered with resentment.

The next two years, however, brought multiple and unpredictable blows for the triumvirate. In 54 BC, Julia, to whom Pompey was entirely devoted, died in childbirth. In the subsequent year it was learned that Crassus's invasion of Parthia had failed. He and the bulk of his army had been destroyed. These losses were at once personal and political, and the dynamics of senatorial power were altered, at first in a small way. Caesar, alert to the new possibilities created by these twin disasters, immediately proposed that Pompey marry his great-niece, Octavia (who would be required to divorce her husband, Gaius Claudius Marcellus, the future consul of 50 BC), while he would divorce Calpurnia to marry Pompey's daughter, herself already married to Faustus Sulla. The sheer complexity of the proposed rearrangements attest to the importance Caesar placed on sustaining his connection with Pompey. But the great man did nothing, for the moment.

Then in 52 BC, owing to political assassination resulting in riot (the senate house was burned down), all of which was unconnected, for our purposes, with Pompey or Caesar – there were after all other troublemakers in Roman society – it become impossible for the government to restore order. The unrelenting turmoil and the current incompetence of the magistrates conspired to make it appear inevitable, to the Roman people at least, that Pompey must be appointed dictator in order to preserve the republic. But Bibulus and Cato devised a novel means of placing Rome in Pompey's hands without resorting to an office so unhappily associated with Sulla. The senate decreed that only one candidate for the consulship should be put before the people and that he should enter office without a colleague. This was done, and Pompey found himself in possession of another unprecedented honor, offered him by a distressed senate at the urging of his longstanding, and now hard-pressed, opponents. Pompey the Great, at once consul and proconsul, was now beyond question the greatest man in Rome – a reality finally given formal recognition by the establishment. And he was far from unaffected by this gesture. He was soon drawing closer to the aristocrats whose past resentment – and resistance – had driven him into Caesar's friendship in the first place. This was not a good thing for Caesar.

It must be remembered that Caesar had very powerful enemies. They included Domitius Ahenobarbus, noble and wealthy enough to raise armies from his own clients and tenants, the Claudii Marcelli, about whom one could say more or less the same thing, and of course Calpurnius Bibulus and the circle centered about Porcius Cato. Here one can hardly speak of an organization with a visible leader: these men were nobles united in principle, usually, and certainly always by their desire to see themselves running the senatorial show. They and their ilk had for more than a decade opposed Pompey at every turn, owing to oligarchic envy and perhaps a genuine worry that he would make himself their master. Caesar they loathed as a criminal thruster who would stop at nothing: there can be no doubting that they hated his contempt, made unmistakably plain during his consulship, for the traditions and values of the senatorial class, what a Roman would have called *senatus auctoritas*, the prestige of the senate. Their most conspicuous spokesman was Cato, notoriously stupid as a schoolboy and supercilious as an adult, which explains his unpopularity with Roman voters (he made it to the praetorship only on his second attempt, and after losing a race for the consulship gave it up as a lost cause). As Caesar rightly observed, Cato resented the success of others, but he cloaked his disappointments in philosophy and in spiteful self-righteousness. For all his truculence and opportunistic moralism, however, he was much admired in the senate. Even Cicero, whom Cato treated poorly, fretted about getting Cato's approval, and after Cato's death he eulogized him to the skies. For the sake of convenience, we shall here denominate this noble faction as *optimates* – the best men – which is certainly how they thought of themselves.

Caesar remained mindful of his enemies. They were relatively few in number, but they were enormously influential. A single illustration will perhaps make this clear: Marcus Claudius Marcellus was consul in 51 BC, his cousin Gaius in 50 BC, and Marcus' brother, also named Gaius, in 49 BC. These were not figures to be trifled with. And by the end of 52 BC it was evident that they were drawing Pompey into their charmed circle (even if they were doing so on Pompey's terms). This need not have shaken Caesar too deeply at this juncture. After all, why shouldn't the *optimates* concede Pompey's eminence? For Caesar the real issue was whether his enemies would also concede *his* hard-earned position in Roman society. Opposition he could predict, but he was likewise also entitled to expect that even the *optimates* must respect his standing as the conqueror of Gaul. By the end of 52 BC, after all, Vercingetorix had been defeated and the Romans' ultimate victory, though not immediate (combat would persist into 51 BC), was certain.

In trying to understand a crisis on the order of the civil war of 49 BC, it is perhaps worthwhile contemplating what ought to have happened as Caesar's campaign drew near its conclusion. Caesar's brilliant personal achievement – he had extended Rome's power throughout Europe, "uniting" Italy with her Spanish provinces, in addition to which he had thrilled the populace of the city by penetrating both darkest Germany and distant Britain – had magnified Roman glory on a scale that perhaps put even Pompey's eastern victories in the shade. The extraordinary quality of

Caesar's conquests had been honored by the senate and people in multiple acts of thanksgiving to the gods – the most extensive in Roman history.

Still, there remained serious work to be done. The Gallic provinces needed reorganization. Allied peoples had to be sorted out in terms of tribute, obligations of service to the Roman army, and restrictions or advancements in their local territories. Administration on this level was complex and potentially lucrative – the participation of Roman *publicani* was both welcome and inevitable – and introduced ample opportunities for shared prestige. For instance, Caesar could have invited the senate to send him a commission to advise and to assist in this great undertaking (something Pompey couldn't be bothered to do after vanquishing the east, and hence his difficulties in getting the senate to ratify his arrangements there). The members of this commission could both lend a helping hand and claim a modest share in the proconsul's accomplishment, cooperation which would have gone a long way toward once again folding Caesar into the society of his senatorial peers. After Gaul had been suitably settled, and the senate could only be patient in this matter, Caesar would return to Rome, celebrate a deserved triumph, enjoy the accolades of the republic, complete his Forum and take his place in the senate as one of its heroes. He would certainly be confident of his immediate election to a coveted second consulship. All of this, to be sure, would have rendered Caesar an exceedingly formidable man. But by no means a figure whom the system of aristocratic competition could not accommodate and thereby manage (even Pompey had been *managed*). And his prestige, like Pompey's, could in no way have put a stop to the robust competitiveness of republican politics. Events didn't happen this way, of course, but this scenario, undramatic in world historical terms, must be kept in mind as we review the actual and cataclysmic events of the late fifties.

Pompey's sole consulship, his third, was a signal moment of greatness. It was not, however, incompatible with Caesar's continued rise. Without question, Caesar had set his sights on a second consulship. As early as 53 BC he had begun negotiating legislation that would allow him to stand for the consulship without actually submitting his application in person and at Rome. The result came in 52 BC, when all ten tribunes of the people joined in putting this measure forward, with the enthusiastic support of Cicero and Pompey. Inasmuch as the bill was veto-proof, it passed securely (Caesar's popularity with the voters was never in doubt) and it is known, imaginatively enough, as the Law of the Ten Tribunes.

Now this is where the technicalities of the Roman constitution begin to bother us (and them). A candidate for office in Rome was obliged to submit his formal application – his *professio* – in person to the magistrate who would preside over the elections. This took place within the *pomerium*, which was the ritual barrier of Rome (not to be confused with the limits of habitation in Rome, which extended farther than the *pomerium*). This requirement once posed a problem for Caesar, when he returned from governing Spain in 60 BC. In that year, Caesar had wanted to apply for a triumph and to stand for the consulship of 59 BC. But here was the bind. The *imperium* of a promagistrate operates only outside the *pomerium*. Whenever he crosses the *pomerium*, his *imperium* evaporates. The sole exception was for celebrating a triumph, in which circumstance the triumphant general's *imperium* was allowed to linger for a single day. To celebrate a triumph, however, one must continue to possess *imperium* on the day. So, in Caesar's case, crossing the *pomerium* to submit his *professio* would cost him his *imperium* – which would make it pointless for him to ask for a triumph. This is why Caesar asked the senate to exempt him from the requirement to submit his *professio* in person (being present at the actual elections didn't enter into it because they took place in the Campus Martius outside the *pomerium*). At Cato's urging, however, the senate refused and Caesar was forced to forgo his triumph.

So the basic idea of the Law of the Ten Tribunes was to save Caesar from a similar bind when he sought his second consulship, which he will have wanted to hold at the earliest possible time. For Caesar that was the year 48 BC (the Sullan constitution required an interval of ten full years between consulships, although Pompey had been exempted from this in 52 BC). Caesar's successor in Gaul, as we have seen, would not be expected to arrive in the province until sometime in 49 BC. A slow hand over just conceivably could delay Caesar beyond the time of the elections for 48 BC (elections ordinarily took place during the summer). Thanks to the Law of the Ten Tribunes, this would not be a problem (he could still be a candidate even while awaiting his successor). If, on the other hand, his return to Rome was timely, he could still anticipate (in 52 BC) that opposition to his triumph on the part of his enemies might keep him camped outside the *pomerium*, the regular practice of generals awaiting a triumph, just long enough to recreate the circumstances of 60 BC. This law eliminated that possibility as well.

What Caesar had in mind goes unrecorded, but is easy enough to divine. He planned to return to Rome in triumph (literally), celebrating his victories while holding the consulship, a dazzling combination unequalled in Rome since the fifth consulship of Marius in 101 BC. Now that was indeed lightning to be outstared, and an unmistakable mark of the *gloria* Caesar judged his due. (His hopes were ultimately frustrated for 48 BC, of course, but in 46 BC he celebrated his *quadruple* triumph *as consul*, thereby surpassing even Marius.) Caesar's aspirations entailed practical benefits too. As consul, Caesar could see to it that his Gallic arrangements were ratified, whatever the degree of resistance put in his way (he knew how to get the most out of executive power: revisit his first consulship). And this meant that he could dispense with consulting the senate about the final settlement of Gaul or with sharing the slightest credit for any of that with anybody (a commission had actually been selected in 56 BC, after which nothing more is heard about it). Furthermore, he could guarantee that his prospects for future glories remained undiminished (again, he knew the drill). The Law of the Ten Tribunes, then, was Caesar's pre-emptive strike against the *optimates*, should they attempt to block him from pushing *past* the boundaries of the high station to which he was, by Roman standards, entitled. No wonder Cato condemned the measure so strenuously.

Pompey's actions during his third consulship, though not dangerous to Caesar in any obvious way, will have added to Caesar's consternation. Appointed sole consul, the great man set to his task with characteristic efficiency. He restored public confidence along with public order. He also took a wife: Pompey married Cornelia, the daughter of the super-noble Quintus Caecilius Metellus Scipio, from the very heart of the *optimates*. Before the year was out, this same Scipio was elected to the consulship as the colleague of his son-in-law. Pompey could claim to Caesar that he was expanding their network of connections, but it had to be clear to the dimmest that he was repositioning himself.

Matters were complicated by a Pompeian law of 52 BC that comprehensively reformed electoral procedures. The measure was sorely needed: elections had been disrupted and postponed in every year since 56 BC (hereafter they were to be both orderly and timely). One provision of this law, however, required all candidates to submit their *professio* in person (which was simply a formal re-enactment of the existing rule). Now this stipulation was plainly inconsistent with the Law of the Ten Tribunes, which it superseded both legally and technically. This was certainly unintended. Roman laws, including this one, were long and detailed documents, often in tedious Latin and usually composed on behalf of their masters by anonymous scribes. Just as modern legislators (and citizens) all too rarely read what they vote for – or against – in its entirety, so too, we can be sure, did the Romans. Not a single one of the tribunes of that year, whose dignity, along with Caesar's privilege, was at stake in the Law of the Ten Tribunes, interposed a veto. The natural reading of the legislation was that it reformed normal practices and was not meant to apply to Caesar's exception. Still, when the inconsistency was pointed out, after the law had been passed, Pompey, insisting that it was far from his intention to deprive Caesar of anything, went so far as to add a codicil to the engraved statute stipulating that Caesar was exempt from its provisions.

This was, on Pompey's part, a remarkable specimen of arrogance, with unfortunate consequences. Although magistrates routinely interpreted laws, they none of them possessed the power to create new laws on their own – not even Pompey. Pompey's codicil had no legal standing, and its relevance to any future understanding of the validity of the Law of the Ten Tribunes depended wholly on the weight of Pompey's personal prestige. Now we can be sure that *that* aspect of this episode was intentional. Pompey's gesture conveyed to Caesar his continued friendship. And it conveyed to the *optimates* his expectation that they should respect his authority. And to everyone it conveyed his dominance. Had Pompey wished nothing more than to reach a genuine clarification, he could have arrived at that by way of a decree of the senate or subsequent legislation re-enacting the original Law of the Ten Tribunes. Instead he was satisfied with his own solution and stood in a position to intimidate anyone who might disagree. But Pompey's action did in fact (as events would demonstrate) leave Caesar vulnerable. Hereafter it was open to his enemies to argue that his right to by-pass an in-person *professio* was no longer valid, against which claim Caesar would be obliged to rely on Pompey's superior prestige, itself an unattractive prospect to the proconsul of Gaul.

Another one of Pompey's reforms, again entirely innocent at the time, contributed to the constitutional crisis that led to civil war. Hitherto in Rome it was the normal practice for magistrates, at the end of their term in office, to set off to serve as provincial governors, a passage from one powerful position to another, the convenience of which had led to bad habits. Candidates resorted to electoral bribery in their race to win a magistracy. Thereafter, they inclined toward corruption when, as provincial governors, they endeavored to recoup their losses and add to their personal fortunes. In order to break this sleazy pattern, Pompey severed the direct connection between office and province: hereafter magistrates would be required to wait five years for a provincial assignment. Because of this change, Rome now had to look for its governors amongst senators who had held higher magistracies years in the past and were currently unencumbered by magisterial duties.

How did this affect Caesar? It meant that, whenever his successor was named, perhaps as early as March in 50 BC, he could immediately go to

Gaul, effectively cutting Caesar's tenure by months and putting more pressure on the validity of the Law of the Ten Tribunes. Although it was not foreseen at the time, this would very soon complicate Caesar's life. Furthermore, this measure created yet another (and even more consequential) political wrinkle. Before Pompey's reform, provincial arrangements had been conducted by the senate without tribunician interference: put differently, no veto was allowed. Pompey's law scrapped that prohibition. This innovation, as we shall see presently, introduced the very pretext that allowed Caesar to invade Italy in defense of the tribunes, in defense of *libertas*. But we are getting ahead of ourselves. Let's return to 52 BC.

The *optimates* launched themselves against Caesar. Cato, like Domitius before him, stood for the consulship, declaring that, if elected, he would recall Caesar and prosecute him for war crimes. The public's reaction is easy to gauge by the flames which engulfed Cato's candidacy. Instead, another of Caesar's enemies, Marcus Claudius Marcellus, was elected, along with Servius Sulpicius Rufus, a learned jurist of independent mind. Taking perverse advantage of the victory at Alesia, Marcellus pressed for Caesar's recall on the grounds that the war in Gaul was finished. But Sulpicius, unpersuaded of the legitimacy of his colleague's position, made legal mincemeat of him, a response that gained political heft from Pompey's complete endorsement. Marcellus' proposal was first voted down and thereafter ignored by the senatorial majority, who clearly saw things Sulpicius' way and who left the consul with little option but to resort to ineffectual ranting.

Scipio proposed instead that the future of the Gallic provinces be debated on the first of March in 50 BC, a suggestion that no one could reasonably resist, although Caesar's friends in Rome complained about it, knowing that on account of Pompey's reforms Caesar could potentially be replaced in advance of the schedule he had devised previously. Still, they had no real basis for their objections. It was all very well but entirely pointless to argue that if Caesar were superseded "early," under the new circumstances of provincial administration, this would in effect deny the popular will as it had been expressed in the legislation of 55 BC: after all, the Roman constitution had no supreme court competent to divine such original intentions. This is why Caesar was now genuinely at risk of being turned out of his province in 50 BC, what for him amounted to a very premature evacuation, one that threatened to spoil the glorious homecoming he had devised. Inasmuch as he could not be consul before 48 BC, his privilege under the Law of the Ten Tribunes would be more or less useless to him if forced to return to Rome in 50 BC. Mind you, nobody could actually drag him into the city. But he would look pretty silly sitting outside the *pomerium* for two years waiting for his big chance to show off. His dignity would demand that he triumph and stand for office in the normal way – lest he become ridiculous.

This was not merely disappointing. It was also dangerous. To explain Caesar's situation, we must once more plunge into the technicalities of the *pomerium* and its neutralizing effect on *imperium*. In the Roman legal system, so long as a magistrate or promagistrate possessed *imperium*, he was immune from prosecution in the courts. Caesar had enjoyed this condition for years. But once he crossed the *pomerium*, and thereby lost his *imperium*, he would suddenly be open to the prosecutions threatened relentlessly by his enemies. Even as consul-designate, he could be charged with a crime. Now it is hard for us to imagine that Caesar, with his riches and reputation, could have been condemned by any jury. But then *we* aren't faced by the likes of Cato or Marcellus, and Caesar never underestimated the clout or the vindictiveness of the *optimates*. Suetonius reports that multiple authorities attributed Caesar's readiness to wage a civil war to his fear of prosecution. Of these, he names only one, the historian Asinius Pollio, who fought on Caesar's side and who claimed to have heard his general insist that "even after so many great deeds, I, Gaius Caesar, would have been condemned in the courts had I not sought the protection of my army." Still, prosecution and condemnation constituted Caesar's worst-case scenario, not his chief concern. It was his yearning for honor as much as his yearning for safety that motivated Caesar. He did not simply seek to avoid disgrace: he insisted on respect.

So Caesar pushed back. If his tenure in Gaul must be, by his own reckoning, cut short, then there must be adequate compensation. He proposed that he be allowed to exercise his privilege under the Law of the Ten Tribunes early – by way of an exception to the ten-year interval between consulships. Thus he could, while holding his position in Gaul, stand for the consulship of 49 BC. He could then still realize his original desire to commence his consulship in Marius-like triumph, with the added bonus of a senatorial invitation to return in glory. This is far from what the *optimates* had in mind, however, and, as it turned out, it also ran contrary to Pompey's plans for Caesar. Again and again the great man made it clear that he was opposed to Caesar's election to the consulship so long as he remained in his province in command of his legions, a position that put him at odds with his former father-in-law. Not that Pompey wanted to force a break with Caesar. When asked in the senate what he would do if Caesar persisted in wanting to stand for office while retaining his province, Pompey gently

133

replied, "What would I do if my son took a stick to me?" Here was a response directed to all parties: Pompey continued to regard Caesar as his friend and ally, whose interests he would respect, but – and this was his message for the *optimates* – he could be counted on to restrain Caesar's wildest ambitions.

Why should Pompey have decided to put himself in Caesar's way? The answer lies in Pompey's determination to keep himself in the superlative station he had arrived at in 52 BC. For the whole of his brilliant career, contrary to the anxieties of the Roman establishment, Pompey had never sought to subvert the superiority of the senatorial nobility. Quite the reverse, it had been his ambition to *lead* the establishment, as its greatest man, not to sweep it away. This dream had been realized in the year of his sole consulship. But it ain't easy at the top. Staying there could be no easy task given the inclination of the *optimates* to envy and unite themselves against anyone who excelled them. Soon the desperation of 52 BC would be forgotten, at which moment aristocratic resentment against Pompey would once again become a luxury the *optimates* could afford. In addition to that, and just as serious, it was clearer to Pompey than to anyone else that his reputation was rapidly being matched by Caesar's. Pompey's tactic against each of these threats was to turn them against one another. The *optimates* feared Caesar as much as they loathed him, but they couldn't stop him let alone beat him without Pompey's aid. And so Pompey needed Caesar to curb the *optimates*. Likewise, Caesar was in a bind. The legality, much less the respectability, of his position in Gaul would become increasingly dubious if he defied the senate and failed to return to Rome in a timely way, but to do so could put both his prestige and his safety at risk. And so Pompey needed the *optimates* to keep the pressure on Caesar, who, in the end, must take shelter under Pompey's shadow. In this way, the solution to everyone's difficulties lay in universal subordination to Pompey the Great.

Caesar, for his part, had decided that, despite Pompey's pronouncements, he *would* be elected consul – be it in 50 BC or 49 BC (his hopes for 50 BC were in fact disappointed without any apparent controversy) – while still retaining his province and army. His strategy was simple: he would deploy loyal tribunes (and Caesar was very good at procuring loyal tribunes) who would veto any senatorial attempt to reallocate the Gallic provinces, a resource available to him courtesy of the same Pompeian reform that had wrecked his proconsular timetable in the first place. This was perfectly legal, if not perfectly proper. Until a successor to Caesar could be appointed and until he could make his way to Gaul, Caesar remained the legitimate proconsul. For its part, the senate was not without resources for dealing with obstructionist tribunes. If unpersuaded by a tribune's rationale for interposing his veto, and the arguments for delaying Caesar's return to Rome can only have been sentimental and not constitutional in nature, the senate could employ its collective prestige in order to overawe the man (this routinely did the trick). If that failed, an obdurate tribune might be intimidated by a threat of violence. Caesar, however, let it be known that he was prepared to lend muscular support to any tribune's veto, a promise it was believed he could keep so long as he continued to command Rome's biggest and best army. The *optimates* had experienced Caesar's enormities during his consulship. For all their own bluster, they remained anxious that Caesar just might possibly turn to civil war if his tribunes were mistreated. And so there were decrees in the senate followed by vetoes from the tribunes, delaying tactics that led nowhere. Which suited Caesar just fine, at least for now. He cared little about angry optimate expostulations – so long as they remained impotent.

This crisis, the point must be emphasized, was entirely manufactured by a tiny senatorial minority. It had nothing to do with the mood of the mob. They adored Pompey and Caesar alike, and as for their attitude toward the residue of the senatorial elite, they were conditioned to defer. However discontented the crowds in Rome may have been, the elite classes, as we saw in the first chapter, knew how to control them, most of the time. Here the historian will find no *sansculottes* boiling with revolutionary rage: the commons of Rome hungered, they sometimes rioted, perhaps they dreamed, but, for all practical purposes, they *did as they were told*. Nor can partisanship be detected amongst the equestrian order or in the Italian municipalities. At the elections in the late fifties, for instance, enemies of Caesar both won and lost (look at Cato) in consular elections: the propertied classes were plainly not polarized along the lines of being pro- or anti-Caesar. Nor did the armies rise up on their own to elevate a single *generalissimo* to supreme power. Even in the senate itself, most members respected Pompey and remained unwilling to see Caesar disgraced. It should be remembered that most senators, ex-quaestors or ex-tribunes, significant men though they were, would never win military glory on the operatic scale of Caesar or Pompey – and could never confuse their own degree of prestige with that of either of these men. It was natural for them, like the rest of the Romans, to admire martial greatness. It took the likes of the *optimates* to resent so intensely the *gloria* of their peers.

Now I have no doubt that had Caesar placed himself under Pompey's protection, he would have gotten every honor. He could have returned to

Rome, celebrated his triumph on his own schedule, gained his consulship – all without a worry about the *optimates*. But by so doing he would have, for all practical purposes, cemented his subordinate status with respect to Pompey, who, with Caesar as his sure resource, could continue in his undeniable supremacy. But this is precisely what Caesar had no intention of doing. In the first place, he claimed to fear Pompeian violence. One contemporary reported that "Caesar is persuaded that he cannot be safe if he returns to Rome without an army," a sentiment that recurs in Caesar's own *Civil War*. In recounting a debate in the senate, Caesar relates that Marcus Calidius and Caelius Rufus asserted how "Caesar was afraid that it was to endanger him that Pompey kept two legions in Rome," a claim that Caesar the narrator does not correct. It was not forgotten in Rome that, during his youth, Pompey had been dubbed *adulescentulus carnifex*, the baby-faced executioner, or that he had a record of letting his friends down when it suited his interests. The great man's ruthlessness was too well known to be overlooked. Caesar's professed apprehensions in fact struck a nerve: it soon became necessary for Pompey to declare in public that he was not acting against Caesar in anything that he did. Even if Caesar had trusted Pompey, however – and this is the second and more important thing – he had done far too much in Gaul for his glory to rely on the favor of somebody else. He could not and would not be humiliated. As he puts it in his *Civil War*, in a long catalogue of wrongs suffered, "in his case and his case only the custom had not been preserved that had always been observed for all other conquering generals, that after completing their great achievements they returned home with considerable honor – and certainly without disgrace – and then they dismissed their armies."

Whatever the exact legalities, most people saw it Caesar's way. At a meeting of the senate in June of 50 BC, when a tribune vetoed a decree to replace Caesar in Gaul, the presiding consul referred the matter of the veto to the senate, a standard way of putting pressure on a tribune to withdraw his veto. In a crowded senate, the consul's proposal was voted down by an impressive margin, with obvious implications for Caesar's position. Caelius Rufus, who was a witness, interpreted the episode this way: "the senate has come to this conclusion: he should be allowed to stand for office without handing over his army and provinces." Of course, most people, at all levels of society, wanted peace at home. As each side escalated its demands along with its rhetoric, a general anxiety about civil war, and about the inevitability of civil war, began to take hold. In a letter written soon after this event, Caelius confessed to Cicero that he expected civil war in a matter of months.

And so Caesar tried a new tack. As he put it later in the *Civil War*, in a passage that is too often selectively interpreted, Caesar conceded that, for him, his *dignitas* had always been more important than life itself (he writes this knowing it is a sentiment that will win approval from his readers). However, despite the insults by which he was threatened by his enemies – the truncation of his command and the requirement that he return to Rome – he could have endured these things with equanimity *rei publicae causa*, for the sake of the republic. It was owing to such sweet reason that he proposed that both he and Pompey should alike surrender their armies. After all, the armies in Italy could have but one purpose – to menace Caesar. Pompey should go to his provinces in Spain, they should both disband their armies, the state should be freed from fear, and government and free elections should be restored to the supervision of the senate. What could be more just?

At first, Caesar did not make the running himself. In February 50 BC, the tribune Gaius Scribonius Curio introduced this stunning proposal. Its appeal was obvious: at one stroke, the oligarchy would be rid of the military threat of Caesar, the elimination of which made Pompey less essential. And Pompey's anomalous pre-eminence could be undone. In other words, Curio's proposal tended to transform what had appeared a confrontation between Caesar and the *optimates* over a matter of legal procedure and senatorial prestige into one between Caesar and Pompey over a contest of personal prestige – as much about Pompey's *dignitas* as Caesar's. Hence the ancient view that Caesar could not endure a superior and Pompey could not abide an equal. But Curio's proposal had the unintended effect of shifting Pompey strongly toward the position of the *optimates*. He now endorsed the opinion that Caesar should leave his province on the Ides of November of 50 BC, after which he must rely on Pompey's protection and goodwill. There was a further (and unofficial) riposte. Various parties – including Pompey – took to grumbling that *on any terms* a second consulship for Caesar would be tantamount to the complete subversion of the republic, an attitude that opened the door to invalidating the Law of the Ten Tribunes and even to a prosecution for the good of the state.

In the summer of 50 BC Pompey fell seriously ill. The people of Italy united in prayers for his health and in rejoicing at his recovery. This unexpected event deceived Pompey, who confused Italy's affection for him with loyalty that could endure even the extremity of civil war. He soon made his famous boast that, at a stamp of his foot, legions and cavalry would spring forth from the earth. In his renewed confidence, he now called Curio's bluff. But Curio insisted that Pompey disarm first, a demand that implicitly criticized Pompey's trustworthiness (and which ignored the fact that, owing to legislation passed in 52 BC, Pompey's command in Spain, unlike Caesar's in Gaul, still had three more years to go). This niggling cost Curio a good deal of his credibility.

In December the senate took a series of votes along the lines of Curio's proposition. The first concerned the question of Caesar's stepping down. It passed. Thereafter the senate voted on Pompey's resignation. This failed to pass. Finally, the body voted on Curio's specific proposal – that each should stand down – and this passed by a margin of 370 to 22. The senators, this vote makes clear, cared more about peace than about either Caesar or Pompey. But no action was taken, and Curio soon left Rome to join Caesar. The *optimates* resorted to pageantry. The consul, Gaius Claudius Marcellus, in company with the consuls-elect for 49 BC, made a display of placing a sword in Pompey's hands and beseeching him to defend the republic against Caesar. The gesture was symbolic, but potent, and Pompey accepted the task – if, he was careful to say, no better solution could be found.

Civil war loomed, but it had not yet arrived, and, even in this atmosphere of pessimism, it is not clear that anyone in Rome genuinely believed it would actually come to that. The *optimates* had absolutely no doubt that Caesar would back down, as did Pompey: each was certain that Caesar had too much to lose if he acted otherwise. Even Cicero remarks in a letter to his friend Atticus: "my only comfort is that, given that even his enemies concede he will get a second consulship and that fortune has given him immense power, I do not believe that Caesar would be mad enough to risk all that." In another letter to Atticus, Cicero reviews Caesar's options in detail, coming to the conclusion that he will probably submit, return without his army and become consul. This shows only that Cicero's sense of *dignitas* was less finely developed than Caesar's. Still Cicero did consider war a possibility. His keen political brain recognized that, if it should come to civil war, Caesar would want a justification. He would find it, Cicero predicted, "either on the pretext of the rejection of his candidature or on the pretext of a tribune's taking refuge with him on the grounds of his veto being overridden by a senatorial decree or on the grounds of his having been forcibly expelled from the city." This is of course what did happen: Caesar's enemies handed him a plausible excuse for striking first.

Now it would be a mistake to assume that Caesar was simply waiting on political events in Rome. In 50 BC the senate was conscripting troops, ostensibly to be shipped east to fight the Parthians. The news from Gaul, on the other hand, was less easy for the senate to come by. It was rumored, and widely believed, that Caesar's troops were wearied and demoralized after a decade of hard fighting and that they looked forward to release. At the same time, stories percolated down the peninsula that Caesar was making ready to invade Italy. Later events demonstrated that these tales were true. The very timely appearance of Caesar's legions during his invasion of Italy suffice to prove that he had given the order to his legions in Transalpine Gaul to march south sometime in 50 BC. This, of course, receives no mention whatsoever in Caesar's own account, who claims to have summoned them only when war became a necessity in 49 BC. But, unless Caesar had stumbled on a Peugeot factory in Gaul, an early march is the only way that these legions could have arrived in Italy as soon as they in fact did.

On the first day of the new year in 49 BC a letter from Caesar was presented to the senate, which give it a hearing only after prompting from the tribunes Mark Antony and Quintus Cassius. It was received as a harsh threat of civil war. A motion was put forward by Metellus Scipio that, unless Caesar dismissed his army before a certain date, he should be judged to be acting against the republic. The motion was passed, but vetoed by Antony and Cassius. On the seventh of January the senate passed an emergency decree, after which Antony and Cassius were warned not to interfere. They fled to Caesar (as Cicero had predicted). Caesar's privilege under the Law of the Ten Tribunes was annulled soon thereafter. Domitius Ahenobarbus was appointed as Caesar's successor. In Rome, the *optimates* and Pompey were alike certain they had won this contest: Caesar must capitulate or try his luck in civil war, which, his enemies were convinced, he could only lose. And yet no real preparations were made for fighting Caesar, although the *optimates* must have foreseen, what had been all too clear to Cicero, that they were delivering Caesar a justification for invading. Which can only mean that they genuinely believed that in the end he would back down. They were wrong.

Caesar appealed to his army, claiming that Pompey had been corrupted by the *optimates*. He asked his soldiers to defend the rights of the tribunes – and to defend their leader's *dignitas*. Everything hung on their reaction. Roman armies are often criticized by modern scholars for their role in the civil war. But it should be clear to everyone that, so far as the peasants who served in the armies were concerned, the issue of constitutional legitimacy had to be uncertain. Granted the senate was owed respect. At the same time, these men believed in the rights of the tribunes – the tribunate was the ordinary Roman's sole protection from magisterial and senatorial excess, and they were an integral element in the

Roman constitution. They also believed, as all Romans did, in the morality of the *quid pro quo*. Caesar had conquered Gaul; he deserved better treatment than this. They, too, had conquered Gaul, hard service for more than a decade, in which their general's merits had been abundantly evident and in which they had prospered by way of the spoils of war. They deserved to march in Caesar's triumph. In short, they had a stake in the preservation of his *dignitas*, not least if they hoped for some security of their own at the end of their service. After all, if a great man like Caesar could be dismissed without his fair desserts – what of themselves?

Roman soldiers, when they put down their arms, sought a pension in the shape of a plot of land that would allow them to return to the farming life whence they had been drafted. Ordinarily, the senate did nothing for demobbed soldiers. Ordinarily, soldiers accepted their fate. Some in Caesar's army, however, may have remembered that it was *their* general and not Pompey who had secured land for the great man's veterans – in the teeth of senatorial hostility. Caesar could be counted on. As for Pompey, he had joined with men like Bibulus and Cato in threatening the tribunes. The *optimates* had once fought against land for Pompey's veterans. No surprise, then, that such men trampled on the tribunes as well. Not even the legionaries will have wanted civil war – the events of the war tended to prove that – but, from their perspective, it was only by following Caesar that they could fight for *libertas*, which for them was not merely an abstract principle. The sensibilities of Pompey and his *optimate* allies did not reach this far, and so they were alike shocked when Caesar led his forces into Italy.

Caesar's invasion of Italy, like his conquest of Gaul, was a war of liberation. And being first in with a serious army, he was quite naturally welcomed as a liberator throughout Italy, whenever and wherever he appeared. And Caesar was diligent in proclaiming himself as a liberator. In his *Civil War* he complains that senatorial freedom of choice had been eliminated by Pompey and by the *optimates*. And, in one of the innumerable instances within the *Civil War* of Caesar's cataloguing his motives, he insists that his invasion of Italy was not undertaken to harm anyone, but instead "to win back his own liberty and the liberty of the Roman people, which had been oppressed by the tyranny of an oligarchic faction." Again and again, he returns to his defense of the tribunate, which leaves it a trifle embarrassing for Caesarian propaganda that, even after Antony and Cassius had fled to Caesar, the remaining tribunes continued to interpose vetoes on other matters of senatorial debate (thus revealing the continuing viability of the institution), a fact of life that Caesar himself records shamelessly. And it is nothing short of hypocritical that, once he arrived in Rome, Caesar threatened violence against the tribune Lucius Metellus, who attempted to prevent Caesar's theft of Rome's sacred treasury. But by then Caesar needed money more than he needed respectability. And liberation is, after all, a marvelously elastic concept.

At least Caesar, unlike so many participants in more recent freedom movements, possessed the candor and the spleen to emphasize the importance of his own prestige and the wrongs done him personally. This is not in any way disguised in Caesar's propaganda. Quite the reverse, he regularly cites the *optimates'* refusal to pay him the respect he deserved and their attempts to undermine his political standing, injuries he adduces as frequently as he does the oppression of liberty. There was nothing selfless in Caesar's representation of himself.

Caesar's elaborate justifications were necessary because he had violated Roman law by leaving his province without authorization and had outraged Roman sensibilities by invading Italy. The devoted Marian had become a second Sulla. This is why, after the Battle of Pharsalus, Caesar, when surveying the fallen nobility, famously remarked, "*they* wished it so." But Caesar did not succeed in shifting the blame for the civil war onto the *optimates*. To some degree this was because Caesar was, in a very real sense, the loser in his struggle with the conventions of oligarchy, and the violent perturbations that followed his death so scarred the Romans that the pretensions and the stupidities of the *optimates* began to appear less unattractive than the general who had defeated them. In the end, imperial literature could see it both ways, and Caesar's bitterest enemy, Cato, who committed suicide rather than be beaten by Caesar, was destined to emerge in the ideology of the empire as the embodiment of what was best in the Roman republic. There was also the reality that Caesar had simply lost the political struggle over the conditions for his return to Rome. Pompey outfoxed him and out-muscled him – in the senate. Any other Roman politician would have conceded this fact. Nearly everyone expected Caesar to do so, and certainly everyone hoped that he would. But they had not reckoned on Caesar, who would not truckle before Pompey the Great. He had been cheated – and he for one would not endure it.

And so Caesar liberated Rome from the tyranny of an oligarchic faction, and soon made himself dictator for life. A grateful senate honored its master by acclaiming him *Liberator*, and further decreed a temple to the goddess *Libertas* in commemoration of Caesar's liberation of the republic. A different faction of oligarchs soon liberated Rome from Caesar – *libertas* was the cry of the conspirators. And thereafter Brutus and Cassius,

Figure 12   Reverse of a denarius of 43–42 BC depicting a *pileus* (a cap indicating freedman status and so an emblem of freedom) between two daggers resting above the phase "Ides of March." The obverse of this coin depicts Brutus. British Museum, London, England. Photo: ©The Trustees of the British Museum.

in their war with Antony and Octavian, were minting coins labeled with the slogan of freedom (Fig. 12). In the end, they would fall to Antony, who in his turn would fall to Octavian, who, as Augustus, would end the cycle of civil war by ending the freedoms that made it a possibility. And, as we should well expect by now, he made liberty the legitimation of his autocracy. In his memorialized *Achievements*, he introduces himself in the language of his deified father: "I raised an army, with which I won back the liberty of the republic when it was oppressed by the tyranny of an oligarchic faction."

The Roman republic did not succumb to the rage of a revolutionary mob, nor to a peasant uprising. Slave revolts counted for nothing, nor did economic crisis. It is silly to speak of the limitations of the city-state. It is less silly, but not really satisfactory, to make animadversions against the structures of Rome's oligarchic society or to the disadvantages inherent in an unwritten constitution. In fact, the cultural structures of Rome's aristocratic society tended *against* autocracy. Roman politics was, from one perspective, the one celebrated in rhetoric and inscriptions, the exercise of *virtus* for the sake of the *res publica* in order to earn glory and praise from one's fellow citizens. From another and less frequently mentioned perspective, however, it was competition amongst the elite for power and prestige, fierce and incessant strife for supremacy within a community of aristocrats whose collective membership was unable to tolerate a superior. These two aspects of political life were hardly incompatible. But it is a basic rule of oligarchy that no individual can excel his peers by too great a margin: every politician must accommodate his own agenda with that of his colleagues even while he struggles to ease the tension between the demands of his own *dignitas* with the loftier values sanctioned by tradition. Otherwise oligarchy becomes autocracy: hence the social benefit of jealousy and small-mindedness, as crucial to the Roman political system as greed is to capitalism. In our period, no one rivaled Pompey the Great: his very eminence, while admired, was a danger to the stability of the republic. As Lutatius Catulus once put it, in a public speech I might add, "Pompey is an illustrious man, but he is already too illustrious for a free republic."

Although figures like Cato and Domitius must seem rebarbative and petty – they *were* rebarbative and petty – they were nonetheless made of the same stuff as Brutus and Cassius and Casca. Their actions were predictable, perhaps even predetermined – to an extent. These men did not change the course of history. They didn't want to. In their small-mindedness they endeavored to sustain the republic by maintaining what for more than four centuries had been the status quo. Their resistance to Pompey and Caesar was inevitable. But there was nothing inevitable about their stupidity, their complete want of statesmanship, or their failure to recognize that it was hardly preordained that their interests should always prevail in every particular. And there was certainly nothing inevitable about Caesar or Pompey. Of impersonal groundswells there is very little evidence in the first century BC. In fact, the lives of most Romans were unchanged by the transition from republic to empire. Farming, trade, begging, soldiering, and prostitution all went on very much as before. The equestrian order and the senatorial order each persisted, and each grew wealthier. Which brings us back to the Thucydidean distinction between the immediate causes of the civil war and its ultimate cause. The immediate causes lay, patently enough, in the area of elite political competition. The ultimate cause was fear, fear resulting in aristocratic aggression. But even in so combustible an environment, there would have been no conflagration but for the unique character and circumstances of two men, one of whom could not bear an equal, the other of whom would not endure a superior.

Further Reading

Few topics in ancient history have attracted more study than the outbreak of the civil war and its causes. In addition to the pertinent sections of the biographies cited in chapter 1, one can usefully consult Mitchell 1991, Beard and Crawford 1985, and Seager 2002. Gruen 1974 remains an important if controversial take on the subject. The best treatment is Brunt 1988. These latter two books, however, are dauntingly learned and make few concessions to anyone not a professional ancient historian.

7

Great Caesar Fell: Philosophy, Politics, and Assassination

It is nearly universally agreed that his death took place almost as he would have wished it. For once, when he read in Xenophon that Cyrus, during his final illness, had left instructions for his funeral, he expressed his disgust at any lingering death and his wish that his own be swift and sudden. And, on the day before he was murdered, during a dinner party at the home of Marcus Lepidus, when the topic of conversation turned to what manner of death was best, he had spoken in favor of one that was sudden and unexpected. (Suetonius)

It will be obvious at once that having supper with Marcus Lepidus was something like having one's teeth drilled. What may be less obvious is the philosophical setting of each occasion for Caesar's remarks on death, though perhaps no one can be surprised to find philosophy so often at the elbow of the Grim Reaper. Xenophon's *The Education of Cyrus* was a philosophical work on the education of the ideal ruler (from the Greek and not the Persian perspective, despite its exotic fiction) and had by Caesar's day become a staple of the classical canon. That Roman table talk had set topics, sometimes literary but very often philosophical, may be less expected than Caesar's perusal of a classic. But it was bad form for senators to spend their evenings in gossip or in discussing the merits of various specimens of salad. *What constitutes a suitable death?* Now that was a virtuous subject for conversation. And what should be the answer? The martyrdom of Socrates? The diseased but serene deathbed of Epicurus? The natural expiration of Zeno? Or perhaps the manly and honorable destruction of a native figure like Marcus Atilius Regulus, a general of the First Punic War. This man, twice consul, had been seized by the enemy and was sent to Rome to negotiate in the senate on the Carthaginians' behalf, a token of their high estimation of their prisoner. After delivering the Carthaginian demands for the restoration of Roman prisoners of war – a category that still included Regulus – he went on to demand that Rome reject her enemy's terms, after which he honorably restored himself into that same enemy's hands and to a painful execution, heroism celebrated in the Roman odes of Horace. That was a good Roman exit. A philosophical death, then, or a patriotic one? Caesar's answer eschews either qualification.

What, one wonders, was Caesar thinking? Romans of his rank prepared for their deaths all of their lives. This is why Romans tended to have memorable last words. Samples include Augustus ("applaud if you've enjoyed my performance"), Nero ("what an artist perishes in me!"), and the unexpectedly whimsical Vespasian ("I think I am becoming a god"). And of course it was a Roman duty to keep one's will, a document presumed to contain one's truest feelings, in excellent and entirely updated repair. The desire for an unexpected death, then, in a society that concentrated so much attention on the manner of one's final exit, seems almost like a betrayal of one's social responsibilities.

In one sense, of course, death can never be unexpected. Like us, however, the Romans often described their losses in just that way. This was most frequent in instances of accidental or of violent demise. The epitaphs of the senatorial order rarely account for the specific cause of death. Not so their more modest fellow citizens, for whom funerary inscriptions remained a poignant vehicle for complaints against gods and men. Roman graveyards commemorate those lost to carelessness – children crushed under carts, young people struck down by falling roof tiles, a Roman soldier killed by friendly fire, death by drowning and, more common than that, death by fire – as well as those lost to wickedness. Here an inscription can provide gratification where perhaps the law could not. One stone cries out that a young woman was murdered by her husband. Another beseeches the gods to punish a mother whose abuse resulted in the death of her baby. Horrific crimes, perpetrated by family members, are monumentalized, as are deaths owing to the assaults of brigands, the subterfuge of poisoners, the enchantment of witches and, more frequent than any of these, the criminal incompetence of doctors. Is this what Caesar looked forward to? Or did he mean to suggest that no death was a good one, in despite of Roman tradition and of Greek philosophy? Is this simply another specimen of Caesar's extreme realism?

It would be a mistake to overlook another version of the unexpected death in Rome. I refer here to the case of premature death – the passing of a child or of a young person. It was a lugubrious Roman reality that death under these circumstances was so routine that it could hardly be astonishing to anyone. The facts of Roman demography were that half of all children died in infancy, before the age of five. And the unhygienic and often dangerous nature of the ancient world meant that a child of five had a reasonable life expectancy of another 35 or 36 years. This statistic does not entail, though the misapprehension is common, that most Romans of a single generation staggered their way through forty or so years only to collapse in a collective and comprehensively deceased pile. But it does mean that, by the time a Roman was in his early forties, he was very probably older than most of the people he knew or encountered in daily life (which is the melancholy condition of university lecturers in college towns). This is why the Romans applied the term *senex*, old man, to men who had attained to their forties. Now, when I began my career as an assistant professor, this seemed entirely sensible to me: once more, the Romans had got it right. Nowadays, of course, I am shocked and disturbed at the Romans' gross insensitivity and conspicuous ageism.

We tend to think of Roman society as a place where old age was venerated, and, in a very real sense, it was. But it was also a society that was, by our standards, populated and managed by the young. To stand for the consulship, with very few exceptions, one had to be not less than 42 years of age – by definition an old man. But that only means that most magistrates, and most military officers, were men in their thirties. The bulk of the senate, then, will have comprised men in their thirties and forties. If one compares this to the relative gerontocracy of the American senate or most modern deliberative bodies, the contrast is nothing short of striking: the Roman senate was a boys' club, in more ways than one. The ancient in Rome *were* venerated – because there were so few of them (there is after all only so much veneration to go round).

And old men were dangerous. The perpetuation of the Roman oligarchy, to some degree, required timely departures by its most eminent members. A talented senator commenced his public career in his late twenties. Service, glory and honor supervened. At the earliest, he was elevated to the consulship in his early forties, after which he was entitled to a provincial command and his final meed of greatness. Thereafter, he was a prince of the state, an honorable personage whose opinion must be asked and must be respected. By then, however, the clock was ticking, and demographic forces soon removed him before he could try the patience of his colleagues – or find the energy or restlessness to re-enter the competition for the very finite quantities of prestige and power that existed. The regular and reliable death of ex-consuls was an important safety valve in the pressurized world of the Roman senate. Now, much has been written about the menace to Roman stability posed by Pompey the Great, because he succeeded so early that it was entirely unclear what he could do as an encore. But, in the end, Pompey conformed to the requirements of the oligarchy. The real troublemakers in the late republic were the men who refused to shuffle off their mortal coils on schedule: men like Sulla and Marius – and Caesar. Had Caesar not lived so long – and there was no obvious reason why he of all people should have done so – there would have been no second consulship to consider, no civil war and no dictatorship. Mind you, Pompey was by then no spring chicken either, and Plutarch goes so far as to say that he and the world would have been happier had he died in 55 BC, the year of his splendid second consulship. It wasn't decadence or luxury or social evils that brought the republic to its knees: it was grumpy old men. And that, I can assure you, is how Caesar's assassins saw it, at least to some degree.

The civil war began in 49 BC. It was hard fought, and the precarious condition of Caesar's regime should never be forgotten. He nearly perished in Alexandria, and after the African campaign and the quadruple triumph of 46 BC, there still remained the threat of the war in Spain, which Caesar nearly lost. Even at the time of Caesar's death, pockets of resistance persisted. All of which means that Caesar's constitutional position and his ambitious legislative reforms were all carried out in extraordinary haste. Only in 44 BC was Caesar in a position for anything like a permanent settlement, intended to secure Roman government until his glorious return from the Parthian War.

By the time Caesar arrived in Rome in 49 BC, the consuls had fled the city. By legislation the dubiousness of which was irrelevant in the face of Caesar's legions, he was appointed dictator for the first time. Now the office of dictator was at once constitutional and a traditional resort in moments of crisis. The history of Rome was littered with dictators, who had defeated enemies both foreign and domestic, or had solved political crises, such as the absence of anyone competent to conduct elections. The office carried greater authority than the consulship, and it was wholly irresponsible: one could not be held accountable for actions taken while dictator. It was designed to be a short-term expedient, but Sulla, after his civil war with the Marians, held the office for an extended term: he had himself appointed dictator for reconstituting the republic, but, while holding that office, he also purged the aristocracy of his personal enemies in a senatorial holocaust so shocking that the Romans never forgot it. Consequently, the office and its powers were looked on warily by the oligarchy (hence Pompey's sole consulship in 52 BC, when the public was crying out for his dictatorship). The crisis of 49 BC made the office a legitimate one – Caesar could hardly be elected consul when each consul was alive even if absent from Rome – and he could hardly manage the city or a military campaign in Spain or in Greece as the proconsul of Gaul. The dictator traditionally appointed a second in command, an office called master-of-the-horse. Caesar appointed Marcus Aemilius Lepidus, with whose depressing supper party we began this chapter.

Hereafter Caesar would never relinquish the office of dictator permanently. His dictatorships did not coincide with the beginning and the end of the official year, so they are not easy to plot, and there are some gaps between them. In the year 48 BC, Caesar was consul (along with Publius Servilius Isauricus), but, after the Battle of Pharsalus, he was again appointed dictator, with Mark Antony as his master-of-the-horse. In 46 BC, Caesar enjoyed another consulship, along with Marcus Lepidus. After he defeated the republicans in Africa, in which campaign Cato famously committed suicide rather than yield to Caesar, he was once again appointed dictator, this time with the provision that he should be re-appointed automatically for ten years (each year being a separate dictatorship but saving Caesar and the senate a good deal of trouble). Lepidus was again his master-of-the-horse. In 45 BC Caesar was consul without a colleague, an obvious and "in-your-face" riposte to Pompey's singular achievement. Thereafter he abdicated, contenting himself with the dictatorship, and in his place were elected Quintus Fabius Maximus and Gaius Trebonius. When Fabius died on the last day of the year, Caesar hastily arranged the election of his friend Gaius Caninius Rebilus, to enormous outrage at this trivialization of the office (Cicero used to joke that no one in Rome ate breakfast or took lunch or even had a nap during the consulship of Caninius). Once more, Lepidus was master-of-the-horse. Finally, in 44 BC, Caesar was consul yet again, with Antony as his colleague. He planned to abdicate and, on the basis of his dictatorship, invade Parthia (Fig. 13). The ever-available Lepidus was once more his second in command, but Caesar had already selected next year's master-of-the-horse, his young grand-nephew, Gaius Octavius.

We shall return to these offices in a moment. First, however, we must briefly survey the dazzling catalogue of honors bestowed on Caesar by his captive senate. By now we are all familiar with his multiple triumphs. But that wasn't all. Caesar was given special privileges in the senate. His statue was placed amongst the kings, another in the Temple of Quirinus (the deified Romulus). He was elevated to superhuman status by way of divine tokens, including the creation of a *flamen Caesaris*. So were his virtues: the senate decreed the erection of a temple to *Clementia Caesaris*, Caesar's

Figure 13 Obverse of a denarius of 44 BC depicting Caesar as Dictator for the Fourth Time. British Museum, London, England. Photo: ©The Trustees of the British Museum.

Mercy. The month of *Quinctilis* was renamed *July* – it still is – and he was granted as his new *praenomen*, *Imperator* ('Conquering Hero'). This was especially degrading for his colleagues. In senatorial debate, after all, one was addressed by one's *praenomen*: this meant that in all subsequent debates, Caesar would be addressed by his peers not as Gaius but as 'Conquering Hero'. He was also awarded the title Father of His Country. And he was granted the authority to nominate future magistrates.

This was difficult medicine for many in the senate to swallow. Caesar intended it to be. Throughout the civil war, a conspicuous distinction between Pompey and Caesar was the latter's *clementia*, his mercy. Unlike Pompey, or Sulla before him, Caesar pardoned his enemies, often more than once. And he continued to practice this policy after his victory. This was not by any means an unadulterated kindness. Rome was a *quid pro quo* society: it was understood how deep an obligation was owed to Caesar when he spared your life or freedom or property. His unparalleled tokens of greatness were all intended to give definition to his total superiority, an absence of peers for the great *Imperator*.

This message was sometimes oblique. Simply owing to his new position as autocrat of Rome, Caesar was a very busy man. It was nearly impossible to get an interview with him, and anyone who has struggled to get an appointment with a dean or a plumber will be well aware that granting and denying easy access is a sure means of reducing the self-esteem of one's inferiors. Caesar was more often in meetings with his equestrian collaborators than he was with his senatorial colleagues, and this rankled greatly. We have it from Caesar's close friend Gaius Matius that this troubled Caesar: "Can I have any doubt," Caesar is supposed to have said, "how much I am hated, when Marcus Cicero is kept waiting and cannot see me at his own convenience? If anyone is easy going, this is the man. But I have no doubt that he hates me." Now this report comes from a man who adored Caesar and who wanted, by reporting to Cicero this very exchange, to convince him that such veneration was the appropriate attitude. Which means that this is the sugar-coated version of Caesar's aloofness. No wonder the aristocracy – especially the nobility – found him arrogant.

Not that Caesar endeavored to disguise his absolute power. According to Suetonius, the action of Caesar that most attracted the senate's hostility was his refusal to rise when he was approached in public by the senate as a body. This contrasted sharply with his attitude toward a tribune named Pontius Aquila, who quite properly did not rise from his tribunician chair during one of Caesar's triumphs, which prompted him to shout: "Go on, then, Aquila, take the republic back from me, you being tribune of the people and all!" And for several days thereafter, Caesar attached to his every undertaking the addendum: "if, that is, Pontius Aquila will permit me." Caesar had more trouble with tribunes. During the Latin Festival, someone placed on Caesar's statue a laurel wreath with a white fillet, this last element being an emblem of royalty. Two tribunes ordered the ribbon removed, a decision which greatly offended Caesar, who removed *them* from office. Some will have remembered the original justification of Caesar's civil war. And many will have recognized that this action went far beyond the appropriate powers of the dictator.

An enduring question is whether Caesar aimed at monarchy. Ordinary Romans often hailed him as king, a title he invariably declined. But on this topic he could not put anyone's mind to rest. Finally, he attempted to eat his cake and have it too. At the festival known as the Lupercalia, a rather rowdy and drunken affair, Antony several times tried to place a diadem on Caesar's head. Caesar refused, to great cheers from the crowd. Finally, he ordered the diadem sent to the Capitol and dedicated to Jupiter Greatest and Best, Rome's true king, as Caesar put it. But this last move ruined whatever positive impression Caesar had hoped to make. He had repudiated monarchy, but by way of a display that demonstrated that he had no need of its eastern trappings – and that made it plain to everyone that the decision was entirely his to make.

What Caesar possessed, and this mattered more than any regal or divine trophies, was the dictatorship and the power to appoint magistrates. For the senatorial aristocracy, as we have discussed in a previous chapter, the purpose of public life was the acquisition of magistracies, especially the consulship, a success which confirmed one's heritage or ennobled one's family forever. But Caesar, despite his standing as dictator, continued to dominate the consulship as well, which was the same thing as keeping others out of the office. Worse than that, aspiring senators could now rise to the praetorship or the consulship or enjoy provincial commands only on account of Caesar's favor. The one-day consulship of Caninius made it clear that this was all as much a matter of Caesar's digestion on any particular day as it was anything else. The majestic apparatus of the nobility was rapidly becoming meaningless because the central attractions of aristocratic competition were all being *hogged up* by Caesar. And for ambitious young nobles for whom the description *senex* was drawing closer and closer, time's winged chariot beat louder and louder. They had only one hope – that Caesar, like Sulla before him, would soon lay down his office and retire into private life.

But this is exactly what did *not* happen. Caesar often joked that by resigning his power Sulla had shown that he didn't know his political ABCs. But his remarks will have meant less than his titulature. It seems, on the basis of scrappy epigraphical evidence, that Caesar's formal title was *dictator for reconstituting the republic*, which had also been Sulla's standing. It was sensible, then, to expect, as the civil war was winding down and Caesar had outdistanced all other Romans in tokens of greatness – and inasmuch as he was now into his fifties – that he would follow Sulla's example. That is, he would step aside and leave it to his loyal adherents to give suitable guidance to the satisfactorily reconstituted republic (and, by doing so, to amplify their own wealth, power and glory). Any expectation along those lines, however, was shattered beyond repair when, early in 44 BC, Caesar exchanged his old title for a new one. He became *dictator perpetuus* – dictator for life.

A dread of one-man rule, of *regnum*, permeated the Roman aristocracy. It was rumored that Romulus had been slain by a senate angry at his waxing autocracy. Lucius Junius Brutus had expelled Tarquin the Proud, and had not spared his own sons in establishing the republic. An often-cited exemplum from the fifth century was Gaius Servilius Ahala, who with his own hand struck down Spurius Maelius when the latter was conspiring for power. In historical times, Publius Cornelius Scipio Nasica, when he was merely a private citizen, led an attack by senators on the seditious tribune Tiberius Gracchus, who, it was insisted, aimed at *regnum*. Later the senate developed the emergency decree, designed to protect the senate and by extension the republic from domination by a faction or an individual. But by Caesar the senate had been reduced to spaniels: the rank and file were *his* appointments; the leadership had either joined him to defeat the *optimates* or, when Pompey was beaten, had accepted Caesar's mercy. Now he had become a tyrant, the sole dispenser of prestige, to whom they each of them owed a debt – a debt of friendship – greater than they could ever hope to repay.

And here lay a serious moral crisis for those who now hated Caesar and his despotism. Amongst senators, there were no political parties. There was only friendship, *amicitia*, and enmity. And these relationships mattered. Unlike our own society, in which the expression "my friend" very often means nothing more than "this person whose name I actually know," Roman friendship was formal and public – and implicated in serious and lasting obligations. To put it concisely, one must help one's friends and harm one's enemies – not the other way round. This constituted the decent and honorable behavior of a gentleman. But by definition Caesar the dictator no longer had any enemies: they had perished at Pharsalus or Thapsus or Munda. The recipients of his *clementia* had made themselves his friends by accepting his mercy. The residue of the senatorial aristocracy, who had acquiesced in Caesar's cause from the start, were already his dependents, his inferiors, which required them, if they wanted to scrape out of the new regime even a smidgen of dignity, to accept the dictator's friendship.

Friendship was a ponderous connection, and could hardly be evaded simply because it was inconvenient. A single illustration will make this obvious. In the months leading up to the civil war, Cicero, in his correspondence with Atticus, deliberated over which side to join: should he take an active part with Pompey or simply reside quietly in Rome (which was all that Caesar asked of him)? Cicero reviews the moral issues, which in his view are entirely on Pompey's side. He also looks at the practical advantages of remaining in Rome (Caesar, he feels sure, will help him to gain a much-desired triumph). In the end, however, and inevitably in Rome, he compares his debt of friendship with each of them. Each is his friend, and he is embarrassed by a generous loan he had received from Caesar. But to Pompey Cicero owed his restoration from exile, an infinitely more compelling obligation. Consequently, Cicero determines that he must find a way to repay his financial debt to Caesar *before war breaks out*. Otherwise his honor will still be compromised. Now if, at a time when Caesar had invaded Italy in a cause Cicero explicitly deemed entirely unjust, Cicero could fret about repudiating the invader's friendship – *because he owed him a few bucks* – then how much greater the moral quandary of senators who owed Caesar their station and their lives. In a *quid pro quo* society, obligations like friendship matter. And favors can become oppressive.

And inspire resentment. In fairness, Caesar's selections for the consulship were not entirely unreasonable: he rewarded birth, talent and loyalty. Even Caninius, who was a new man, could claim the last two of these qualities. The consuls designated for 43 BC, Hirtius and Pansa, two more new men, also demonstrated ability and were entirely trustworthy. They could be counted on to govern responsibly in Caesar's predicted absence. Likewise the consuls-designate for 42 BC were Decimus Junius Brutus – rich, noble, a brilliant and trusted officer who had been with Caesar since Gaul – and Lucius Munatius Plancus, another new man whose capacities Caesar did not overlook. Although we do not actually know with certainty whom Caesar had designated for the consulships of 41 BC, there can be little doubt that they were Marcus Junius Brutus and Gaius Cassius Longinus.

But the residue of the nobility, though they might applaud the appearance of the Junii and of Cassius, cannot have been pleased by the preference accorded so many new men – whatever their capacities. Worst of all, however, was Caesar's fondness for men of no proven capability. Caesar had decided that, after he abdicated his consulship in 44 BC, his place should be taken by Cornelius Dolabella, who was too young for the office and in any case was so disreputable that even Antony threatened to block his election. And it will have been widely known that Caesar's teenaged kinsman, pimply-faced and sickly and on no account deserving, was destined to become master-of-the-horse. This was all much too much, and Decimus Brutus soon persuaded Cassius that Caesar had to go. They, in turn, recruited Marcus Brutus, whose moral stature gave the project respectability adequate to ensure the complicity of leading men. And soon it was a conspiracy of more than sixty senators, all of them beneficiaries of Caesar's dictatorship.

But how to justify this violation of friendship and base ingratitude to the figure to whom they owed all? Although it was true that Caesar had achieved *regnum*, they had done the heavy lifting for him and they unquestionably shared in his culpability. Each of them had supported the current regime in arms and in the senate. For this, too, they blamed Caesar – and one another, hostilities that remain patent in our sources. How, then, could Caesar's friends find the means to translate their personal ambition and selfish jealousies into noble behavior? Enter Greek thought – and especially Greek philosophy, which had to be good for something.

Of the known conspirators, some were followers of Pompey whose fortunes and reputations had been restored (but whose animosities were thereby aggravated) by Caesar's mercy. Others were disappointed loyalists. The patrician Servius Sulpicius Galba, for instance, was resentful at having been passed over for a consulship for the sake of new men and of sensualists like Antony and Dolabella. Lucius Minucius Basilus, himself a new man, had sought a provincial command, but the dictator had deemed him not up to scratch. Men like these were perhaps less deterred than others by the moral impediments to acts of violence against a friend. Courage more than moral cover will have been their deficiency. Which directs our attention to the leaders of the conspiracy, of whom three stand out.

Posterity has forgotten Decimus Brutus, though he was the principal figure. His excellence in service to Caesar was rewarded with a consulship, to be followed by the governorship of Cisalpine Gaul, Caesar's old province. The dictator knew its strategic importance. Only his most trusted allies were eligible. And the degree of their friendship's bond was demonstrated in Caesar's will: should the dictator ever produce a son, Decimus must be his guardian. This is why, in the aftermath of Caesar's assassination, it was he who was most detested by the Caesarian party for what they regarded as the man's appalling treachery. Cassius emerges into history as Crassus's quaestor in his ill-fated Parthian War. Out of the ruins of this Roman defeat, Cassius, a capable soldier, soon restored Rome's borders and her security. His connection with the circle of Cato took him to Pompey's side in the civil war, but after Pharsalus he was pardoned and promoted by the man whom he jokingly referred to as his "old and merciful master." And, finally, there is the noblest Roman of them all, Marcus Brutus. This man was adored by his contemporaries. His nobility of birth was unsurpassed. He was a talented orator and an intellectual. And he was passionate in politics: "whatever this young man wants," Caesar once remarked, "he wants very much." That he was prickly and vain will offend our sensibilities more than Roman ones. But it must be observed that the noblest Roman of them all was often involved in sordid business dealings, lending money to foreign cities at 48 percent annual interest and pressing provincial governors to employ their soldiers to shatter the appropriate kneecaps of anyone slow to pay up.

These three men were all of them winners in the Caesarian scheme. Their disillusionment can have had little in common with the likes of a Galba or a Minucius Basilus. Never the less, these men could no longer endure the unlimited authority of Caesar's perpetual dictatorship. He had made his point – Caesar had beaten Pompey and tamed the nobility. Now it was time for him to move aside for the new generation of aristocrats, who hankered after *authentic* and not delegated station and power. That was why they had followed Caesar in the first place. It had not been to remain forever in his shadow. It short, it was their turn.

Not that *that* could be their rallying cry. We have seen enough already to recognize that the conspirators were numerous enough, and diverse enough, to be stimulated by an array of personal motives, no doubt in varying combinations of daring and poltroonery, principle and expediency, public spirit and outright selfishness – all of which would find its justification, like so many other political actions, in the concept of liberation. But inasmuch as these Liberators were so thoroughly implicated in the dicatorship of Caesar, and all of them united with the man by public affirmations of loyal friendship amplified by their acceptance of Caesarian favors and preferments, they found themselves in a bit of a moral bind. In this instance, Roman traditions could only be satisfied by an accommodation of philosophical theorizing.

The Romans believed that their second king, Numa, had been a student of Pythagoras, which was patent nonsense to anyone with an education. Still, there was an ancient statue of Pythagoras in a corner of the forum. From very early on, the Romans will have known that philosophy was an accouterment of Greek society, like drama or sculpture or rhetoric or the symposium. And perhaps they will have known that philosophy was an expression of elite Greek society, hence at least part of its attraction to the nobility.

We tend to think of the ancient Greeks as philosophers by nature, in the way we imagine that every Frenchman is a gourmet or every Italian is a stunning lover. Granted it *was* from the Greeks that Europe first developed the idea that the world is intelligible, as is human society, and that it is worth exploring the normal and the normative relationship between these two things. It was also the Greeks who emphasized the primacy of language as the vehicle for this exploration, a habit of mind imitated by modern analytical philosophers. Just as modern philosophers privilege English and its idiosyncrasies, so the Greeks, and later the Romans, tended to regard Greek as the only available means of thinking philosophically (this was not least owing to the profound differences between Greek and Latin). But, for

156

the typical Greek, philosophy was rubbish. Aristophanes's *Clouds*, a comedy for popular consumption, represents Socrates as a grubby, smelly and completely self-absorbed *Luftmensch* whose sole contribution to society is subversive – in other words, a university lecturer. That this was how most people viewed Socrates can hardly be doubted. The Athenians put him to death, after all, not least because his best students, men like Alcibiades and Critias, had managed, more than once, to overthrow the government. Thereafter in Greece philosophy always played second fiddle, even in an elite education, to rhetoric, a gap which lessened as philosophy branched out into grammar, geography and history. Still, the early Romans, and not exclusively that large subdivision of them we sniffily refer to as the mob, were simply following in the steps of the Athenians when they used the (originally) Greek word *philosophus* to mean *quibbler*. Young aristocrats, on the other hand, found philosophy alluring, which was disturbing for their seniors, for whom philosophy was hard to understand and for that reason (so they supposed) dangerous, like hip-hop.

By the second century BC, however, things had changed – amongst the upper classes anyway. Intellectual curiosity, and an appreciation for dialectic's usefulness in improving one's debating skills, will have been the original impulses for Romans to study philosophy and to cultivate Greek philosophers. Soon the Roman aristocracy went so far as to embrace philosophical investigation itself. By the late republic, it was natural and normal for Roman senators to possess a deep and technical familiarity with philosophy. Roman aristocrats traveled to Greece to study rhetoric and philosophy, and most housed at least one philosopher in their Roman and Italian estates. Antiochus of Ascalon lived with Licinius Lucullus, Philodemus with Calpurnius Piso (the remains of whose library in Herculaneum is at the center of current research into Hellenistic philosophy), Cicero's philosopher in residence was Diodotus. These philosophers served more than one purpose. Obviously they were available for technical study and consultation, and obviously they lent their patron a certain cachet. But they were also regarded as confidential moral advisors, the philosopher as therapist, since ethical philosophy, at least, was concerned not with logical problems but with the betterment of one's soul, be it mortal or immortal.

Until very late in the Roman republic, philosophy was conducted entirely in Greek. The learned Varro once insisted that there was no point in discussing philosophy in any other language. Then it suddenly became important to develop a Latin philosophical vocabulary, which was in fact a monumental intellectual achievement without which Greek philosophy would have withered on the European vine. There can be no clearer signal of the extent to which philosophizing was being naturalized by the Roman aristocracy than the Latinization of Greek philosophy. This was accomplished largely by two figures from the first century, the poet Lucretius and the politician Cicero. But they were hardly alone in their technical mastery of philosophy. They were reacting to the urge of their contemporaries, for whom philosophizing was fast becoming a sound Roman attribute.

The late republic constituted the acme of the Romans' philosophical attainments, and it is safe to say that there has never been a political elite more devoted to philosophical inquiry – or to philosophers themselves, whom the Roman aristocracy lionized. That, however, was a state of affairs that did not last. Philosophy continued to be studied, but it soon returned to the domain of specialists, usually but not exclusively Greeks, who, reverting to the Socratean model, dressed oddly (by which one means badly), wore their beards and hair in a characteristic and idiosyncratic style (that is, they were an absolute mess), and who elevated all forms of philosophy to the impracticable abstractions they remain today (practical philosophy, at least in American universities, has for the most part fled to departments of medicine, economics or law; ethicists nowadays prefer logical hairsplitting, which is of course their privilege, to the project of actual moral improvement, which they distrust). Consequently, the philosophical lifestyle, inasmuch as it had become untethered from what most of us might call "real life," became unacceptable for the elite classes. Tacitus, in his biography of his father-in-law, Julius Agricola, tells us that:

> when he was a young man, he would have imbibed philosophical study more keenly than is appropriate for a Roman of senatorial ambitions had the prudence of his mother not restrained his fiery, passionate spirit. Soon maturity calmed him, and he managed to take from philosophy a sense of moderation, which is a supremely difficult thing to do.

This prejudice, however, did not obtain amongst the political elite of Caesar's generation.

Three schools of philosophy dominated the Roman scene. The most conspicuous and most glamorous was Epicureanism, which promulgated an atomistic physics and a moral philosophy that emphasized pleasure and friendship and retirement from public life. Mind you, the pleasure of Epicureanism was the pleasure of acting virtuously, not of spending every Saturday night zipping from one sensational party to the next – not that these need to be incompatible actions I suppose (only if you're lucky). It remains a curious and unexplained phenomenon that Epicureanism was so popular with Roman senators, not least because the master had specifically insisted that a good Epicurean ought not to engage in politics. Yet Caesar seems to have been an Epicurean, and Cassius certainly was – and so were many others. It is obvious, from the poetry of Lucretius as well as other sources, that Roman Epicureans were very much attracted by the technical problems of atomistic physics, especially explanations of vision and of the properties of the mind. These topics are debated and joked about, in a highly informed way, in Cicero's correspondence with his Epicurean friends. This is perhaps not what we expect of the Roman aristocracy: we tend to want to represent them as stupid. But this was intellectual discourse at a level that might well challenge the capacities of even a professional philosopher. Epicureanism was relatively easy to master, however, by comparison with the bulky commentaries of the Stoics, the second of our philosophical denominations, which reveled in disputation and revision. Cato was an adherent. Fortunately for us, Cicero was an exponent of the Academy, and this is the third of our schools, the skeptical Platonism associated with Philo of Larissa, with whom Cicero had studied. This was a view that encouraged a close examination of the likelihood of any proposition, the chief effect of which was that it encouraged eclecticism. This matters to us because the philosophical writings of Cicero constitute our most important source for Hellenistic philosophy, and Cicero, owing to his Academic inclinations, covered a good deal of ground.

Ethics always constituted the Romans' chief interest in Greek philosophy. This is so obvious that it is easy to overlook. The letters of Cicero and his friends teem with bromides like "virtue has supreme value" and "consciousness of behaving virtuously is sufficient for extreme happiness" and "what is right and what is useful must always coincide." These banalities can find their expression in just these formulations only owing to the Romans' familiarity with Greek philosophy – no one has ever talked that way without being taught to do so – and it is of crucial importance for understanding the Romans to appreciate that they felt obliged to conceptualize the moral code of *mos maiorum* in terms of the principles and formulas of Greek ethical discourse. They simply could not resist their impulse to philosophize.

This dimension of the aristocratic mentality is stressed here for a single reason. The circle of men who conspired to assassinate Caesar, to a remarkable extent, communicated with one another, recruited new members to their conspiracy and justified their actions by resorting to the principles and arguments of Hellenistic philosophy. The evidence for this is extensive, and it was accumulated and interpreted for less perceptive Roman historians (like me) by a distinguished professional philosopher, David Sedley, the Laurence Professor of Ancient Philosophy at the University of Cambridge. The conspirators' decision to employ philosophical argumentation as a central medium for their intrigue is as extraordinary as it is unmistakable. As we shall see, it was far from disinterested, nor did it result in a case that was persuasive to everybody.

From its origins, Greek political literature had provided frightening representations of the tyrant, a term which originally referred simply to an autocrat who was not a king, but which went negative when so many early tyrants proved to be wicked men. The standard example was Phalaris of Agrigentum, in Sicily, who, in the sixth century, made it his custom to roast his victims alive in a brazen bull. Tyrants were evil because they put themselves above the law, and, in so doing, suppressed the best men of their cities. From Xenophon and Demosthenes through the traditions of Greek declamation, the tyrant remained the ultimate expression of wickedness. Consequently, the tyrannicide became the ultimate hero. Never the less, even within the rhetorical tradition, the motives of the ostensible tyrannicide were scrutinized. The true tyrannicide resorts to assassination only for the sake of his community. If, on the other hand, he was motivated by a desire to regain his property, to preserve his safety, or even by a thirst for glory, his credentials are spoiled. Tyrannicide was not an exclusive property of the popular morality of public oratory. Moral philosophy also took notice, and offered commentary and qualification.

Even before the civil war Cicero referred to Caesar as a Phalaris. Once he had been tamed by Caesar's clemency, however, he publicly denied, in speeches delivered during Caesar's dictatorship, that his friend was a tyrant. Other senators shared Cicero's cowardice even if they couldn't match his eloquent hypocrisy. On the statue of the republic's founder, placards were surreptitiously posted that read: "would that Brutus were alive" and, in case he didn't get it (the name *Brutus*, by the way, means "stupid"), "Brutus, are you sleeping?" Now Marcus Brutus was not in fact descended from the famous Brutus, nor does he seem to have been connected in any close way with Servilius Ahala. But, just as Caesar early in his career had co-opted Marius, so Brutus had claimed these two men as his ancestors. This pose on Brutus' part directs our attention to one of Cicero's dialogues on oratory, entitled *Brutus*, dedicated to Marcus Brutus and featuring him as one of the work's interlocutors. The *Brutus* is a history of Roman oratory from its beginnings to its culmination, predictably enough, in the career of Cicero himself. One of its themes is the relationship between public speaking, in the courts or the senate or before the people, and the proper functioning of the Roman republic. The essay was published in 46 BC and, although it (naturally) has very nice things to say about Caesar's rhetorical talents, it closes with a depressing account of the limited opportunities available to orators under Caesar's dictatorship:

> It pains me, Brutus, when I look on you. Your youthful career has been showered with praise and glory, as if it had raced along in a speeding chariot. Now, however, the wretched misfortune of our state has, as it were, toppled your successful career.

Cicero goes on in a provocative, if not instigative vein:

> It is my desire that you realize the full potential of your noble excellence. I hope that you will enjoy the kind of republic in which you can restore and even enhance the reputation of the two great families from which you descend.

The pressure here stems from *mos maiorum*. But Caesar was Brutus's friend.

The conspirators' desire to rid themselves of Caesar could not be adapted to traditional Roman paradigms without introducing embarrassing complications. Obviously matters could not be put plainly: the conspirators could hardly justify Caesar's assassination by proclaiming to the public that the time for Caesar's handing over the reins of power to themselves had gotten to be past due. Nor was their situation easily aligned with that of the original Brutus or of Scipio Nasica. These men, by tradition innocents themselves, were provoked to action by outrages perpetrated by novel menaces to liberty. The conspirators, by all too clear a contrast, had made themselves Caesar's friends – and his collaborators. Each was too implicated in the dictator's regime to appear anything other than a hypocrite at best should he strike too pristine a republican posture. Hence the attraction of Greek moral philosophy, the importance of which in this episode of Roman history has for too long been dismissed. Here was an ideology, fresh but by now satisfactorily Romanized amongst the elite, that evaded the question of the conspirators' shared responsibility and the requirements of old-fashioned Roman *amicitia*. That it was convenient for the conspirators to take up philosophy at this moment does not mean that it was inconsequential or mere window dressing.

Now it is undeniable that all three philosophical schools make it possible to accommodate tyranny without tyrannicide. For the Epicurean, there is retirement to private life, where one can tend one's garden in tranquility. For the Stoic, it was a principle that no culpability attends coercion, and in any event suicide was the ever-available solution to an untenable moral situation. And, for the Platonist, there was the example of Socrates and of Plato himself, each of whom endured tyranny without rising against its apparatus. We can only speculate on the arguments by which Cassius and Brutus brought themselves around to action. However, we can still read the moral arguments adduced by Cicero, who of course never acted on them. In his essay *On Friendship*, he makes it a fundamental rule that we must terminate our friendship with anyone who urges us to undertake base actions. This was a banality with which no one could disagree, but it ignores the problem of pre-existing obligations. He is more fulsome in his important treatise, *On Duties*, composed after Caesar's assassination. There he investigates the problems of practical morality explored by the Stoics Panaetius and Posidonius. The discussion often centers on potential conflicts between what is honorable – *to kalon* – and what is advantageous – *to sumpheron*. Again and again, Cicero returns to the problem of tyrannicide:

> What crime can be greater than killing someone who is not simply a fellow man but also a friend? Still, there is no crime – is there? – if anyone kills a tyrant, even if the tyrant in question is a friend. Has what is advantageous conquered what is honorable? By no means! Instead, what is honorable has been entailed by what is advantageous [*and the analysis carries on in just these terms*].

More than once, Cicero refers specifically to the assassination of Caesar as an example of an action that properly combines the advantageous with the honorable. That, of course, was easy for him to say: someone else had already restored his freedom. Still, Cicero illustrates the continuing attractions of the philosophical case for taking out Caesar.

That philosophical argumentation was the means by which initiation into the conspiracy was attained seems undeniable. Recruitment was by way of philosophical debate. As Plutarch puts it in his biography of Brutus:

> Of his other friends, Brutus excluded Statilius, an Epicurean, and Favonius, an admirer of Cato [*and thus a Stoic*]. This was because earlier, in the course

of their engaging in dialectic and joint philosophizing [*note how this was a common social activity*], he put each of them to a test in a roundabout way [*viz. he raised the issue of one's obligations when confronted with tyranny*]. Favonius replied that civil war was worse than an illegal monarchy, whereas Statilius said that it was not a duty for one who was wise and intelligent to take risks and suffer perturbation on account of people who were bad and stupid. But Labeo, who was there, spoke against both. At the time Brutus said little, observing only that the argument involved a difficulty which was hard to decide. But later Brutus shared the plot with Labeo.

Clearly Brutus felt he could only make himself vulnerable to those who had arrived at a philosophical rejection of tyranny (and even that, of course, could hardly guarantee that such a resolution would trump friendship or faintheartedness). These negative arguments may help us to get at Cassius's and Brutus's positive ones.

As I said earlier, it is difficult to see how a senator could reconcile politics and Epicureanism. But unless one simply assumes a bumper-sticker mentality on the part of Cassius, and his letters to Cicero render that entirely unpersuasive, he must have embraced an actual principle. Perhaps it resided in virtue: Cassius stressed to Cicero that it is only through virtue that one can find pleasure and tranquility. By now we are aware of the inescapable political implications of *virtus* in Latin. Another possibility derives from the Epicureans' emphasis on friendship and its necessity for a pleasurable life. Now Epicurean friendship was a more elastic concept that one finds in Greek culture generally. Interestingly enough, this same elasticity obtains in Roman politics: "during an election campaign," writes Quintus Cicero in his handbook on campaigning for a magistracy, "the definition of the word *friend* is broader than what it is in the rest of life." Because the Epicurean is enjoined to run risks, even at the hazard of his own life, for the sake of friendship, public service to one's fellow citizens, one's friends, and certainly to one's fellow aristocrats, finds its way in. It seems to me, as David Sedley has suggested, that this is the very interpretation of friendship that Statilius is rejecting. For Cassius, however, this may well have been his basic and principled justification: his friendship to his fellow oligarchs and his debts to them outweighed his obligation to Caesar. He must rescue them from his old and merciful master.

Brutus, who was a Platonist, had a response to give to Favonius, who preferred tyranny to civil war. In Plato's *Politicus*, lawless monarchy represents the worst form of government, because it is the hardest to live with. So there is something worse than a civil war. In a speech that he delivered in 52 BC, during the debate over whether to make Pompey dictator or sole consul, Brutus had evoked this very idea but in stronger language: "it is possible to live a moral life without having political power, but there are no terms at all on which you can live with enslavement." If the moral life is impossible under a tyranny, suicide remains the Stoic option. But Hellenistic Platonists were ambivalent about suicide, not least because one had responsibilities toward the happiness of others. Since neither morality nor happiness is possible when one has been reduced to slavery – and by now we know how easily the Roman oligarchy divides political reality between mastery and slavery – doesn't this constitute an obligation to humankind that outweighs one's debt to a single friend? Such reasoning on Brutus' part, if that was Brutus' actual reasoning, ennobled and legitimized the conspiracy. No surprise, then, that the assassins portrayed themselves as the Liberators.

Not everyone could bring himself to buy this bill of goods. One of Caesar's closest friends, already encountered earlier in this chapter, was the equestrian Gaius Matius, who was also, as we have seen, an old friend of Cicero. It was to Matius that Caesar had penned his famous *veni, vidi, vici* report, and the dictator relied heavily on Matius's acumen and advice (as we have seen, Matius had easy access to Caesar whereas Cicero didn't). Matius was a true believer in Caesar's reforms, and he could prove it by observing that one of their results was the diminution of his own wealth. Unlike the Liberators, his collaboration with Caesar had come at a personal cost, in the hope of restoring what Matius had come to believe was a failed republic. In a letter written by him to Cicero in the aftermath of the assassination, his comments carry a very Roman and very exasperated edge:

> The hostile comments leveled against me since Caesar's death are well known to me. It is regarded as a moral deficiency on my part that I am so sorely disturbed by the death of a man who was my friend and that I remain outraged because a man I loved has perished. My critics say that our country should come before friendship, as if they have already made a convincing case that his death was advantageous for the republic. But I shall not engage in cunning argumentation: I confess that I have not attained to that level of philosophizing. I was not one of Caesar's followers in the civil conflict. But nor did I forsake my friend, even when I recoiled from what he was doing. I did not approve of the civil war or the events that led to it. In fact I did my best to extinguish it before it caught flame. Furthermore, when my friend came out the winner, I was not captivated by the sweet allure of high office or wealth.

Philosophical flummery had no hold on the hard-headed and old-fashioned Matius. For him, the morality of Roman friendship and of making personal sacrifices for the greater good of the republic was not easily trumped by highfalutin' or specious sophistries.

But the decision to assassinate Caesar was also motivated by traditional political impulses, stimulated by the ideals and expectations of the senatorial aristocracy. Caesar had excelled all others in violating the fundamental code of the oligarchy by winning what was meant to be a perpetual contest. He had to go. Roman conventions of friendship, however, stood in the way. It is nothing short of astonishing, however, that the champions of the republic resorted to Greek ethical doctrines to discover justifications powerful enough to motivate their bold conspiracy. Rarely has philosophy mattered so much. It was the only avenue around Caesar's clemency and friendship. But as a means of justifying Caesar's assassination it carried risks. Not everyone outside the ambitious circle of the senatorial elite had the same motives for letting themselves be persuaded by the Liberators' approach to dialectic. In the view of a man like Matius, and in this he was hardly alone, Greek philosophy had in this instance violated Roman constancy.

On the Ides of March, it was only with effort that Decimus Brutus could persuade Caesar to come to the senate. He was not well on that day, and his wife suffered from disturbing premonitions. As Caesar entered the senate's chambers, Trebonius delayed Antony's entrance by engaging him in conversation outside, lest Caesar's formidable colleague come to his rescue when the violence commenced. When his assassination came, it was sudden and quick, in accordance with Caesar's stated preferences (Fig. 14).

These Liberators, like their more modern manifestations, believed that they would be welcomed with joyful celebrations. They had intended to drag Caesar's body to the Tiber and to declare him a public enemy, after which the proper workings of the republic would be restored effortlessly. Instead, the senate fled in panic, something that should have been easily predictable. After all, the men in the senate were by now *Caesar's* men – and they could hardly know how many were marked out for destruction. They did not immediately recognize in Caesar's demise a gesture of patriotism, philosophically inspired or otherwise. In a panic of their own, the Liberators took refuge on the Capitoline Hill – while the world waited in frightened suspense.

"He often remarked," Suetonius informs us, "that it was not so much in his interest as in that of the republic that he remain alive; he had long

165

Figure 14 Vincenzo Camuccini's *Assassination of Julius Caesar*. Galleria Nazionale d'Arte Moderna, Rome, Italy. Photo: Scala/Art Resource, NY.

enjoyed the full measure of power and glory, whereas, if he should perish, the republic would be plunged into civil war and into a considerably worse condition." Caesar failed to understand the extent of his friends' resentments and hatreds. But of their capacity for destructive factionalism, he possessed a perfect understanding.

Further Reading

Lively and opinionated (in the most attractive sense of the word) accounts of Caesar's assassination are Parenti 2003 and Woolf 2006. Yavetz 1983 assembles and examines Caesars' legal actions and positive reforms during his brief domination. A thorough discussion of Roman ideas regarding friendship can be found in Konstan 1997. The important paper by David Sedley exploited by me in this chapter is Sedley 1997. Excellent introductions to the Roman philosophical scene and its background include Griffin and Barnes 1989, Powell 1995, Barnes and Griffin 1997, and Sedley 2003.

8

The Evil That Men Do: Caesar and Augustus

Caesar
Is a god in his own city. First in War,
And first in peace, victorious, triumphant,
Planner and governor, quick-risen to glory,
The newest star in Heaven, and more than this,
And above all, immortal through his son.
No work, in all of Caesar's great achievement,
Surpassed this greatness, to have been the father
Of our own Emperor. (*Metamorphoses*, translated by Rolfe Humphries)

This is how the Roman poet Ovid introduces the last metamorphosis of his epic, the catasterism of Caesar, a cosmic event justified by the dictator's supreme accomplishment, his parentage of Augustus. Not even the gods, Ovid informs us, could prevent Caesar's assassination, the event which was necessary in order for Rome to enjoy her two Julian benefactors, Caesar *and* Augustus, whose advent and reign advanced Rome to what for Ovid was her current state of perfection – a state of affairs in which the poet prospered and luxuriated, until he was relegated to exile on the Black Sea for offending Augustus, either owing to his obscene poem, the *Art of Love*, or to his subversive interference in palace intrigues. Ovid, a better poet than he was either patriot or politician, got what was coming to him – not least (if you ask me) on account of the precious truckling perpetrated in his *Metamorphoses*.

The assassination of the dictator resulted in fear and outrage. When the senate dispersed in panic, the Liberators lost their nerve, anxiety that metamorphosed into terror when the people, who adored their hero, took to the streets in violent excitement. The abuse of senatorial prestige had meant less to the populace than did Caesar's *gloria* – and less than did Caesar's administrative acts and legislative reforms. His games and public building reinvigorated the city's economy (he was so successful in this regard that

167

he could introduce a means test to the dole without risk of unpopularity). His legislation eased (though it did not solve) the problem of debt that threatened to ruin Romans of moderate means. He even fixed the calendar, which was months out of whack and a complete absurdity. The people's fury was directed at the Liberators themselves, one of whom was the patrician Lucius Cornelius Cinna, a praetor and Caesar's former brother-in-law (he had also been a son-in-law of Pompey). Alas the man in the street, as even the populists amongst us must concede, tends to be less than entirely discriminating (or in any case poorly informed), the result in this instance being that the Roman mob mistakenly attacked and lynched, not the guilty Cinna, but instead the loyal Caesarian tribune and poet, Gaius *Helvius* Cinna, whose lesser family had filched the famous *cognomen* of the patrician Cornelii only to suffer this unfortunate outcome. The guilty Cinna survived the perturbations to come, and his son, yet another Cinna, lived to reach the consulship in 32 BC. So much, then, for the collective wisdom of the common crowd. Never the less, this lesson in mistaken identity was not lost on the Liberators themselves, who fortified themselves on the Capitoline Hill. And yet, the Liberators must have contemplated, the urban populace was less formidable than the armies. What Caesar's veterans would do remained unclear. They were pensioned off on land provided by *Caesar's* legislation, a reality not to be overlooked by these champions of senatorial preeminence. As for the men still in arms, they were astonished by their leader's betrayal. Truculent, they waited for orders.

The Liberators, it is regularly charged by modern historians although the pattern began with Cicero, were naïve. Despite their obvious and genuine republican passions, they lacked an exit strategy, as if they were motivated by the simple, but by no means disarming belief that, once Caesar hit the ground with a thud, they themselves would be greeted by the masses for the liberators they plainly were, and the republic would be restored easily and immediately. In modern parlance, they were hapless ideologues instead of being practical realists.

This criticism is not entirely fair. But it was certainly true that the Liberators underestimated popular feeling, the recurring fault of the Roman aristocracy. And the nobility once again failed to appreciate the zeal amongst lesser senators and Roman equestrians for the security afforded by peace and stability, all of which was threatened by the Liberators' boldness. Their first action, as Caesar hit the floor, was to cry out the name of Cicero, who was by now the senior consular and a venerable icon of senatorial prestige. The death of Caesar, this gesture makes clear, should have restored *senatus auctoritas*. This, however, was a move that Cicero, although he relished his iconic status, later criticized. Instead, he insisted, they ought to have *killed* *Antony* as well as Caesar. In this instance, and not for either the first or the last time in his life, Cicero got it wrong.

The condition of the city in fact now depended on the reaction of the remaining consul, Mark Antony. He alone had legal authority, but in the bewilderment of the Ides the constitution was momentarily forgotten. Publius Cornelius Dolabella, Caesar's designated successor, did not wait for his election but immediately and opportunistically assumed the insignia of the consulship. More significantly, and far more dangerous, Marcus Lepidus, although his position as master-of-the-horse had evaporated with the dictator's demise, remained in command of Caesar's troops and introduced them into the city on the morning of the 16th. This of course represented a far greater menace to the Liberators than the hostility of the mob. Consequently, Brutus descended to the Forum and addressed the people. Unfortunately, he flopped. With what richer and more successful emotion, Cicero later boasted, would *he* have swayed the populace. The famous orator, however, was nowhere to be found. It was Antony who acted.

He secured Caesar's papers from Calpurnia. He consulted in secret with the residue of the Caesarian leadership. He agreed to tolerate Dolabella, and by dint of his personality – and no doubt his personal standing amongst the legions – he won over Lepidus, to whom he promised the recently vacated office of *pontifex maximus*. It began to appear that a junta would take command of the city. Supervening events proved otherwise. On the 17th, Antony convened the senate, where he rejected the proposal that the Liberators be honored, but supported their pardon. He went on to insist that the acts of Caesar, the *acta Caesaris*, past and planned, possess the force of law. With this last demand nearly all were in sympathy, although such a move went a long way toward legitimating the dictator's tyranny. Nevertheless, most of the senate, including most of the Liberators, owed their present and future positions to Caesar's decrees. Furthermore, it was owing to Caesarian legislation that the veterans were pacified and that the army could anticipate honorable retirement. Not everyone will have wanted to validate Caesar's unpublished acts, but this was the price of the Caesarians' compromise with the Liberators. In other words, the senate, in one meeting, voted that the assassins were honorable men and that their victim was the legitimate legislator of the city. Cicero, so often the champion of the status quo, endorsed the deal, with flourishes of rhetoric in praise of peace and concord, which on this day cannot have been mere pretexts.

On the 20th, Antony delivered Caesar's funeral oration, a usurpation of family right by a man who was Caesar's friend but by no means his kinsman.

Of course, as the son of a Julia he may have, in imitation of his master, stretched the point. A talented orator, scion of a household celebrated for its eloquence, Antony managed in his speech to inflame the crowd without incurring blame for treachery. The mob rioted, while the Liberators barricaded themselves in their houses. In the forum an altar was hastily erected by a populace keen to worship Caesar as a god. Cicero, Rome's supreme rhetorician, was one of the few who appreciated Antony's power over the people as well as over the troops (hence his later complaints that though the tyrant was dead the tyranny lived on). The consul would very soon quell the crowds and restore order: but he had made his point. Neither Brutus nor Cicero could hold things together – nor could Lepidus without troops. Antony's personal superiority – his *dignitas* – had been made manifest to everybody.

History has not been kind to Antony. That he was a valiant warrior and masterly general is not in doubt. His political skills, however, remain underrated. What is almost universally ignored is that it was *he* and not the Liberators who restored the republic. They shed Caesar's blood. Antony restored the senate. This is masked in our record by imperial historiography, in which Antony, the enemy of Augustus, must by definition be a bad man. Plutarch, for example, justifies his biography of Antony by stressing the moral benefits of studying examples of vice. And, more influentially, Antony is consistently denigrated by the contemporary speeches and letters of Cicero, who detested Antony like the Gates of Hell. So far as Cicero was concerned, there was nothing Antony could do that was right.

A single and trifling matter suffices as an illustration. One of Cicero's personal enemies was a certain Sextus Cloelius, who had been an ally of Clodius Pulcher, the man who drove Cicero into exile. After Clodius's murder, Cloelius had suffered a like fate, having been condemned for political violence. Now consul, Antony was pressed to secure the man's pardon by the Claudii and by his own wife, Fulvia, who was once married to Clodius (and who had participated in the violence for which Cloelius was prosecuted). Naturally, Antony had sufficient influence to pull this off all on his own. However, he preferred not to do so without Cicero's consent, which the orator could hardly refuse, an empty gesture but not an inconsequential one. And so he wrote to Cicero:

Mark Antony, consul, to Marcus Cicero

My responsibilities and your sudden departure from Rome have conspired to prevent my taking this matter up with you personally. On account of this,

I fear that my absent self will strike you as less substantial than would my present one. Still, if your characteristic good nature corresponds with the opinion of you I have always held, then I feel certain of gaining satisfaction. [*He then makes his request at some length, concluding*] I hope you will recognize how important it is to me to have the prestige of your approval on my side and for that reason you will be more inclined to yield to my request.

To which approach Cicero responded with unbridled fury – in a letter not to Antony but to his friend Atticus:

Mark Antony has written to me regarding the restoration of Sextus Cloelius – with what degree of deference to me you will detect in his letter (I am sending you a copy). You will also easily measure how sleazy, how base and how wicked his letter is – so much so that sometimes I long to have Caesar back.

Mind you, in his rejoinder to Antony, the orator was the embodiment of graciousness:

Cicero to Antony, consul

There is a single reason why I should have preferred your raising in person the matter contained in your letter. For then you could have recognized my affection for you not merely in my words but also in every expression of my face. Indeed, your letter, composed with so much affection and esteem, has moved me so deeply that I seem not to be granting you a favor but instead receiving one from you.

In this period more than any other, the historian must read *through* Cicero in order to get at the history he meant to dominate and to *misrepresent* for contemporaries and for posterity. He has been very successful. After the compromise of the 17th, Antony, as consul, exploited his influence to the full to secure his own political position. He deployed Caesar's acts, sometimes with brazen dishonesty. He championed the veterans and the legions to win their loyalty. He secured for himself and for Dolabella extraordinary military commands of five-year terms. He did not devote himself to looking after Cassius or Brutus or any of his enemies. No harm came to them on his initiative. But they were all of them *on their own*, free to rise or fall according to their own political capacities. The law of the jungle, the struggle for oligarchic pre-eminence, was back.

Does any of this sound familiar? There is a term for this unrelenting and exacting political contest: *the Roman republic*. What did the Liberators expect? What did Cicero expect? Did they equate liberty exclusively with their own domination of senatorial affairs? Perhaps so. In which case it was *their* job to rally the senate and people of Rome to *their* side, or to give way. But the remnants of the nobility, and to some degree this now becomes true of Cicero their new leader, were men who, although they had fulfilled the duties of the oligarchy, had for too long failed to take seriously what it meant to perform the functions of government. This was their moment – to disintegrate once again into factionalism or to meet the great challenge of their nation. They failed, dismally. They chose the *easy* path, but, like all weak men, to steal another aphorism from Disraeli, they preferred to dignify their weak actions by calling them strong measures. The senior statesman of the senate now lavished all his considerable ability on the destruction of Antony, a narrow purpose he recklessly identified with the salvation of the republic.

It is time to meet Caesar's heir. Gaius Octavius was the son of a rich new man, who had reached the praetorship before succumbing to a natural death. His wife, Atia, was the daughter of a modest senator derived from an Italian municipality and of a Julia, a sister of Caesar. Atia mattered. Her second husband was the consul of 56 BC, Lucius Marcius Philippus. One of her daughters married a consul of 50 BC, while her son caught the attention of his great-uncle, the dictator. Social advancement followed. Octavius was enrolled by Caesar amongst the patricians, and on the Ides of March he was master-of-the-horse designate for the campaign against the Parthians. He was 18 years old, of fragile health and poor complexion – and implacable ambition. It is regularly reported that his intellect and talents must have been already in evidence for him to have attracted Caesar's favor. Perhaps, but Caesar was also very fond of Lepidus and Dolabella. It will have counted more in Octavius's favor that he was (for what he was worth) the dictator's closest male relation.

The boy who started his life as Gaius Octavius ultimately became Augustus Caesar, and, as such, the recipient of a tradition of encomium that traces itself back to antiquity. Augustus selected the sphinx as his signet, and the man remains a puzzle. But it will perhaps be as well to essay a few remarks on his talents and his character, not least because these are so often misrepresented even by modern historians who should know better. Augustus was far more ruthless in the pursuit of power than was the man he called his father, and far more successful. His rise to power was immediate, and his life extended until AD 14, by dint of which longevity as well as his

172

political acumen he established an age and a system of government that endured longer than the republic. Yet it will not do to equate his success at sustaining autocracy with genius in his fingertips and toenails. The metamorphosis of Octavius into Caesar and thereafter into Augustus was not an easy glide, which in fact makes it all the more impressive.

And there is some utility in comparing him with his mortal enemy, Antony. Posterity has tended, with Plutarch, to make of Antony a drunken sexual adventurer with little savvy and less polish, a depiction which renders his ultimate failure a wholesome and perhaps even gratifying object lesson for all of us who imagine ourselves polished or even savvy, however concomitantly sober or lonesome by way of melancholy compensation. Now it is true that Antony *did* know how to exchange coarse jokes with his soldiers, and Antony was without question a party animal. More than once he carried on with his magisterial duties while suffering with a terrible hangover, taking advantage of the odd recess to vomit up the remains of a previous night's excesses. Once again I believe it says all too much about the joyless and bloodless life of modern classicists that they find it incomprehensible that someone can be at once a sensualist and a statesman, of which breed Antony was neither the first nor the last.

Augustus, on the other hand, is normally endowed with all the qualities of the Augustan age, as if he were personally responsible for every Horatian ode, every architectural wonder, every successful military campaign (the great bulk of which was carried out by others). But even in the historical tradition that subsists, we can detect a very different figure. His sickliness kept him from martial valor, through no fault of his own, though his enemies accused him of cowardice (which is nonsense: if nothing else, Augustus possessed redoubtable physical courage). More intriguing are the reports that he was neurotic about lightning, and that, when he suffered from insomnia, he was scared of the dark. Augustus, though a patron of the arts, was no intellectual. His favorite pastime was observing the lower classes brawl in the streets, though this might be forgiven as the best ancient Rome could do to come up with a reasonable facsimile of rugby. What actually stands out in *this* regard is Augustus's regular reliance on manuscripts for public oratory, because, unlike his contemporaries and more like us, he lacked the necessary fluency for extemporaneous speaking. And this was true not only of his public performances: whenever he had conversations with his wife, Livia, he carried with him note cards, to help him to stay on track. Furthermore, Augustus was, by the standards of his social class, incompetent in Greek literature. He begins to sound more like Ronald Reagan or a swaggering Texan, for each of whom crushing their political opposition constitutes their main substitution for talent or education, than he does his adoptive father, or his infamous rival.

Antony, by contrast, was in actuality an accomplished literary man, very much at home in oratory and in the complicated world of Alexandrian poetry. It was his fondness for Greek culture, after all, that was in the end to prove his undoing. We ought not to be surprised by this. Antony had enjoyed a proper education, whereas in the very years in which Augustus should have been studying rhetoric and philosophy in Greece, he was ruling the western Mediterranean world. How he did that is a subject bigger than this chapter, but the answer must lie somewhere in his total resolution. More than any Roman who ever lived, Augustus grasped the meaning of *real* political power in the context of a jealous oligarchy. Here was something the republic had never before seen.

But we must return to the year 44 BC, long before there was a hint of Augustus. The reading of Caesar's will indicated ample benefactions to the army and to the urban populace, rewards that, in the conventions of Roman law, must be paid by the dictator's principal heir, if he elected to accept the legacy. That heir was Gaius Octavius, who could only inherit if he took Caesar's name. But that is what Octavius principally wanted. Here we enter territory that is both technical and controversial – and permanently shrouded from historical recovery. Any handbook in any language will tell you that Octavius was *adopted* by Caesar's will, a phenomenon denominated as *testamentary adoption*. Now there is no question that Octavius changed his name in accordance with the practice of adoption: by accepting his inheritance, he became Gaius Julius Caesar Octavianus (this is why modern scholars call him Octavian, though his contemporaries eventually referred to him as Caesar, which was after all his name). And young Caesar never stopped invoking the late dictator *as his father*.

Yet it is far from obvious how Octavius became Caesar's son, which was a very different matter from taking his name. In the first place, there is no such thing as testamentary adoption. Roman law admits two species of adoption: in each case, one individual becomes another's son because he is placed in that person's power, in his *patria potestas*. Romans did not suffer modern emotional perturbations on the subject of adoption: an adopted Roman had two fathers to whom he owed his loyalty – his biological parent and his legal one. So far as society was concerned, each tie was binding, but if anything the legal one trumped the natural one. Because *patria potestas* dissolves at death, one cannot be adopted by a dead man. What one finds in wills is something very different, what in Roman law is "the condition of accepting the name" (*condicio nominis ferendi*): the testator offers his

174

fortune to an heir but only on the condition that the heir accept the testator's name.

This was a common practice within related families when a rich man lacked a son. For instance, Marcus Junius Brutus, because he accepted the estate of his uncle Quintus Servilius Caepio, also bore that name, and is regularly indicated in contemporary sources as Quintus Caepio Brutus. The uncle is never mentioned as anything but his uncle. And the proof that this legal condition is not equivalent to adoption is found in the fact that women could require male heirs to accept their name: a certain Livia named Dolabella as an heir under this condition. Women did not possess *patria potestas*, for obvious reasons, and so were incompetent to adopt. Yet Octavius both took the name and made the claim that Caesar was his father. That claim was resisted, but it had strong supporters. Cicero, for one. And of course the populace and soldiery, who appreciated young Caesar's generosity in fulfilling the mandate of the man they were content to accept was his father. At some stage, we must postulate, there was legislative intervention to clarify and ground Octavian's standing as Caesar's son. It will have been highly irregular, and perhaps that is why we never hear of it.

The advent of Octavius found Rome in its natural condition of stress and strife and grudging political coexistence. The compromise of the 17th had restored Rome to an order of sorts, one sufficiently republican to render a brilliant career impossible for Caesar's heir, whose self-awareness made it instantly clear to him that he lacked the qualities to ensure himself a consulship in two decades' time – if, that is, his delicate health gave him the years his biological father had been denied. At first Octavius paid court on Antony, who condescended to meet him but who treated him with nearly open contempt. Another Roman, and let me emphasize that in 44 BC Octavius was *18*, might simply have folded. Not so the future Augustus, whose penetrating political instincts instantly recognized that his political advancement depended entirely on his wrecking the peace and fomenting crisis.

Now although Antony's administration had minimized the possibilities for crisis, the inevitable political volatility inherent in republican Rome prevented their complete removal. At once Octavius understood the mood of the people and the mood of the army – and the mood of many Caesarians who were less willing than Antony to move on from Caesar's dictatorship. Octavius accepted his legacy, denominated himself Caesar – though Antony persisted in dubbing him by his original moniker – and began to demand revenge for the death of his father. Just as in America, greed is good, so, as we have seen, in Rome, *vengeance* is good. A son was expected to punish his father's enemies (traditionally by prosecuting them in court if that could be managed, but certainly by resisting them in politics), and young Caesar made it clear that that was his new purpose in life. This was nobility itself, and a masculine embodiment of *pietas*.

Young Caesar's agitations created a rift amongst the Caesarian elite and riled the masses. Antony's position was compromised, a reality that could not escape the attention of Cicero, who discovered in young Caesar the stick with which he could beat Antony to death. Not that Cicero planned to abandon the Liberators, who objected to the orator's sudden fondness for this dangerous young man, ostensible affection that he bolstered by advancing young Caesar's claims to early political advancement. The senior statesman was certain that he had this boy wrapped around his little finger: he was to be praised, the orator was careless enough to say more than once, he was to be elevated – and he was to be disposed of. For his part, young Caesar responded by doting on Cicero, referring to him as *father*, and pretending to take his advice in everything. Cicero's inflation of Antony's enemy was effective, and Antony's attempts to deflate his new and increasingly worrisome foe were hampered by the mixed loyalties of his own supporters.

The new Caesar managed to raise an army of his own, from his father's veterans and with the residue of his inheritance, a criminal action on which Cicero heaped encomium and eventually gave legal cover by a senatorial decree. But the men loved Antony and young Caesar alike. The dictator's former officers demanded that the two of them reconcile. The Caesarian troops made it clear that they refused to raise their weapons against either Antony or Caesar's heir. Then, fatefully perhaps, when the games in honor of the victories of Caesar were being performed in Rome, a comet appeared in the night sky, spontaneously applauded by the masses as proof of the apotheosis of the dictator. Caesar could now style himself *divi filius*, son of god (Fig. 15). A frustrated Antony complained correctly that this was a boy who owed everything to a name.

The destabilizing influence of Caesar's heir, the recklessness of Cicero, and the failure of the senate to sustain its authority, led to collapse. Soon Antony and Lepidus and Caesar had formed the Second Triumvirate for the Regulation of the Republic, a legal dictatorship divided amongst the three of them. Their recognition of the failure of Caesar's *clementia* to ensure future loyalties prompted them to re-introduce Sulla's sanguinary expedient, the proscriptions. Hundreds of senators, including Cicero, and thousands of knights were butchered, a bloodbath that put Sulla's excesses

Figure 15   Obverse and reverse of a bronze coin of approximately 38 BC. The obverse depicts Octavian described as "Caesar, son of god." The reverse depicts Caesar as *Divus Iulius*. British Museum, London, England. Photo: © The Trustees of the British Museum.

in the shade, terrified Italy, and suppressed whatever virtue remained in the senate. Thereafter Philippi, the deaths of Brutus and Cassius, and Caesar's vow to construct a great temple to Mars Ultor, Mars the Avenger, the god who destroyed Caesar's enemies. Lepidus was soon dropped, and for ten years the world was ruled by Caesar and Antony, until their great confrontation, in 31 BC, at the Battle of Actium, produced, once again, a single autocrat. The fate of Rome stood in doubt till the final moments, when Marcus Agrippa, the new Caesar's trusted commander, demonstrated his military superiority over Antony and Cleopatra. Victory was declared, over Egypt, and Antony was processed into a non-person whose memory was largely obliterated.

The world was jubilant, not because conquering Caesar was especially beloved, but because at last there was a chance that the incessant and destructive strife that had racked the world since 49 BC would go away. The violence of these years and the disintegration of the republic were quite naturally constructed as the victory of freedom over the forces of oppression. The theme of liberation was lifted straight from the text of Caesar's *Civil War*. The *Achievements of Augustus* begins with the boast that:

> At the age of nineteen, at my own initiative and at my own expense, I raised an army, with which I won back the liberty of the republic when it was oppressed by the tyranny of an oligarchic faction

To this was added vengeance:

> The men who murdered my father I drove into exile, avenging their crimes through legitimate tribunals. And afterwards, when they waged war against the republic, I twice defeated them in battle.

And the result was the restoration of the republic:

> In my sixth and seventh consulships, after I had extinguished civil wars, when with universal consent I was master of everything, I transferred the republic from my power to the administration of the senate and people of Rome.

Naturally, the senate handed it all back immediately, and added to Caesar's luster by inventing the name *Augustus*, a new name that suggested superhuman superiority (Fig. 16). Augustus reigned from 31 BC until his death in AD 14, during which time he thoroughly transformed the Roman aristocracy, to the degree that one may legitimately speak of a revolution, if not perhaps the revolution of Ronald Syme's famous and influential book.

The perceptive Augustus had no intention of being removed in the style of his father. Now in some respects he enjoyed advantages that excelled his predecessor. The world was exhausted and very willing to pay nearly any price for restoration. More importantly, the senatorial class had by now seen proscription and more than a decade of complete if shared tyranny. Most of the traditionalists were dead by now anyway, and the remainder were house trained. Which is not to say that there were not plots against Augustus – there were. But Rome's new master understood well how to share power and how to share prestige without losing the primacy that allowed him to continue as an autocrat no less powerful than his resented predecessor.

Augustus defined himself by way of the traditional offices and powers of the republic, styling himself *princeps*, first citizen, not because he surpassed other senators in power but because he was their superior in

Figure 16 Augustus as *Pontifex Maximus*, a contemporary portrait. Museo Nazionale delle Terme, Rome, Italy. Photo: Koppermann, Neg. D-DAI-Rom 1974.1565.

auctoritas, in prestige. This is too often represented as a trick, as if there was anyone in Rome who failed to realize that Augustus was their absolute master. That is simple nonsense. Augustus never disguised his or his family's supreme status. But Augustus deployed familiar and acceptable relationships between himself and the rest of the governing class. He realized the secret of the empire. Like modern university administrators, he knew that he must share with his inferiors the work of running the empire but very little of the actual power. Augustus put the senate to work, and until the late empire it remained a vital center of administrative and military expertise and a focus of the state's majesty. In exchange for their labors, which by the way gave them power enough over the lives of humbler folk, senators were rewarded with prestige and with wealth. Imperial senators were far richer than their republican counterparts, and, when their dignity was dented, they could count on the emperor to defend it from provincials and from the lower orders. Under Augustus, they were free to express their views, even to insult the *princeps* with impunity. In fact, we find in the late writer Macrobius the remains of what must have been something of a joke book, wherein witty equestrians regularly get the better of Augustus.

For instance, when the emperor sees a knight at the games eating and drinking in the grandstand, he sends him a note: "when *I* want to eat, *I* go home." To this the knight rejoins, with a note of his own: "*you* are not afraid of losing your seat." A young equestrian visits Rome and it is soon appreciated how very much like Augustus he appears. The youth is sent for by his *princeps*, who, after inspecting him, asks of him with a smirk: "Tell me young man, did your mother ever visit Rome?" "No," the young man replies, "but my father did – often" (Augustus had been born in Rome). And so it goes. Augustus in fact vetoed laws that would have restricted free speech on the part of the elite classes. He grasped that, for most people, the freedom to say what they think matters far more to them than the freedom to act on it.

The Age of Augustus, then, was a Rome in which everyone was a winner. In the person of the emperor, the lower orders enjoyed some protection from their superiors, as did the provinces. Opportunities for wealth and status were increased for equestrians and for senators. And all enjoyed the benefits of peace, by means of which Augustus seduced the whole of the world. And peace is unquestionably a good thing. Peace was certainly the key to the empire. At all costs, men of every class agreed, civil war must be avoided, and the Augustan settlement, not unattractive in itself, seemed a bargain.

Augustus set the imperial pattern. Thereafter emperors were expected to be congenial senators and were soon obliged to take on the lion's share of the work of the empire. The emperor, though increasingly the source of Roman law, was expected to subject himself to it. He was not at all a despot or a potentate. As Pliny put it in his panegyric to the emperor Trajan: "you desire to have no more rights than we do [*we senators, that is*], and the result of this is that we would like you to have more." Every emperor swore his fidelity to the laws of Rome and was in duty bound to exhort his senatorial colleagues to share with him the administration of empire.

One of the myths of the Roman empire is that emperors were idle and decadent. Instead, they were more frequently crushed by their workload, which obliged them to tend to matters ranging from foreign policy and commerce to a provincial dispute between neighbors over which of them owned a tree situated between their houses. An anecdote told of the emperor Hadrian is typical: while journeying through the provinces, his procession was approached by a peasant woman who begged for his attentions. "Madam," said Hadrian, "I am simply too busy to stop." "Then quit being emperor," she returned, at which fair complaint Hadrian unpacked his full court in order to hear and to resolve her problem. All citizens, as the experience of the apostle Paul illustrates, had the right to appeal to Caesar. Consequently, the emperor had to devote his talents and, what was a greater bane, his *time* to all the responsibilities of empire. He was hardly free to skirt his duties and enjoy lengthy holidays at his ranch, in the style of modern democratic leaders. Not every emperor succeeded equally well – some of them suffered Caesar's fate – but the imperial conduct of Augustus determined the expectations of future generations, so long as the aristocracy dominated in the senate and in the palace.

Every citizen must be loyal to the *princeps*, because it was the *princeps* and only the *princeps* who protected the republic from lapsing into civil war. The memory of the civil war between Caesar and Pompey was not permitted to be forgotten. This was the crime that destroyed the old republic and required the ministrations of the principate to repair. Consequently, the legacy of Caesar remained more complicated than the legacy of Augustus. Already in the time of Augustus, historians were encouraged to debate the question of whether it was a blessing or a curse that Caesar had been born (we have seen Ovid's answer to this). Augustus was the remedy to the aristocratic ambition that animated his father and Pompey the Great. This is not to say that Caesar was shunted aside during the principate – far from it. His images were everywhere, and each year magistrates continued to swear to uphold the *acta Caesaris*. But, in ideological and practical terms, Caesar's genius was deemed to be something other than an unqualified good thing.

There are many instantiations of this, but none is richer than Virgil's epic poem, the *Aeneid*. In the sixth book, the hero, Aeneas, founder of Rome and of the Julian line, descends to the underworld in order to seek wisdom from his father, Anchises, a mission that enacts the *pietas* of which Aeneas is the living embodiment. This is the Roman adaptation of Odysseus's similar declension in his epic. But whereas the Greek hero seeks out the blind Tiresias as if he were little more than a divine travel agent, in the *Aeneid* Anchises reveals to his son the destiny of Rome. It is a vision of greatness but also of conflict, suffused by the ever-current danger of civil war (herewith David West's prose translation):

Do you wish to see now the Tarquin kings, the proud spirit of avenging Brutus and the rods of office he will retrieve? He will be the first to be given

181

authority as consul and the stern axes of that office. When his sons raise again the standards of war, it is their own father that will call them to account in the glorious name of liberty. He is not favoured by Fortune, however future ages may judge these actions – love of his country will prevail with him and his limitless desire for glory.

Even the origin of the republic lay in civil war. The original Brutus (like Augustus an avenging force) overthrew the monarchy in the cause of liberty, allegiance to which he did not shirk even in the case of his own sons' royalist treason. The demands of the republic, Brutus' example makes clear, transcend even a father's love, a representation of patriotism that punctuates the perversity of Caesar's destructive relationship with Pompey, to which the poet then turns:

> Those two spirits you see gleaming there in their well-matched armour are in harmony now while they are buried in night, but if once they reach the light of life, what a terrible war they will stir up between them! What battles! What carnage when the father-in-law swoops from the ramparts of the Alps and his citadel of Monaco and his son-in-law leads against him the embattled armies of the East. O my sons, do not harden your hearts to such wars. Do not turn your strong hands against the flesh of your motherland. You who are sprung from Olympus, you must be the first to show clemency. Throw down your weapons. O blood of my blood!

And so Anchises beseeches Caesar not to initiate the civil war. Because only an enemy of Rome would rise against her, any challenge to the republic, not least internal rebellions, put everything in peril, as Roman history between 49 BC and the Battle of Actium sufficed to demonstrate to everybody. Augustus, as second founder in the mold of the original Brutus, had saved the republic – had restored liberty – by means of violence. Now, at all costs, and this is the prevailing ideology of the principate, let there be domestic peace.

This mentality had implications for the future fabric of aristocratic society. The responsibility of the first citizen to correct the moral failure of the civil war was not a theoretical abstraction. Augustus restored Rome's temples and her religious practices, including obsolete institutions. He demanded virtue, not least by passing legislation that, well in advance of the impositions of the Church, regulated and sought to restore lapsed family values, a startling (and much-resented) intrusion of the state into Roman private life. Henceforth citizens must marry, or face serious economic and social consequences. And because families exist, in the view of Augustus as in the view of the fierce modern right, for the purpose of begetting legitimate offspring, each family must prove itself fruitful by way of multiplication. What, one might well ask, constitutes the suitable number of children in a proper Roman household? A topic for sociologists and demographers perhaps, but Augustus had his own answer: *three*. More and you get bonuses: not a paltry payout on the order of modern Austrian or Australian baby-making incentives, but rather lasting privileges at the games and in electoral contests. And, of course and most important, the approbation of the first citizen himself, who had only one child and whose second and permanent marriage, to Livia, produced no children at all. But to complain about that was to miss the point entirely, as every Roman realized.

The supremacy of the imperial family could never be questioned. The acceptance of this reality was a central dimension of a citizen's loyalty to the established order. Each year, the citizens of the empire swore a dire oath. We cannot recover the full text of this oath, and we know from epigraphical evidence that there were regional variations. We possess enough, however, to get the essential idea. Herewith the oath sworn to the emperor Caligula, which was sworn first by the consuls, then various magistrates, after which the senate, the soldiers and the people:

> I solemnly swear that I will be an enemy to those who I learn are enemies to Gaius Caesar Germanicus. If anyone brings or shall bring danger to him and his welfare, I will not cease to pursue him with arms and deadly war on land and on sea till he has paid the penalty to him; I will hold neither myself nor my children dearer than his welfare; and I will regard as enemies of mine those who have hostile intentions against him. If I knowingly swear or shall swear falsely, then may Jupiter Best and Greatest and the deified Augustus and all the other immortal gods cause me and my children to be deprived of fatherland, safety, and all good fortune.

You needn't actually love Big Brother, but you must be his friend and his ally.

Now it has been suggested, by Matthew Roller in his stimulating book *Constructing Autocracy*, that "these oaths perpetuate in contemporary society the divisiveness" of republican factionalism, that "in short, the civil war never ends." In my view this gets it wrong. These oaths ingrain into the consciousness of every citizen the reality that the civil war is past – but

183

not for that reason relegated to the realm of the impossible. The preservation of peace remains a struggle, but one that is sustained by the institution of the principate – an institution that must take priority over all else. Deference to the imperial house, senatorial subordination that far exceeded anything demanded by Caesar the dictator, became an expression of *virtus* – in the new order.

How, then, to become a Great Man in the empire? This was a problem taken seriously by the aristocracy, for reasons all too obvious. The imperial senate was aware of its republican predecessor. Every general, and Roman senators still served as generals, could compare himself with Marius and Pompey. Indeed, their images and trophies were conspicuous enough in the city's public spaces. Every orator, and Roman senators still gave speeches in the courts and in the senate, was well aware of Cicero, who became the classic model. But those days were gone – evidently for good.

This is revealed in two compositions by the Roman writer, Tacitus, a leading orator and politician who prospered under Domitian and flourished, principally as a historian, in the reign of Trajan. In his biography of his father-in-law, Julius Agricola, he depicts the successful career of a senator whose type did not really exist in the republic, the *vir militaris*, the military man, whose service combined the responsibilities of officer and provincial administrator. Agricola's career was smooth, respectable, and honorable. His military command in Britain remains a focus of schoolboy and schoolgirl study in that nation, and Agricola was ultimately rewarded with the insignia of a triumph, the highest accolade available to a general outside the imperial family (unsurprisingly only the emperor and his relations might celebrate an actual triumph). Never the less, Agricola's talent attracted the jealousy of Domitian. A prosecution was mooted, then dropped, mysteriously. Agricola courteously requested of his emperor the privilege of refusing a newly proffered proconsulship, in order that he might retire into private life, a favor that was generously granted. The moral is made explicit by Tacitus: it is possible for a good man to be a great man even under a bad emperor. This form of greatness, however, demands compliance and restraint, *obsequium* and *moderatio* – requirements that could only have sounded hideously out of place to Scipio Africanus or Pompey or Caesar.

In Tacitus' dialogue on oratory (imaginatively entitled *Dialogue on Oratory*), and this is the other composition we want to have a look at, the principal topic is the *decline* of oratory under the empire. To be fair, one of the participants rejects the reality of such a decline, but subsequent discussion relies on the premise that imperial oratory is inferior to its republican antecedents. The speaker usually taken to be the voice of the author, Curiatius Maternus, insists that the cause does not lie in the inferior natural talent of contemporary orators, but instead in their historical circumstances. The political oratory of the republic had been made great by the turmoil that inspired it and which it was intended to quell – or to incite. Nowadays, however, this perilous state of affairs has been eliminated by the institution of the principate, which, because it protects Rome from the dangers of factionalism, likewise removes the necessity for that degree of greatness in speechifying. This very dialogue, like the reputation of its author, makes it clear that even in the empire oratory can make a man's career. Only now he must reconcile himself to the fact that he will never – can never – be a Cicero. And is that a bad thing?

Lest you carry away the impression that this perspective was simply an effect of Tacitus' congenital grumpiness, let me draw you into the world of ancient Greek literary criticism, few works of which are more famous or more influential than Longinus's, or better pseudo-Longinus's, *On the Sublime*. This is an essay which attempts to isolate the features of great prose and great poetry – including, fascinatingly, a discussion of the *Book of Genesis* – that contribute to the heightened effect the author indicates by the term *sublimity*. The work concludes with a miniature debate, which attempts to explain the worldwide dearth of sublimity in the imperial period. A certain but unnamed philosopher has put forward the view that freedom (*demokratía*) is essential to literary excellence, but moderns (imperial moderns that is) live in a state of "righteous servitude" (*douléia dikaía*) that inhibits greatness. Pseudo-Longinus disagrees. In his view, it is the moral corruption of the present age that destroys talent. But he agrees with his philosopher friend on the righteousness of their inferiority to a political master:

> It is perhaps better for men like ourselves to be ruled rather than to be free, since our appetites, if let loose without restraint upon our neighbors like beasts from a cage, would set the world on fire with deeds of evil.

The emperor remains the bulwark against disaster and social breakdown.

The empire brought the Romans unparalleled peace and unparalleled prosperity, at the cost of unparalleled boredom and mediocrity. The ideology of the principate had a profound effect on the public and political identity of the aristocracy. To illustrate this, let us compare two senatorial mausoleums. First, and this amounts to a second visit for us, the Tomb of the Scipios, which we encountered in our first chapter. These are the earliest specimens of aristocratic self-representation that we possess. I submit to you two inscriptions commemorating splendid men who, in the end, failed in their quest for the all-important consulship:

(i) Lucius Cornelius Scipio, the son of Lucius and the grandson of Publius.
Quaestor, military tribune. Died at the age of thirty-three.
His father conquered King Antiochus.

(ii) Gnaeus Cornelius Scipio Hispanus, son of Gnaeus.
Praetor, curule aedile, quaestor, military tribune twice, decimvir for judging lawsuits, decimvir for making sacrifices (*a major priesthood*).
By my good character I added to the virtues of my family. I begat a family and I sought to equal the achievements of my father. I upheld the reputation of my ancestors, with the result that they rejoice that I was born to their line. My honor has ennobled my family.

Our first inscription makes the reason obvious: an early death. But Lucius was well on the way, and the inevitability of his consulship is asserted by the notice that his father had won the Syrian War, the implication of which for Lucius's *virtus* is patent. The second inscription offers no excuse for Gnaeus's failure, and so we should not assume premature death. This inscription is an exercise in ambiguity: its author blurs the distinction in Latin between *honor* in the sense of an actual office and honor the personal endowment. But for our purposes it is significant that Gnaeus basks in his family's glory and insists upon his own excellence entirely in terms of his own family's reputation and its embrace of his less than stellar career. The Cornelii matter – to the Cornelii, and, owing to that and that alone, to Rome.

Let us turn now to the mausoleum of the Plautii, established by the consul of 2 BC, which commemorates a family from the imperial aristocracy. Here is a single example of a Plautius who did not make it to the consulship, though it is uncertain whether this failure owes itself to an early death or to some other impediment. His message to posterity, it will be clear in an instant, is radically different from that of either Lucius or Gnaeus above:

Publius Plautius Pulcher, son of a triumphant general (*i.e. a general who had won triumphal insignia from the emperor*).

Augur, triumvir aere argento auro flando feriundo (*an official at the mint*), quaestor of Tiberius Caesar Augustus when he was consul for the fifth time, tribune of the people, praetor, aedile at the treasury, friend of Drusus the son of Germanicus, uncle of Drusus the son of Tiberius Claudius Caesar Augustus and enrolled by him, when he was censor, amongst the patricians, chosen curator for the paving of roads, chosen by the neighborhood associations on the authority of Tiberius Claudius Caesar Augustus Germanicus, proconsul of the province Sicily.

Two aspects are immediately clear and unmistakable. Plautius's memorial is far far wordier than his Scipionic predecessors. Most of this verbiage, however, is taken up not with his own career or with the glory of his own house, but instead with his personal connections to the imperial family. Plautius was a Roman noble. His father had been a distinguished general. But here, in place of inherited *mores* and inherited *virtus*, we find his claim to eternal fame lying in the friendship, the kinship and the *auctoritas* of the emperor. This is a very different Roman nobility from anything Caesar could have recognized in his own day. The emperor has become fully implicated in the self-representation of the senatorial order, for whom the very concept of senatorial greatness has changed.

If one believes that the best form of government is the one that provides the greatest good to the greatest number, then one must prefer the empire to the republic. The empire brought peace, stability, and prosperity to a degree that could not be duplicated, much less surpassed until the great revolutions in British industry and in French politics severed antiquity from modernity. But there can be no escaping the undeniable fact that the *pax Augusta* removed the stimulating properties of conflict: the genius of the late republic, like the splendor of the Augustan age, all fed on perturbation and uncertainty. When peace of a truly permanent sort arrived in Rome, when stability was changed from an aspiration to a reality, life got, well, boring. Under the empire, every incentive was against the ambition and the talent of a Julius Caesar, the likes of whom must be thwarted. As Cicero conceded, and the practice of later generations is sufficient to prove that they did not disagree:

A passion for office, command, power and glory exists in men possessing the best minds and the most brilliant talents. Consequently we must be all the more careful not to err in ambitions of this kind.

Peace and prosperity yield expertise and competence, but not brilliance, however much we endeavor to fool ourselves. Of course, very few societies get to make their own choice. But, I must say, were I ever to be asked to weigh my views in this balance, to judge between the unavoidable dullness of peace or the excitement and genius that only destructive conflict can nurture, then without hesitation I should speak … in praise of mediocrity. Perhaps we can call it moderation. The Augustan poet Horace was all too right to insist that "the tallest towers are the ones that experience the heavier fall," an apt admonition against the very real dangers of aristocratic (and not only aristocratic) overreach. The harm of them that fell from high degree, alas, is rarely restricted to themselves. In their crash, they too often take down too many of the rest of us. Too many Caesars are definitely not a good thing.

Further Reading

Osgood 2006 provides a recent and excellent account of the civil war and its cultural and political reverberations. The rise of Augustus is viewed in an almost comprehensively negative light by Syme 1939, still an important account. For a celebratory assessment of the man and his age see Galinsky 1996. Galinsky 2005 offers a broad and valuable survey of the period. Bowman, Champlin, and Lintott 1996 provides a detailed and thorough scholarly treatment.

Important Dates

100 BC Birth of Caesar.

88   Sulla's first march on Rome.

87–83   Cinna's domination of Rome.

82–79   Sulla's domination of Rome.

73   Caesar admitted to college of pontiffs.

69   Caesar is quaestor, serves in Spain. Funeral orations for Julia and Cornelia.

63   Catilinarian Conspiracy. Caesar elected *Pontifex Maximus*.

62   Caesar is praetor.

61–60   Caesar governs Further Spain.

59   Caesar's consulship.

58–49   Caesar's campaigns in Gaul.

52   Revolt of Vercingetorix. Rioting in Rome leads to Pompey's sole consulship.

49   Caesar invades Italy. Campaigns against Pompeians in Spain.

48   Pompey defeated at Pharsalus, thereafter murdered in Egypt. Caesar puts Cleopatra on the Egyptian throne.

48–47   Alexandrian War.

47   Battle of Zela.

46   Battle of Thapsus and suicide of Cato.

45   Battle of Munda. Caesar becomes dictator for life.

44   Assassination of Caesar. Caesar deified.

43   Formation of Second Triumvirate.

42   Battle of Philippi.

31   Battle of Actium.

30   Suicides of Antony and Cleopatra.

27   Octavian "restores" the republic and is granted the honorific Augustus.

Bibliography

Ashton, S. 2007. *Cleopatra and Egypt.* London: Blackwell.

Atkins, M. and Osborne, R. (eds) 2006. *Poverty in the Roman World.* Cambridge: Cambridge University Press.

Badian, E. 1968. *Roman Imperialism in the Late Republic.* London: Blackwell.

Balsdon, J.P.V.D. 1963. *Roman Women: Their History and Habits.* New York: John Day Co.

Balsdon, J.P.V.D. 1967. *Julius Caesar: A Political Biography.* New York: Athenaeum.

Barnes, J. and Griffin, M. (eds) 1997. *Philosophia II: Plato and Aristotle at Rome.* Oxford: Oxford University Press.

Barton, I.M. (ed.) 1989. *Roman Public Buildings.* Exeter: University of Exeter Press.

Batstone, W.W. and Damon, C. 2006. *Caesar's Civil War.* Oxford: Oxford University Press.

Beard, M. and Crawford, M. 1985. *Rome in the Late Republic: Problems and Interpretations* (2nd edn. 1999). London: Duckworth.

Beard, M. North, J. and Price, S. 1998. *Religions of Rome,* 2 vols. Cambridge: Cambridge University Press.

Bowman, A. Champlin, E. and Lintott, A. (eds) 1996. *The Augustan Empire, 43 B.C.–A.D. 69,* vol. 10 of *The Cambridge Ancient* History, 2nd edn. Cambridge: Cambridge University Press.

Brunt, P.A. 1988. *The Fall of the Roman Republic and Related Essays.* Oxford: Oxford University Press.

Burstein, S.M. 2004. *The Reign of Cleopatra.* Westport, CT: Greenwood Press.

Champion, C. (ed.) 2004. *Roman Imperialism: Readings and Sources.* Malden, MA: Blackwell.

Christ, K. 1994. *Caesar: Annäherungen an einen Diktator.* Munich: Verlag C.H. Beck.

Crook, J.A. Lintott, A. and Rawson, E. (eds) 1994. *The Last Age of the Roman Republic, 146–43 B.C.,* vol. 9 of *The Cambridge Ancient History,* 2nd edn. Cambridge: Cambridge University Press.

D'Ambra, E. 2007. *Roman Women*. Cambridge: Cambridge University Press.

Dixon, S. 1992. *The Roman Family*. Baltimore: Johns Hopkins University Press.

Dixon, S. 2001. *Reading Roman Women*. London: Duckworth.

Dowden, K. 1992. *Religion and the Romans*. London: Bristol Classical Press.

Earl, D. 1967. *The Moral and Political Tradition of Rome*. London: Thames & Hudson.

Feeney, D. 1998. *Literature and Religion at Rome: Cultures, Contexts, and Beliefs*. Cambridge: Cambridge University Press.

Ferrero, G. 1933. *The Life of Caesar*. London: G.P. Putnam's Sons.

Flower, H. 1996. *Ancestor Masks and Aristocratic Power in Roman Culture*. Oxford: Oxford University Press.

Flower, H. (ed.) 2004. *The Cambridge Companion to the Roman Republic*. Cambridge: Cambridge University Press.

Galinsky, K. 1996. *Augustan Culture: An Interpretive Introduction*. Princeton: Princeton University Press.

Galinsky, K. (ed.) 2005. *The Cambridge Companion to the Age of Augustus*. Cambridge: Cambridge University Press.

Gardner, J.F. 1986. *Women in Roman Law and Society*. Bloomington: Indiana University Press.

Gelzer, M. 1968. *Caesar: Politician and Statesman*. Cambridge, MA: Harvard University Press.

Goldsworthy, A. 1996. *The Roman Army at War, 100 B.C.–A.D. 200*. Oxford: Oxford University Press.

Goldsworthy, A. 2006. *Caesar: Life of a Colossus*. New Haven: Yale University Press.

Gradel, I. 2002. *Emperor Worship and Roman Religion*. Oxford: Oxford University Press.

Griffin, M. and Barnes, J. (eds) 1989. *Philosophia I: Essays on Philosophy and Roman Society*. Oxford: Oxford University Press.

Gruen, E.S. 1974. *The Last Generation of the Roman Republic*. Berkeley and Los Angeles: University of California Press.

Harris, W.V. 1979. *War and Imperialism in Republican Rome 327–70 B.C.* Oxford: Oxford University Press.

Harris, W.V. (ed.) 1984. *The Imperialism of Mid-Republican Rome*. Rome: American Academy in Rome.

Hemelrijk, E.A. 1999. *Matrona Docta: Educated Women in the Roman Elite from Cornelia to Julia Domna*. London: Routledge.

Jones, P.J. 2006a. *The Last Pharaoh*. Cairo: Haus Publishers Ltd.

Jones, P.J. 2006b. *Cleopatra: A Sourcebook*. Norman, OK: University of Oklahoma Press.

Kamm, A. 2006. *Julius Caesar: A Life*. London: Routledge.

Kleiner, D.E.E. 2005. *Cleopatra and Rome*. Cambridge, MA: Belknap Press of Harvard University Press.

Konstan, D. 1997. *Friendship in the Classical World*. Cambridge: Cambridge University Press.

Liebeschuetz, J.H.W.G. 1979. *Continuity and Change in Roman Religion*. Oxford: Oxford University Press.

Lintott, A. 1999. *The Constitution of the Roman Republic*. Oxford: Oxford University Press.

MacMullen, R. 1974. *Roman Social Relations, 50 B.C. to A.D. 284*. New Haven: Yale University Press.

MacMullen, R. 1981. *Paganism in the Roman Empire*. New Haven: Yale University Press.

Marincola, J. (ed.) 2007. *A Companion to Greek and Roman Historiography*. London: Blackwell.

Meier, C. 1982. *Caesar: A Biography*. New York: Basic Books.

Mitchell, T.N. 1991. *Cicero: The Senior Statesman*. New Haven: Yale University Press.

Mommsen, T. 1894. *History of Rome*. London: R. Bently.

Morgan, M.G. 1971. "The Portico of Metellus: A Reconsideration," *Hermes* 99: 480–505.

Morgan, M.G. 1973. "Villa Publica and Magna Mater: Two Notes on Manubial Building at the Close of the Second Century B.C.," *Klio* 55: 215–46.

North, J. 2000. *Roman Religion*. Oxford: Oxford University Press.

Osgood, J. 2006. *Caesar's Legacy: Civil War and the Emergence of the Roman Empire*. Cambridge: Cambridge University Press.

Parenti, M. 2003. *The Assassination of Julius Caesar: A People's History of Ancient Rome*. New York: New Press.

Powell, J.G.F. 1995. *Cicero the Philosopher*. Oxford: Oxford University Press.

Price, S.R.F. 1984. *Rituals and Power: The Roman Imperial Cult in Asia Minor*. Cambridge: Cambridge University Press.

Riggsby, A.M. 2006. *Caesar in Gaul and Rome: War in Words*. Austin, TX: University of Texas Press.

Roller, M.B. 2001. *Constructing Autocracy: Aristocrats and Emperors in Julio-Claudian Rome*. Princeton: Princeton University Press.

Rosenstein, N. and Morstein-Marx, R. (eds) 2006. *A Companion to the Roman Republic*. London: Blackwell.

Russell, J. 1980. "Julius Caesar's Last Words: A Reinterpretation," in B. Marshall (ed.), *Vindex Humanitatis: Essays in Honour of John Huntley Bishop*. Armidale: University of New England Press, pp. 123–8.

Scullard, H.H. 1959. *From the Gracchi to Nero: A History of Rome from 133 B.C. to A.D. 68*. London: Methuen.

Seager, R. 2002. *Pompey the Great: A Political Biography*, 2nd edn. London: Blackwell.

Sear, F. 1982. *Roman Architecture*. London: Routledge.

Sedley, D. 1997. "The Ethics of Brutus and Cassius," *Journal of Roman Studies* 87: 41–53.

Sedley, D. (ed.) 2003. *The Cambridge Companion to Greek and Roman Philosophy*. Cambridge: Cambridge University Press.

Stamper, J.W. 2005. *The Architecture of Roman Temples: The Republic to the Middle Empire*. Cambridge: Cambridge University Press.

Strasburger, H. 1938. *Caesars Eintritt in die Geschichte*. Munich: Neuer Filverslag.

Strasburger, H. 1968. *Caesar im Urteil seiner Zeitgenossen*, 2nd edn. Darmstadt: Wissenschaftliche Buchgesellschaft.

Strong, D.E. 1968. "The Administration of Public Building in Rome During the Late Republic and Early Empire," *Bulletin of the Institute for Classical Studies* 15: 97–109.

Syme, R. 1939. *The Roman Revolution*. Oxford: Oxford University Press.

Taylor, L.R. 1931. *The Divinity of the Roman Emperor*. Middletown: American Philological Association.

Treggiari, S. 1991. *Roman Marriage: Iusti Coniuges from the Time of Cicero to the Time of Ulpian*. Oxford: Oxford University Press.

Ulrich, R.B. 1994. *The Roman Orator and the Sacred Stage: The Roman Templum Rostratum*. Brussels: Latomus.

Wardman, A. 1982. *Religion and Statecraft among the Romans*. Baltimore: Johns Hopkins University Press.

Warrior, V. 2006. *Roman Religion*. Cambridge: Cambridge University Press.

Weinstock, S. 1971. *Divus Julius*. Oxford: Oxford University Press.

Welch, K. and Powell, A. (eds) 1998. *Julius Caesar as Artful Reporter*. London: Classical Press of Wales.

Whittaker, C.R. 1993. "The Poor," in A. Giardina (ed.), *The Romans*. Chicago: University of Chicago Press, pp. 272–99.

Woolf, G. 1998. *Becoming Roman: The Origins of Provincial Civilization in Gaul*. Cambridge: Cambridge University Press.

Woolf, G. 2006. *Et tu, Brute? The Murder of Caesar and Political Assassination*. London: Profile Books.

Wyke, M. 2002. *The Roman Mistress: Ancient and Modern Representations*. Oxford: Oxford University Press.

Wyke, M. (ed.) 2006. *Julius Caesar in Western Culture*. London: Blackwell.

Yavetz, Z. 1983. *Julius Caesar and His Public Image*. London: Thames & Hudson.

Zanker, P. 1988. *The Power of Images in the Age of Augustus*. Ann Arbor, MI: University of Michigan Press.

Index